In And Out Of Madness

In And Out Of Madness

N.L. Snowden

This book is dedicated to Teddee Jordan—my daughter, my best friend and the person who pushed me, pulled me and encouraged me.

This book was first published by Sneakaboard Press in 2009. This is a new edition with a rewrite and a different ending published in 2015.

"N. L. Snowden's debut novel In and Out of Madness is a searing and brutally honest story of sexual obsession and chronic mental illness. Lee, the protagonist, is vividly portrayed, and the pain and agony of her struggles against her demons—and her ultimate triumph over them—will remain with the reader of this powerful novel long after the last page is turned."
—William Cobb

He is a Pulitzer Prize nominee and the 2007 winner of the Harper Lee Lifetime Achievement in Writing Award.

In her enthralling, compelling narrative, N.L. Snowden, giving voice to her heroine Lee, performs wondrous exorcisms. Lee has a chilling, terrifying early start in life: Big Maw, her grandmother, her mother's mother. Big Maw pinning Lee down in a tub of deep water, rubbing Lee raw in all her tender places, dragging her naked into a room full of strangers, spreading her out naked on the bed, splaying her legs.
"Please don't make me stay with Big Ma," Lee later begs her mother. "Something bad happened."
Lee is perhaps seven when she is able to make this plea. Her mother's answer is to whip Lee mercilessly. Not simply to whip her, but to whip her in front her friends, who look on with horror and hilarity. Lee, her mother pronounces, is telling a story, a lie.
So Lee's tale, Snowden giving voice to Lee, begins. And the tale is a whopper, intense and compelling. The voice, brave,

authentic, real, never ceases to surprise
and delight. It tells no lies.
—Samuel Pirro

Acknowledgments

First would be my daughter, Teddee, who never gave up believing that someone would publish my book one day. When depressed or frustrated, she always knew what to say to liven things up—putting me in a mood to write another page. She had no pity on me and never allowed me to moan or to quit trying.

Thanks goes to all the varied people who helped inspire the story.
I'd like to thank these BETA readers: Allison Miles, Danny Garland, Marsha Miles, Cathy Hackney, Chris Crowhurst, Joe Sieber, Mary Ann Taylor, James Hamilton, Susan Hopkins, Darrell Ewing, Andrea Briggs and John Copeland.

Of course a big thanks goes to William Cobb, Samuel Pirro, Cassandra King and Moe Armstrong who did my book blurbs for me.

I'd be remiss to forget you, the reader, who chose to make my book a success.

Chapter One

One of us must die.

Bright lights flickered as red spots on my closed lids. I went in and out of reality. A searing pain awakened me the same as every morning, but this time it hurt worse as they removed the NG tube from my nostril.

I thought to myself, this is the first time I'd had my stomach pumped, and it hurts like hell. Horrific anguish from the endless tubes vexed every orifice. I had no idea where I was or what was going on. Groggy was an understatement.

I remembered sitting in my recliner when the phone rang. Jolly, my daughter, calling me. My mind worked, although the rest of me felt paralyzed.

"Tholly. . .I. . .uh luf. . . youfth.

I heard Jolly's voice, but I couldn't understand what she was saying. Soon, another vaguely familiar voice sounded loud in my ear as he shook me awake.

"Lee, wuh-wuh-wake up, can you hear me?" I recognized the voice as belonging to Tom, our local town cop whose number my daughter kept on her phone's speed dial.

Thinking I was sipping a glass of tea, I sensed a prick and a burning sensation in my arm. That part I did remember, though I thought it had just happened. Turns out it was when the EMTs found me passed out in my chair. The pain had awakened me the night before for a few seconds. Life wasn't fair, even in death.

I tried to open my eyes. They were too heavy to open all the way, but I squeezed one into a slit. A blinding light assaulted me, and the red spots faded. There were strangers leaning over me. The strong smell of alcohol burned my nose as a nurse unhooked the IV and pulled it out. She cleaned the stick and bandaged it.

"You know, you are wuh-wuh-one lucky lady."

The voice I heard sounded like he screamed at me from far away. Tom's voice again. I managed to open my eyes and look at him, and he was there this time.

"Have you returned to take me to a mental hospital?" I asked.

"I'm here mainly as a wuh-worried friend, Lee, but, yes, if the doctor decides to send you back by ambulance to Birmingham, my job is to see that you go agreeably."

"How did I get here? What happened?"

"Jolly called me last night and said you'd taken an overdose. Wuh-wuh-when I got to the house, you'd locked all of the doors. She had you on one phone and me on her cell phone. She gave me permission to kick the doors in to get to you. I kicked in the outside studio door then the locked pantry door. You wuh-wuh-were out but still breathing. The ambulance arrived shortly after I did, and the EMTs wuh-worked on stabilizing you. They brought you to the hospital here in LaGrange. Her call saved your life."

I was too drugged to make much sense out of what he was saying to me, but I comprehended that I'd nearly killed myself and Jolly had saved my life. The thought of Jolly was the only thing that made me grateful to be alive.

The aftermath of the self-hatred still clung to my spirit. I wasn't sure that getting saved had been what was really best for me. Then I thought about what I'd almost done to Jolly. In spite of the brain fog, my thinking was clear enough to feel a deep shame.

At last, no machines induced their rhythmic check on my life. A young doctor came in and assessed my situation with a brief question.

"Do you still want to harm yourself?"

"No." That was the truth. I'd learned my lesson by coming so close to taking my life. "Are you going to put me in a mental hospital? I have an appointment with my psychiatrist in Birmingham tomorrow afternoon."

Because I had the appointment the next day, they let me go home. Tom drove me back to Senora, Alabama in the police car. He was kind and helped settle me.

"Tell me about two nights ago, Lee," said Dr. Hopkins. "When you had to go to the emergency room."

"I don't remember too much. I know I was mad as hell at Joe. I vaguely remember wanting to kill myself. God, earlier in the week I'd asked my neighbor, who'd been keeping my daddy's gun, to let me have it back. She refused to give it to me. I don't understand why she refused to let me have the gun."

He leaned back in his chair, and his mouth twitched in a nervous tic. He spoke in a fast monotone that was often hard for me to understand because of my hearing problem. For a man of sixty-three, he was still quite attractive. I'd heard rumors that he was Birmingham's best catch.

As I talked, I shook my right foot in figure eights.

"I only wanted it for protection, now that I'm a single woman." I looked up and spoke in rapid-fire sentences. "You know, I wish I'd gotten that damn gun back. God, I would kill him. In fact, if I could think of a way, I'd do it right now. No, I wouldn't kill him. Uh-uh, I'd shoot him in his dick and paralyze him. I'd stand there and watch the fear in his eyes as I aimed the gun at his beloved crotch."

I uncrossed my legs and stretched both feet toward the doctor, kneading the air with each foot, back and forth.

"Then I'd laugh as he screamed in agony," I said, "and I'd gloat over the blood as it drenched his hands. I'd stand there for a minute and listen to him plead with me to call for help. He'd watch me unplug all of the phones, grab his cell phone and take them with me. I'd leave him in pain, begging me to come back and help him. I'd laugh all the way back to my car. I'd drive with the convertible top down, radio turned up, and cruise home smiling to myself."

Dr. Hopkins's face looked pale. In a sad but frustrated voice he said, "You have certainly complicated things now. I'm required by law to write orders for your commitment to the mental hospital."

"No! I don't want to go to the hospital."

Suddenly, my inexhaustible joy turned into a deluge of tears and slurps as I realized he was going to lock me up. I begged him not to make me go. He summoned his office manager, Marilyn, and they called the unit to prepare a room for me. She wanted to drive me, but I told her I could drive myself, since I'd need a way to get home once the hospital released me. I kept protesting that I didn't have any clothes, toothbrush, etcetera, and no one to take care of my pets. The look on their faces told me that I was a lot sicker than I realized. I shrugged and followed Marilyn out to the parking lot.

We drove to the unit, and things were different from the other times I'd been there. First, I was going right on in, there would be no long wait in the emergency room. Second, Joe was not there letting me know that he'd take care of everything for me. The worst sense of loneliness since we'd split up overwhelmed me.

I watched a nurse look at her watch and log me in at three fifteen on May 5, 2003. They handed me papers to sign. The first one she gave me would allow them to file for the insurance. Well, since Joe had recently burned me by not paying my medical bills, I read this paper carefully. Sure enough, in small print were the words that signing on the line below meant that I would be responsible for the bill. I pushed the paper back, refusing to sign it.

"Why don't you call my son-of-a-bitching ex-husband to sign this? He's the one who is mandated by the court to pay these medical bills."

They tried to humor me by saying that it was okay and that I didn't have to sign it. One of the nurses asked the other if she needed to go through my purse. By this time, Marilyn had returned to Dr. Hopkins's office. When I heard that they were going to lock up my purse, an eerie feeling came over me. That was my last and only possession, and I'd be damned if I was going to let them take it.

"Last time I was up here, a lady had things stolen out of her purse," I said desperately.

"That's impossible. They are locked up in a safe."

In the past when Dr. Hopkins had hospitalized me, Joe always took my purse home with him. He brought me books, some clothes, and I knew he loved me, would miss me, call me and visit me. Normally, he would be happy to see me when I got well. This time I'd be alone. Jolly was too far away and couldn't miss school. Joe wouldn't give a shit anymore. Besides, Jolly hadn't told him I'd nearly killed myself. She'd handled it all alone, sure that Joe wouldn't want to help.

The nurse walked toward the door that would bring her out to get me and take me up to the floor that had power locks and double sets of doors. I'd be strip-searched, given one of those bare-butted gowns and not be allowed to drink when I was thirsty. No, I couldn't do this!

As the nurse reached for the door handle, I picked up my purse and my keys off the check in counter and ran for the front door.

"Lee, come back! Let us help you. Now stop, we can help you!"

I heard the panic in her voice. They had goofed and allowed a seriously psychotic patient to escape. I kept on running and quickly unlocked my car's door and darted in, rapidly relocking all of them. By then she was at my window.

"Come on, Lee. Don't do this."

I turned the key, started the car and backed out. I gave it a little too much scoot juice, and it made like a wave as I sped away. My heart pounded. I was afraid they'd have a guard or the police coming after me. I knew not to speed and draw attention to myself, so I settled down and headed for home. Once I got out of Birmingham's city limits, I became frenzied. It was drizzling, but I pulled off the road and let my top down. Driving in the rain—in that air bubble of protection from the wet—made me bold as I accelerated. Feeling invincible and fearless on the slick roads, I blasted it to eighty and made it back home in record time.

On the way home from seeing my doctor I stopped again at Jessica's house in hope that I could wrangle the gun out of her this time. Jessica and Boyd were private people and didn't tell my business to anyone. Both of our families were Senora's out casts.

I ambled up the brick walkway to the old antebellum home. The smell of the Confederate Jasmine vine filling my nostrils with such a sweet scent, made me pause, and I almost reconsidered things. Then I thought of all the times Joe had promised me, when we sat in our gazebo by the pool, that he loved me and would never leave me. What a liar! Anger again fueled my resolve. I heard the wooden porch creak from a loose board as I walked up and knocked on the right double door.

"Who is it?"

"It's me, Lee. I need to talk to you." I heard the television going in their front bedroom. NPR, the only thing they'd allow themselves to watch.

"Hang on just a minute. I need to get dressed. I'm in my nightgown. Do you know what time it is?" I heard a shade of irritation in her voice.

"No, I don't. I 'm on the way back home from my doctor in Birmingham."

The door opened, and Jessica glared at me for interrupting her peaceful evening.

"Hey, I'm sure you heard about my latest suicide attempt by now?"

"Yes. Lee, I don't know what to think. You've got to get over that sleazebag. All he ever did was hurt you. He is not worth taking your life. That is what he wants you to do."

She was right. That was basically what Jolly told me.

"Listen, my sister is here from Meridian. She is going to stay with me a couple of days. She asked me to stop and pick up Daddy's gun so she can take it back with her. Since she is big into genealogy, she wants it to stay in our family."

"Lee, I don't know. I don't trust you. Can I call your sister? I need to talk to her about a stained glass project."

"Sure."

"Let me get the gun and take it home to her. Give me time enough to get home and settled in and call. But don't wait too late. She's one that goes to bed early."

"Okay. I'll get Boyd to get it for you. Come on inside. Can I get you a glass of tea or water while you wait?"

"No thanks. I'm sure it won't take long. I'll just stay out on the porch enjoying the scent of the Jasmine."

Jessica left, and I heard murmuring. Soon footsteps ascending the stairs to their attic let me know my plan was working. I walked over to the porch swing and sat down. I hated lying to Jessica. But I knew what I had to do tonight, and anything at my disposal was not off limits. The door opened, Boyd appeared and handed me Daddy's Colt 45. For a minute I felt a pang of guilt, but not enough to make me stop.

"Thanks, y'all. Margaret will be so happy to have it back in our family."

Because I was frenetic and angry, I fishtailed my silver Miata into the driveway. Slamming the door in frustration, I glanced at my watch. It was five after six. Walking back from the mailbox, I thumbed through the bills and junk mail without interest until the invitation addressed to Joe and Lee Thames appeared. Word we'd split up hadn't made it to that circle of friends yet.

"Damn you, Joe! I'm going to get you for what you've done to me."

I said this to summon the courage I needed for what I had in mind when he got off work—I planned on killing him. I just needed to lure him back to my house tonight and wasn't sure how to do it, since our last face-to-face conversation had ended in a physical fight two nights ago. I felt aghast and thrilled by my thoughts, but not enough to stop these overwhelming urges—even as another part of me wanted to wash such thoughts away.

I needed to go inside my house and lock the doors—I'd just eloped from a psychiatric inpatient facility and knew the police would be looking for me.

I opened my glove drawer and put the gun into it, feeling the cool metal as it slid underneath the soft kid leather. I knew no one would think to look in my bedroom for a gun. Since I was mentally ill, I couldn't purchase one. Only Jessica, Boyd, Jolly and Joe knew I had inherited my dad's gun.

Touching its smooth surface gave me a sense of power. I knew I'd find a way to fix the pain Joe caused me. I'd tried to forgive him and let go of the past, but he kept doing things like lying to me, flaunting his women and generally treating me like shit, even though he lived thirty minutes away from me in his own apartment. These things forced me to focus on confronting him and trying to control him. Now my moment of looking into his lying eyes and watching him suffer drew near. My destiny called me as I shut the drawer and heard that grating, squeaking sound a dresser makes when it is too old for its drawers to open and close easily. A cut-glass vase of wilted yellow roses stuck out on the dresser. Although I'd cut them only the day before, they appeared to have given up—like me.

I felt my pulse increase as I remembered what had inflamed me enough to want to act in a way that I shouldn't. God, how far had we come, how low had we stooped, and how wretched was my life? Right now, on this fine spring day, I didn't care about anything. I didn't care about Joe or me, not even my daughter Jolly. I didn't care that I'd probably lost Dr. Hopkins, my psychiatrist in Birmingham. What I was doing to my good friend didn't bother me either. I didn't care that I was fixing to mess up my life. All I cared about was stopping this madness and pain.

By now, an APB probably chattered on every police radio in the state. The drive from Birmingham to my home in Senora had taken less than three hours, since I'd raced home in my sporty coupe as though I were the next Triple Crown winner. Although a drizzle had shrouded the road, I'd enjoyed the mist on my face. My freedom from the mental hospital invited me to live dangerously. I was high.

Although realistic enough to expect a knock on my door at any minute from our only local police officer, Tom Vanguard, who would cuff me and drag me back to The Pit, as we crazies called it, I still made plans to wreck my life. Senora is a little hamlet on the far eastern side of Alabama—a small town with less than two hundred fifty people, including those in our cemetery.

Despite the risk, I stayed home. All I could think about was that smirk on Joe's face. I wanted to slap it off. No, I didn't want to slap it off; I wanted to blow it off.

Would this be over in record time like my drive home? I thought about the gun in the drawer—I'd worked hard lying in order to get it back. More pressing to me was my anxiety about losing my doctor.

Worrying about losing Dr. Hopkins almost made me rational, then the voices started again, and I acknowledged what I had to do. Damn! It was only six fifteen.

I knew there were only two solutions to this problem. One was to kill myself, and the other was to kill Joe. The voices told me that my only hope for serenity was to be ready when Joe got home from work so I could bait him into coming to my house.

The phone rang. I jumped.

"Damn telemarketer!"

I remembered my father's gun in the drawer. At that moment, I cherished the illusion of taking it out, aiming all my frustrations on the ringing phone. I fantasized about hearing the answering machine pick up, and as I heard one of their familiar mispronunciations of my name, pulling out the gun and blowing the telephone into blue dust.

My own voice on the answering machine interrupted my dark sentiments: I'm writing, or I'm out horsing around. Please leave your name, number, and a brief message, and I'll get back in touch with you, unless you're my ex-husband or a telemarketer.

I heard the low beep.

"Mom?"

I lunged to pick up the phone, nearly tripping over the bed in the process. I answered the phone slightly out of breath.

"Jolly, don't hang up. I'm here."

"Are you okay? I've been worried sick. You told me Dr. Hopkins ordered a room for you at South Park, then you called and said you'd run away."

"Jolly, I'm fine."

"Mom, do you want me to call Tom and let him take you back up there? I'm afraid. I'm worried that you're going to kill yourself."

"No, Angel. I'll be okay. I needed to come home."

I sat down on the bed, untwisting the telephone cord while listening to Jolly. I heard a waver in her voice. I felt guilty for upsetting her again, especially after two nights ago when I'd ambitiously tried killing myself. Now I was pulling this stunt on her. Jolly was my best friend in the world because she stayed level-headed and remained calm in a crises. She'd proven she could handle a very difficult situation—saving my life from three hours away.

"You know, Mom, you almost succeeded the other night. God, please don't leave me alone. I love you. Daddy's not worth losing your life."

Good, she seems to understand that he has to be the one to die.

"I was upset with your dad, not suicidal."

I heard her gulp as she bravely tried not to cry and upset me.

"You are a wonderful mother and a talented person. You have to realize that you don't need Daddy to be happy. I know it's hard now. One day you'll

7

realize you are better off without him."

"Angel, I'm fine, really I am. I just couldn't bear the thought of going into a mental hospital alone. Your dad went with me every other time. His strength encouraged me not to be afraid."

"Mom, he's not good for you now—try to grasp that."

"But he always stayed with me until they took me up on the lockup floor. He called me and he visited me. Jolly, he was good to me when I needed him the most.

"Angel, I knew that the loneliest feeling in the world was realizing they were going to lock me up and no one would be there. You're too far away, and you can't afford to miss any of your classes. I wouldn't have had a soul on visitation days."

Just thinking that literally had my heart hurting. For a minute, I wondered if I could die from a broken heart.

"They were going to lock up my purse. Without it, I wouldn't have had a way to call. If I couldn't call you and give you my PIN number, you couldn't have called me."

"Mom, Dr. Hopkins wouldn't have put you in the hospital unless he thought you were sick."

Ignoring her words, I went on. "God, I froze with pure fear. I realized I was crazy. Going to a mental hospital would have made me sicker, not better. Returning home saved me. I needed to calm down."

Looking around the room as I talked, disgust welled up within me that my bedroom was nasty. Housekeeping was low on my agenda now, although I'd always kept my house picked up and neat. On a beauty kick, I had surrounded myself with china, crystal, silver, and fresh cut flowers from my yard.

"I promise you, sweet girl," I said to Jolly, "I'm not going to try to kill myself. Why, I'm back here in the bedroom right now fixing to go to bed. I'm okay. Really, I am."

"Mom, please don't do anything stupid. It's hard to trust you."

I tried to reassure her in my most convincing voice. "I'll call you first thing tomorrow morning. I'm about to take my sleeping pills and grog out."

"How many will you take?"

"I swear to you I'll only take the two prescribed by Dr. Hopkins. You get on back to studying."

"Yeah, right. That'll be easy to do now."

"I'm going to e-mail Dr. Hopkins while I'm lucid and see what he says to me," I added. "I hope I haven't screwed things up to the point that he won't be my doctor anymore. After I hear from him, I'll e-mail you and let you know what he says. I know he was legally obligated to have me committed to the hospital, but I don't believe he personally thought it would have been the best thing for me. I know coming home was the right thing for me to do."

I knew Jolly would gauge that I was a little too peppy, which meant trouble, so I slowed my speech down, trying to sound normal. "Night, night, sweet Angel. Mommy loves you."

"Night, Mom, I love you too. I'll call you tomorrow morning as soon as I get up. Go on to bed and take it easy. Take care of yourself." There was a pause. "Mom . . ."

"What, Angel?"

"Oh, Mom, please don't do anything to hurt yourself again. I couldn't stand it if I lost you. Try to remember how much I love you and need you."

"I swear to you I will never try killing myself again. Go on and do your thing. I'm okay. Talking to you has helped me." I paused then said, "And, Jolly . . . thanks for saying that you needed me. I thought right now that I needed you, and you didn't need me anymore. That does give me some hope that I'm not a total fuck up."

I hung up the phone with a sense of sadness in my heart.

I knew I needed to take some Lithium to calm down. I poured myself a glass of milk and took a dose. Then I started running my bath. I knew the hot water would help the Lithium to work better. Wanting to relax in a hot bubble bath, I lit some candles as the tub filled. Lilac-scented candles cast their soft light and sedated me. The hot steam soaked through my skin, however it didn't come close to warming my icy heart.

I listened to the water as it lapped the edge of the tub each time my hand moved, cutting a heart shape aimlessly. The hot liquid etched itself into my fingers. The bubbles piled up like white gloves with open fingers, one bursting on my nipple with a soft phffft sound.

Then I remembered when taking a bath had terrified me.

Chapter Two

I hated my grandmother's large bathtub, the ugly thing with claw feet. I'd always felt as if she were going to drown me in it. She ran the water deep, and ever since I was young—possibly only two or three—her baths had scared me. Fear of sinking down the large drain as the water gurgled away in a whirlpool used to make me cry. I wanted her to hold on to me. At the same time, I couldn't stand her touching me.

I remembered the way her face froze in a grin as she washed me. She was always rough, rubbing me hard in tender places. Her breathing sounded rushed and heavy, and if I listened real close, I could almost still hear it. I had always hated even more what would sometimes happen next. She'd march me out naked into the bedroom filled with strangers. Her bedroom always smelled of snuff and cheap flowery perfume. She would pick me up, lay me on the bed, look down at me and smile. Then she would force my legs open. I winced at the memory of how I covered my face with my hands and screamed No!

I pushed the memory out of my mind, except for a quick flashback with no details. The Secret Keeper split off deep inside my soul. Only later did I discover the truth about another incident that happened during the summer of 1956 when I was seven years old. Now, at fifty-four, the memory was as fresh as if it had happened within the past year of my life.

"Please don't make me stay with Big Maw Maw. She scares me, Mama. Something bad happened. I didn't have on my panties. Somebody held my legs apart. I don't want to go back to Big Maw Maw's house."

I'd cried and grabbed my throat as I said this, trying to stop the crawling sensation on my neck. It had been four years before I finally told my mother the truth.

"Don't you lie. Why on earth would you say something like that about your grandmother?" My mama, Laura Snowden, glared at me, spitting the words out with venom. "Who hurt you?"

Softly, I whined. "I don't know."

"If you don't know who did it, then I know you're lying, you little turd.

Nina Lee, I'm going to spank you if you don't stop that. You are going up there this weekend, and you will spend the week with your grandparents. Your daddy and I have planned this trip for months. We're flying to the Caribbean on Saturday, and we're not calling off the trip because of your foolishness."

She narrowed her eyes into snake-like slits. Whenever she did that, I knew what was coming—a whipping with a switch. I started shaking with dread. Despite what I knew my mother would do, I feared going to my grandmother's house even more. I pleaded with her.

"Please let Mrs. Cowan stay with me. Don't make me go. Please!" I started to cry louder because I knew the answer.

My eyes misted at the vividness of the memory that made it seem as if I were still that little girl, begging my mama not to make me go.

I sank deeper into my tub, allowing the scent of the candles to diffuse the tension. I grabbed my goat's milk soap and tried scrubbing off all my offenses, which smelled of Mama. She had always reeked of a mixture of cigarettes, bourbon, and Youth Dew perfume. To this day, the smell of bourbon makes me nauseated. The strange thing was that I also wore Youth Dew because I loved how it smelled. Santa always stuck a bottle in my stocking at Christmas.

I shuddered as the memory continued.

"Go find me a switch. I'm tired of your mess. It had better be a good one too." Mama stood in the open door and called all my friends to line up. "I'm fixing to tear Lee up for lying to me. I want y'all to watch what I do to bad girls." She would actually have a grin on her face as she hissed those words.

The whole neighborhood played at our house in the fenced-in back yard. She couldn't just whip me for a falsehood I hadn't even told. That hadn't been good enough. No, she had to be sadistic—humiliate and torture me. Fear traumatized me at the thought of returning to my grandmother's house.

I got the switch and took it to Mama. Across the back of the old woody station wagon stood my friends, like trees on the horizon. The white dust from the cement plant had changed the car from an evergreen to a marsh green. Instead of beautiful polished wood on its sides, it had a dull, cotton-gin brown color to it. The stench of the paper mill hung in the air despite the fact that it was ten miles away. Drawn up in pinched smiles of horror and hilarity, my friends watched Mama's hand move in a blur as she whipped me. She held my arm, and I tried to turn a flip as I attempted to jump around and dodge the sharp stinging of the switch. I screamed. The embarrassment overwhelmed me.

"Mama, please stop! I didn't tell a story. Stop!"

"Shut up, you little shit. Quit saying that. Quit crying."

"Ouch! Mama, stop!"

"Now, did you tell me a story or not?" She switched hard as she asked the question.

"It's not true, nothing happened!" I begged for mercy. "I'm sorry I told a story."

That day, I stopped loving my mother. Who could I trust if my grandmother molested me, my mother called me a liar, and now my friends would all think I was some horrible storytelling jerk?

My childlike voice reverberated as my mind wandered back to the present. My bath water was cooling down as my temper heated up.

Reluctant to leave the mellow haven I found, I couldn't keep my thoughts from drifting back to that day once again. My own mind had only remembered the whipping in front of my friends. The reason my mother had whipped me had always been a mystery until Dr. Diamond, my psychoanalyst, had helped me retrieve those memories when he hypnotized me and regressed me to age seven. Had I lost the ability to remember because pathetic, depressed Nancy had split off that day? Nancy had told Dr. Diamond about the incident. Although he had tried to take me back in my subconscious mind to the age of the bath, he had been unsuccessful because the Secret Keeper refused to talk to him. I chose to remember what he had discovered. Remembering made me understand why I had become such an honesty freak.

The only lie I had told was when I said I'd fibbed so she would quit spanking me. That lie soon became the truth, save for a flash memory. I stayed confused. Soon after my whipping, I forgot that I didn't care for my grandmother. On an odd plane, I was the only one who had ever shown her affection. I still never enjoyed being at her house, though. It was dirty and full of strange people. I'd never cottoned to strangers, but I learned to deal with the fact that time with her was inevitable.

Because I was my grandmother's namesake, she'd always favored me. Part of me loved her, and part of me abhorred her. She gave me a Swiss wristwatch when I was eight. It never did keep time on me. It kept perfect time on my sister. I often wondered about that. Of course, Big Maw Maw noticed when I quit wearing it. She felt my mama was behind it, because she knew my mama hadn't cared for her. I'd let her believe that lie. I'd seen her anger and didn't want her mad with me. I'd heard stories from my dad about the closet.

My grandmother used to lock my daddy in the closet when she had company because he was fat, and she was embarrassed for people to see him. I shuddered, remembering the pained look in Daddy's eyes when he told me what she did to him. He wasn't really all that fat. She was just mean.

By six twenty-two, I felt waterlogged. I never had been one for long baths. I always felt as though it wasted too much time. I got out of the tub, clean but covered with the memories.

When I was twelve, Mama traumatized me again when she took me to a new doctor in town to have a pelvic exam. I remembered having some kind of odd rash on me. My twelve-year-old personality, Dee Dee, had talked to Dr. Diamond during hypnosis and told him about how Mama had humiliated me in front of a doctor in 1961. Dee Dee carried that memory in my head, but Dr. Diamond retrieved it. I chose to remember what Dee Dee said during the hypnosis. I always thought of Nancy and Dee Dee in the third person rather than being a part of me.

I'd awakened that morning with bloodstains in my panties—not enough to think I'd started my period, but enough to know something was wrong. I hated to go to my mother, yet I had been more afraid of the terrible itch and yellow mucus in my panties that now had a faint pink color to it denoting blood.

"Mama, can you come here a minute? I'm in the bathroom." I was sitting on the commode with my panties down.

She took one look at my panties and demanded that I let her examine my "toodle woodle" as she called it. Hung up, she hadn't even been able to call my privates by their proper name. I stood up, leaned back, and felt her opening me up. Shame had blanketed my emotions.

"I'm going to have to take you to the doctor. You're too young to have this kind of problem. What have you been doing, Lee?"

"Nothing, I promise."

I hadn't been about to admit that I sometimes touched myself down there in a pleasurable way. I thought maybe whatever was wrong with me was my punishment.

"There's a new doctor in town. I don't want our family physician to know about this. Come on and get dressed. Bathe yourself real good down there. Put these same panties back on. I want him to see this discharge you have."

We'd walked into the doctor's office and, because he was new, it hadn't been busy. We went right on back. He was young and very attractive. I figured he'd listen to my chest, do my ears and mouth, then we'd show him my panties. I'd never heard of a pelvic exam. Mama never took the time to explain what was going to happen.

"Hi. I'm Dr. Fritz. What's your name?"

"Lee."

I was shy and felt very self-conscious because I was going through puberty and had maybe six pubic hairs and egg yolks for breasts—way behind in development compared to most of my peers.

"Well, Lee, I need you to undress and get up on the table for me."

"No! I'm not going to get naked. Not in front of a man."

"Lee, he's a doctor," Mama said. "Stop your foolishness. Take those clothes off right now or I'm going to whip you right here in front of him."

That had humiliated me as much as getting naked. I'd reluctantly done as I was told, keeping my legs tightly together. Back then, they didn't cover you with a sheet. Mama had sat down at my feet rather than up at my head. I remember the hot embarrassment I felt over having her see me naked. I started crying.

"Shut up! You're acting like a big baby. Quit crying or I'll give you something to cry about."

I heard an odd sound as the doctor brought the stirrups into position.

"Scoot down to the end of the table and place your feet in these," he said.

"No! I don't want you looking at me down there. And I especially don't want my mama to see me." This I'd screamed in anger as Dee Dee split off, my personality of anger and spite.

The doctor grabbed my legs and pushed them open as Dee Dee screamed at him. He placed a foot in one of the stirrups. She'd immediately snatched it out as he grabbed the other.

"You leave me alone! I'm not putting my feet up! Mama, you can shut up!"

Mama had jumped up, and slapped me in the face. Distracted by that, the doctor had placed both feet in the stirrups and held my legs open.

"I'm not going to hurt you. I just need to check you to make sure you are okay." He said this in a winded voice as Dee Dee put up one hell of a fight.

Mama took over the job of holding my legs apart while he inserted the speculum.

"I hate you! That hurts! I'm going to get you for doing this to me. You just wait and see."

Mama gritted her teeth and said, "As soon as the exam is over, I'm going to whip you with a belt in front of the doctor."

Dee Dee didn't give a shit. She had been mad as hell and flailed her arms in an attempt to hit Mama and knock her away from holding her legs. In the meantime, the doctor took a swab and put it on a slide for a microscope. Dee Dee knew she had nothing to lose, so when Mama let go of my legs, she kicked the slide out of the doctor's hand. It landed with a clink on the tile floor.

Mama yanked me off the table and borrowed the doctor's belt. She whipped me naked in front of him. Normally, I would have screamed and been scared to death, but Dee Dee had glared with hatred in her eyes and refused to shed a tear. Mama kept hitting me over and over. I guess she had been trying to get Dee Dee to cry, to no avail.

"Can you use the slide?" Mama asked. "Or do we have to go through this again?"

"Luckily, it fell specimen side up. You can do whatever you wish, just get her out of my office and never come back. I'll call you and give you the results."

By the time I'd gotten dressed, I was crying because Dee Dee had withdrawn back inside of me. Lucky for me, I didn't remember any of it. After the doctor had asked me to slide down to the end of the table, my memory had gone blank, and Dee Dee had taken over. I didn't know what had happened, I just knew I was glad it was over.

14

Remembering that now made me want to pour myself a glass of tea, which always soothed me. I walked by the nice computer I now owned thanks to Dee Dee. Its clock said six thirty. The time was going by far too slowly. These memories had haunted me for years, but seeing them through my adult eyes helped me come to terms with them.

I had no childhood memories of my mother making cookies with me or being a homeroom mother at school. I do remember her locking me out of my house for hours when she took her nap. I remembered feeling alone, unloved, and as if I were a bad person. I'd go to my friends' houses and watch their mothers interact with them in such a loving way. I had to be the worst human being on the face of the Earth to have a mother who had turned against me.

My friends, Lisa Smith and Jenny Mackie, had mothers who loved me more than my own mother did. I was so jealous of both of them for having their wonderful mothers. Both of these mothers encouraged me to draw because they were amazed at my artistic ability. At age three, I could draw a horse even though I couldn't print my own name. My parents never put one piece of art on their refrigerator or framed any of my work, even when I was in college or art school doing some very nice pieces. They never praised me for this talent or acted proud of me. To this day, when I remember my childhood—what little I haven't suppressed—I get a slumping feeling inside me.

One Christmas Eve had been especially bad. When I was sleepy and tired, I began whining to go home so Santa Claus could come. Instead of Christmas being for my sister Margaret and me, my parents drank, socialized, and ignored us. My whining had incited a whipping in front of another set of friends, this time with a belt. My childhood was empty.

That flash memory still haunted me. I never did remember what had actually happened. I recalled how defective I'd felt whenever that flash would enter my conscious mind, and I could remember wanting to mutilate my own genitals because they were at the root of all that angst. Those feelings later turned into depraved sexual fantasies. In them, men always used me, abused me and exposed me in a demeaning way. Despite the demented nature of my fantasies, they ended up getting me off. I knew it was crazy and felt contaminated. Still, I was unable to have an orgasm without them—except with Joe, my lover and later my second husband.

I think my desperate need for love was part of the reason I'd married my first husband, William, after he was in a wheelchair. Because of my empty childhood, I was starved for love. After Vietnam, I'd been afraid of losing him. William Peterson had been my puppy love. Even with that, life had thrown me down that mountain because, in the end, he'd given me up—at least that was how I felt. Not even a man in a wheelchair could love me. Then Joe Thames had come along and filled me up. Eventually, he too had switched his heart and left me stranded in an emotional hell.

My heart sped up at these memories. After nearly twenty years of marriage, Joe had decided he didn't love me anymore. He'd secretly posted on Match.com that he was divorced and looking for someone to date in a serious relationship. When I caught him cheating in 1998, I'd fallen for his insincere tears, yet he'd plotted more cheating as he waited for our daughter to go to college in 2002. Although we renewed our vows in 1999, he broke the second set with a friend of mine. I never meant anything to him. It was all just a game. Well, all good games have a winner and a loser. Joe might be ahead now, but I'd soon have the victory when I killed him.

Chapter Three

Joe had been gone for four months, yet the scent of his Stetson cologne still lingered. I tried to remove all physical traces of him. There are some things that houses tend to hold inside that no amount of cleaning, throwing away, or dog cussing could erase. We'd shared this place since 1992 and our bed since 1982.

Our broken dreams permeated the walls, our muffled laughter echoed off the now half-empty rooms where we'd been civil and divided things up between us. Our particular soft scents found refuge in the cracks and crevices of the oak floors and rough-paneled walls. I was keenly aware of the contrast between the rough walls and the smooth metal of the gun in my drawer as a metaphor for my life.

Our bedroom insisted on remaining dismal, no matter how many lamps I turned on. Even the overhead light couldn't quell the depressing nature of the room. The umber-colored oak floors beneath the dark wall paneling produced a dreary atmosphere. My nose constantly dripped because the cottage cheese ceiling sifted a steady supply of white powder onto everything. No matter how often I vacuumed or dusted, within five minutes I could sign my name to my clean-up job. Even the furniture's dark mahogany color added to the gloom.

The room reflected my mood perfectly. Individual planks slapped down over a few cross pieces on top of a slab moaned with each step. The refrigerator or air conditioner kicked on at odd times, and the floors fussed whenever they were disturbed, be it a person, a temperature change or other stranger reasons. In fact, we had been convinced we had a ghost living in our house.

I glanced at Jolly's senior portrait on the dresser. I needed something to do to keep my mind occupied, otherwise I might chicken out of what I had to do. Pride for my daughter filled my heart. Her real name was a combination of our names—Jo Lee, a good Southern tradition of giving her a double name. However, I'd broken that tradition after my amniocentesis had shown I was carrying a baby girl. I decided to call her Jolly, because I knew she would make me happy.

I studied myself in the portrait's subtle reflection and assessed how normal I appeared. Although my image was smoky in the reflection against her portrait's dark background, I knew what stared back at me. The same hurricane-colored eyes, short dark brown wash-and-wear hair, thin lips set in a beginning dewlap of wrinkles. At fifty-four, I didn't look my age, although wrinkles did give me away to some degree. I didn't have any gray hair. Okay, that was a lie. I did have a few sprigs around my right temple. Never fat, I'd recently dropped too much weight—twenty pounds in two months. There's nothing like the "infidelity diet" to slice those extra pounds right off. Although I looked exceedingly thin, it wasn't so bad. I could wear my teenage daughter's sexy clothes. However, my butt cheeks flattened the same as two deflated balloons, and my boobs had disappeared.

Just six months earlier, a professional photographer had posed me nude, spending five hours taking shots of me at various angles with a slow processing digital camera. Being an artist myself who specialized in doing nudes, I'd had no qualms about undressing in front of him. In fact, I'd considered it an honor that he wanted to photograph my imperfect fifty-three-year-old body—no waist, small hips, and even smaller breasts. Having worked out daily on a Bowflex, things had been firm that fall. He'd appreciated the beauty of my boyish figure, like Phillip Pearlstein's nude paintings of ordinary people. To be honest, posing in the nude had been the hardest, most tiring thing I'd ever done. I held a twisting torso for seven takes and stood perfectly still while he checked the shot, demanding too much from my muscles. I'd sweated for five hours doing isometrics.

Normally, my weight went up and down according to my medications. Some of the meds tended to plump me up, while others tended to thin me down. It didn't take a genius to imagine which ones I liked the best. Although my eyes still sparkled with mischief most of the time, the rest of my face currently displayed the residual tense look of not forgiving my husband. Tonight, my eyes had a mechanical look to them. This assessment made me realize I'd aged more in the past six months than I had in the previous ten years.

Jolly's portrait beckoned me back to study it once more. God, I was lucky to have her for a daughter. That thought calmed me. Thinking about her always made me smile with gratitude. It would help keep me sane as I waited to get the job done.

I glanced back at her portrait, realizing how Joe and I had marked her genetically. There she was in the portrait in her all black gothic garb—lipstick, nails, and clothes—a pagan and a beautiful girl. By looking at her, no one would guess she was a card-carrying Republican. She had more conservative values than her dad or me. Unlike most teenagers, she'd never rebelled against us. Jolly was unique.

During her sophomore year in college, she had joined the Air Force

ROTC. She'd had an uber-liberal English Lit professor who had given her a C for the class, even though she had made A's on all her papers and tests, because she had to wear her fatigues to his class whenever her ROTC class met on a Thursday afternoon. She'd reported him to the dean, but he'd high-tailed it out of Alabama with her final exam in tow. That was when she had learned that life was not fair. She hadn't even bought the literature book for class, because she'd read all the original stories as primary sources. Her photographic memory was the reason she'd made all A's on the tests. Of course, I'd known how intelligent she was as a baby.

I remembered with a bittersweet smile the time she was only sixteen-months-old and had erased her first birthday party off the VHS tape. We'd had the old style camcorder that plugged into the VCR, carried around in a shoulder bag. The night before, I'd set the camera to video her putting an ABC puzzle together—saying the letters, recognizing them and placing them in their proper spot on the puzzle. She'd been only a baby, yet her mental age was four.

I should have checked before I started recording. The next morning, nothing looked out of place to let me know she had gone in and opened the cabinet door, turned on the VCR, hit the rewind button, turned it off, then closed the door. Most babies would have never backtracked their steps and would have left a tell-tale sign. Not Jolly! Without checking, I'd videoed for about thirty minutes. I had totally erased her first birthday party. I wanted to cry for the loss, yet there had been this great awakening in me as to how gifted she was to have pulled it off without leaving evidence behind that she knew how to work our VCR. That was back in the day of a blinking 12:00 spelling disaster, as all clocks had been very hard to reset. VCRs had personified the most difficult equipment back in 1984.

Thinking about that era when Joe, Jolly, and I had been so happy and in love almost mellowed me out. It softened me as I continued to think about how Joe and I were a formidable team as parents.

We had always encouraged Jolly never to cave in to peer pressure. We felt that was our strongest weapon in the war on drugs. It had worked too. There was one incident where she hadn't succumbed to peer pressure, yet living with us and our different lifestyle had cost her big time. I'd been sound asleep when the phone had awakened me after midnight.

"Mrs. Thames?"

"Yes, this is she."

"I'm Patricia Collins of the Alabama School for Gifted Children, and I'm calling to tell you that your daughter, Jo Lee Thames, has been—"

My mind supplied the words in a nanosecond: killed, raped, mugged, in a wreck. When the woman on the phone said arrested, I screamed, "Thank God!"

I laughed out loud thinking about how that must have sounded to the lady who'd called me. Then I remembered the bad aftereffects of what had transpired that night of the call.

Jolly had been fifteen and attending the school for gifted children in Mobile. Mardi Gras parades had been going on at the time, and Jolly had gone to one with her friends. She'd been wearing a see-through blouse and her strapless bathing suit top, along with hip-hugging leather pants and a multitude of beads hung around her neck, thrown by the people on the floats. While Jolly was sitting on the shoulders of her boyfriend, one of her friends reached up and unfastened her bathing suit top, pulled it off and ran away with it. Since Jolly had a conglomeration of beads hanging around her neck, nothing had really showed.

When the last float approached her, a flamboyant young man on board fingered the signal for her to flash him for his armful of beads. Normally, she was very modest, but she was also as uninhibited as me. We both swam nude in our pool back home. It was a night parade, the lighting was poor, and the beads acted as an ox yoke around her neck. She quickly lifted her see-through blouse and flashed her perfect Victoria's Secrets sized breasts. The next thing she knew, a SWAT team surrounded her and made her kneel down as they handcuffed her. SWAT, used for crowd control during the parades, came charging in because she was with a group of students. Without protest or resistance, they carried her off to the Mobile County Juvenile Center.

I'll never forget that night as long as I live. I knew my child and knew the incident was totally out of character for her. I took her to Dr. Hopkins, who administered the MMPI that proved Jolly had been manic that night. I felt all kinds of guilt for the trouble she'd gotten into with the school because of her genetics.

When I got the phone call, the school had already picked her up from the Juvenile Center and called us to come and get her, since they'd suspended her for the next three days. Missing three days of classes at that school and falling behind was the equivalent to missing two weeks at any other school. It wasn't good. What made it worse was that she'd have to go before the school disciplinary committee and face expulsion. She relayed all this to Joe and me on the ride back home from the school, a six-hour round trip.

Three days later, when I returned Jolly to her classes, I decided to meet with the head of discipline. He welcomed me into a spacious office filled with vintage photos.

"Mr. Moore," I said, "I am not one who thinks my kid can do no wrong. I realize Jo Lee made a huge mistake. I am begging for mercy, as I have contributed to this situation because I am an artist who specializes in nudes. We just don't make a big deal about nudity in our house. Jolly . . . er, Jo Lee and I swim nude all the time."

He fixed me with a gaze that seemed to have lust in his eyes as he imagined the two of us naked.

"Besides," I went on, "I had her looked at by my doctor, and she is now medicated for being manic."

"Don't worry about it," he said. "My wife and I have the same European outlook on nudity. However, since she was taken to the Juvenile Center, it causes considerable problems for our school's reputation."

I nervously licked my lipstick off as he said that last sentence.

"I'm not asking you not to punish her," I said, "and I will back up one hundred percent anything the school hands out to her if you will please remove expulsion as an option. We also punished her the three days she was home with us. I've explained to her that not everyone is as cavalier about nudity as we are, and there's a time and a place where it is and is not acceptable. Please keep this in mind when you hand down her punishment."

On the way home that Thursday, I turned on the radio to WRAB for some soft rock. Instead, I heard a Mardi Gras update that said the police had arrested a juvenile for indecent exposure the previous Monday, but the rest of the week had been calm. God, if I'd left five minutes later, I never would have heard it. What an embarrassment to realize they were talking about my child! The disciplinary board planned to meet the next day on Friday. I did a lot of praying in the meantime.

They banished her to her room for the rest of the semester instead of expelling her. For nearly three months, she could not leave campus or her bedroom except to go to class or to the cafeteria. That was a harsh sentence, but both Jolly and I accepted it. Nearly finished with her sophomore year in a school that didn't use Carnegie units, she would've had to repeat the tenth grade if they had expelled her.

She couldn't even leave to go buy personal items, so I was required to drive the three-hour trip and stock her up once a week. At least the school allowed me to visit her in her room. We accepted this over expulsion graciously. One time in March, the basement of the girl's dorm flooded, and Jolly was down there working very hard to clean up and get the water out. Mr. Moore was so impressed with her willingness to help the school while on punishment that he changed her restrictions to allow her one day a week when she could leave campus before five o'clock and stock up on her personal items.

Realizing that Joe and I were no longer a team enraged me again, yet pride in my daughter brought me back into the present as I continued looking at her portrait. Very thin, with long chestnut hair the color of her daddy's instead of my brunette, she reeked self-confidence in spite of us. It made me feel at peace that our mess hadn't screwed up her self-esteem. Jolly's face, narrow with a square jaw and high cheekbones similar to mine, seldom erupted into the rages and fits that I had. We both fixed people with our unblinking stares that blasted them into oblivion. Joe never looked anyone in the eye except during sex, which he often started days before he consummated the act.

Joe's cheekbones were cliffs casting bronze triangular shadows under his eyes, while Jolly's and mine sloped gently toward our noses. I thanked God that Joe's huge, wide nose hadn't planted itself on Jolly's face. We were throwbacks to our Native American ancestors. She didn't have Joe's big round head, but he had stamped her with his high forehead. My forehead was almost Neanderthal. I'd always prayed there wasn't a correlation between small foreheads and lack of intelligence.

Jolly had attended a high school for gifted children and had gotten her smart nature from my daddy, who was in MENSA. Similar to me, Jolly had a love for deep conversation and studying things in depth. Joe hated debates or, as he called it, arguing. I can remember my mama saying the exact same thing to my dad. Jolly had inherited Joe's Germanic coloring and his laid-back, pragmatic approach to life.

Joe was a loner and didn't have friends. Jolly tended to be the same, one reason her punishment had not been as bad for her as it would have been for typical teenagers. Now living in an apartment while attending the University of South Alabama, Jolly had already rescued a python and a coyote pup and managed to gentle them both down. Her love for animals and her willingness to stand up for what was right were things I knew she'd learned from me. Joe was a pushover who always ate the food cooked wrong or an order mixed up at a restaurant rather than sending it back as Jolly and I would do.

I was too sick to understand the consequences of killing Jolly's dad. I was aware of how trying to kill myself affected her. Killing him hadn't registered because my boardroom of right decisions had recessed.

I shook off thoughts of my daughter and moved to the computer in my den. It dawned on me that, with my preoccupation of doing Joe in, I hadn't checked my e-mail. Paranoid that Joe would somehow get into my computer and find out how often I hacked into his, I had both a BIOS password and a Windows password. Jolly knew both of them.

It took a few minutes for all my programs to load. Since I was having an episode, it seemed to take fifty-five forevers. Soon I became engrossed in reading the e-mail messages. There was the usual assortment of forwarded jokes, which I immediately deleted. I wasn't in the mood. There was a message from Jolly asking me to call her as soon as I got in. Since we had already talked, I deleted it. Her e-mail is under her given name and not her nickname. I almost mistakenly deleted a message from Joe.

What could that bastard want? We barely spoke anymore. Had Dr Hopkins called to tell him the good news about my wanting to kill him? I was tempted to delete it without reading it; my curiosity won. What a surprise to find that he was talking to another woman!

Dolly,

Right now, I know that maby this is the only type relationship that you and I can have. To much has happened between us. It will never be what it once was. But I do feel if we work at it, we can straighten things out between us. All I can do is continue to tell you what you mean to me and how much I love you. If you'll give me a chance, I'll try my best to prove to you that if you come up here to live with me, I'll do all in my power to take care of you and show you how much I love you.

I felt my usual embarrassment for Joe when he misspelled the word maybe and misused the word to for too. Since I had often hacked into his e-mail and read their correspondence, I knew Dolly was a college professor. I wondered if she, like me, cringed each time he wrote her. The funny thing was that in our twenty-plus years, I had never once corrected Joe. Jolly and I would laugh at his letters behind his back.

I know you aren't the kind of woman that expects much out of a man. You are a good woman, Dolly. I also know there isn't anything I don't love about you. All I ask is you give me a chance to prove it to you.

I love you,

Joe

Those words killed me. I wanted to get up and take every pill in my kitchen cabinet. I pushed away from the computer and went into the kitchen. I opened the cabinet door and started with my anti-convulsive meds, guaranteed to cause a massive convulsion that would take me out. Then I remembered my promise to Jolly. Why give Joe the satisfaction of letting him know that something he did on purpose would cause me to kill myself so he'd be done with me?

I poured the pills back into the bottle and decided to channel the hurt into anger. What a sleazy bastard he was to send me another woman's mail. I knew for sure I was going to blow his fucking head off tonight. I needed to simmer down before I worked myself into a psychotic state. I poured myself a glass of tea and went back to the bedroom.

"Oh, well, Lee, old girl," I muttered, "your days of glory and bloom are gone. Do you walk around now like some used-up slut trying to look thirty, or do you bow out and age gracefully?"

This nasty habit of talking to myself as if to debate my own thoughts had always annoyed Joe—although he did it more often than I did. As I spoke, I felt the chill associated with Ray, our ghost who resided in this house. Yeah, that sounded crazy as hell for us to believe, yet he'd made himself known in ways that were unexplainable. Ray didn't resemble my childhood ghost stories.

That thought sent me spiraling back into my childhood—how lonely I'd been. My parents were more involved in building their business and climbing the social ladder than being concerned with me. All their photo albums showed them with their friends at various get-togethers or pictures of their material possessions. We'd always had the latest gadgets offered for the post-World War II up-and-coming families, thus I'd grown up in the early fifties with an electric washing machine, a dishwasher, a television, and air-conditioning.

In their albums, I was at best an out-of-focus figure in the background. I thought about all the maids and nurses I was closer to than my mama. One—Juanita—was the reason I ran away and hid anytime there was a highly charged emotional crisis.

Chapter Four

"Miz Leeeeeee, you better come back right now or I'm gonna switch you! Where you hiding this time? Child, you gonna be the death of me!"

Juanita puffed out the words as she shuffled along, dragging her feet because the heels were worn, causing her shoes to flop around like fish thrown up on a bank. She tried to find me before my mother got home from the beauty shop. I heard her long earrings tinkling like wind chimes. As she passed me, I smelled the garlic necklace she always wore to keep the evil spirits away. The garlic mingled with the smell of the fried chicken she had cooked, which clung to her white apron. As always, that smell alerted me to when she was sneaking around the corner of the house. The pungent odor of a strange concoction in her corncob pipe warned me too. It didn't smell like my neighbor's pipe when he smoked, nor did it smell similar to my parents' cigarettes.

My five-year-old brain couldn't comprehend Juanita's age. Because she was thin, she had the appearance of the dancing skeletons we'd all feared in 1952. Juanita wasn't bald-headed, although she looked that way. She had gray fuzz so fine you could see her scalp through it. Scary lights reflected on her prominent cheekbones, reminding me of the character who represented death coming for a soul. The large, smooth head and the large rounded cheekbones made me freeze in fear. I knew I was looking into the eyes of evil.

She wasn't affectionate with small kids, especially me, because I looked for trouble. I always found it too. As usual, she carried a switch in her gnarled hands. There was no way I was going to come out of hiding. To say I feared her was saying nothing at all.

I had a nighttime nurse named Thelma that I loved more than my mother. My mother stayed gone most of the time. If I dared to disturb her between one and three o'clock every day, she scolded and often whipped me. She never spent any time with me or showed me any affection. I was afraid of my mother when I was young and disliked her as I grew into my teens. She always threw my sister Margaret up in my face and tried her damnedest to change me into a clothes hound or beauty queen. Margaret didn't love me because I embarrassed her. But I knew Thelma loved me unconditionally.

Thelma was young, pretty, sweet, and kind. Both she and Juanita were as black as moon shadows, which was normal for nurses in the South in the fifties and early sixties. Mainly, though, Thelma played with me, held me, kissed me and sang songs to me. Whenever I saw Thelma, I'd run as fast as I could, jump into her arms, kiss her, and hug her. Then we'd sing our special song to each other. I never feared Thelma.

Juanita was completely different. When Juanita walked in, I'd start shaking because I never knew what she was going to do to me each day.

"Girl, I gonna tear you up," she said the day I hid from her. "Gonna switch you all the way to the door and then some more when you get inside. I gonna switch the meanness out of you. You know I will."

I hunkered down under the small shrubs at the corner of our house, even though I was afraid of the mossy corner where snakes and frogs often rested. I could smell my own fear mixed with the dank smell of this never-dried-out Black Belt soil. With my imagination, I smelled and heard a slithering snake or a hopping frog. As scared as I was of both those creatures, Juanita seemed to be the bigger threat.

I couldn't remember why I hid from her that particular day. I just remembered what she did to me when I came out of my hiding place after I'd gotten thirsty. Running away and hiding became my habit. It followed me into my adulthood. Whenever I felt overwhelmed by life, I'd run away, hide, and ignore anyone looking for me. I know I caused many people to fear for my safety when I disappeared. Sometimes I hid for a long time. As I aged, I perfected this coping mechanism. I began climbing trees, which put me out of sight quickly—giving the illusion that I had literally disintegrated.

Thinking about this led to thoughts of another incident when I was fifteen, back in the fall of 1964.

"If you don't stop that, I'm going to tell Mama and Daddy. You'll be grounded for the rest of your life."

I watched my sister's mouth move and gradually turned down the volume knob on my mental television, slowly making the words disappear. Her mouth continued to flap open and closed, giving it a Charlie Brown comic strip feel.

I sat there in the car never saying a word, like some defeated chunk of plasma. Margaret was a senior in high school, and I was just a skinny fifteen-year-old freshman. She apparently figured she had me put in my place, and I pretty much thought the same thing.

Although I stayed quiet, I'd gotten angrier and angrier. I felt my pulse increase and suddenly heard a voice telling me to jump out of the car. When I heard it, things looked as though they were happening in slow motion. I have since learned this was my mind thinking in high speed as my sensory input processed everything so easily, making life seem to crawl to a halt. The voice telling me to jump was strangely clear, so it felt as if I had no choice but to do as it said. Actually, it wasn't even a matter of listening and doing or choosing. It was simply a thought merging into an action that seemed controlled by a brain other than mine.

I looked over one last time and watched Margaret's red lips bounce up and down, and I noticed her clenched hands on the steering wheel. Lisa Smith, my best friend, sat shivering in the back seat. I knew she was just as afraid of Margaret as I was.

As I looked out the window, the gravel stopped blurring as I focused on the road and looked for a spot of sand rather than sharp gravel. I knew a place and, as we approached it, I put my hand on the door handle, ready for the right time. As I cast my gaze downward, surveying the roadbed, the trees seemed to be dancing ribbons in my upper peripheral vision. I could see the beautiful olive greens outlined in rust, and sometimes they had a spot or two of bright yellow and even red. My hands sweated in anticipation. Like an army private following a general into war with his gun clutched in his hands, I clutched my means of fighting my way out of this hell.

I was scared, but mostly I was mentally up. I wanted to get it done. Seeing the perfect spot, I pushed the door handle down with a ringing snap and thrust myself out of the car. I managed to land without hurting myself. I jumped to my feet and ran toward the woods. I remember hearing the screeching sound of the brakes along with the sand paper sound of the tires as they locked up on the gravel.

Margaret called out my name as Juanita had done long ago—driving me farther away. There she was—the favorite child, the beauty queen and cheerleader, popular in school—and I was the social dud. She loved people and loved being the star. I hated most of them and wanted to melt into the background. I thought about her perfectly coiffed blonde hair getting messed up when she tried to catch me. I imagined the incensed anger in her blue eyes turning to fear as she realized that she'd pushed me over the edge that morning, and maybe I would never come back. She knew I was crazy enough to do something that impulsive and stupid.

"Come on back now, Lee! Please don't do this. I promise to leave you alone. Don't make me have to tell Mama and Daddy that you jumped out of the car. It will be our secret, I promise you. Where the hell are you?"

Margaret hadn't been slow. Neither had she called me in a labored, out-of-breath voice the way Juanita called me. Margaret was wired and frantic. Juanita always moved slowly and yelled at me. Worse than that, she whipped me almost daily. I couldn't go to my mother about it, because she would have sided with Juanita and whipped me again.

At least Margaret didn't whip me, although she loved to threaten me. There was one time she had chased me with a long tuning screwdriver and hit me with it. It left a huge welt on me. Did she get in trouble? No! I did for provoking her. We were both much younger then. When we got into our teens, her threats to tell on me scared me enough.

While Margaret chased me, I let myself through a barbed wire fence and made straight for a thicket of hardwood trees. The pines were too straight and tall for me to climb. I wasn't that athletic or strong. Then I saw the perfect tree. I was afraid of heights and didn't relish the idea of climbing it, but the thrill of my escapade gave me the courage to climb a sycamore. Soon I heard Margaret and Lisa calling me. The tone of Margaret's voice was changed. Bargaining had failed, so she was using her usual tactics to control me now.

"You'd better come back right now! Mama and Daddy are going to whip your butt. Just wait 'til I go home and tell them what you've done."

Oh, Margaret tried to sound mean and in charge, but I heard the panic in her voice. For once, I had her squirming in fear. I think that little episode sealed my fate, because the outcome had been so wonderful. Oh, that doesn't mean I didn't pay for it, because I sure did. Mama whipped me, then Daddy, and then Mama whipped me again. My parents grounded me for a solid month from television, the phone, riding my horse, and of course from seeing all my friends or going on dates. That didn't matter though. As I sat up in that tree, laughing in my head because no one thought to look up, it was worth every bit of the punishment.

I released a huge amount of anxiety that day. I also experienced the sensuous taste of revenge, although it hadn't been my plan. That incident established my maximum meltdown coping mechanism. Whenever life chased me into a corner, I was fifteen again with an older sister who was letting me have it, and I would resort to my trump card and buy myself some temporary peace. The bad thing was that I always paid the price for it later.

I remembered how it had all started with Juanita. When I came out of hiding, she'd used a belt on me. Mama came home that day, and when she heard I'd run away, she whipped me with a belt too. You'd think that would have broken me of the habit. No, it made me more determined to hide and stay hidden and ignore any logical voices in my head.

The consequences of my behavior were terrible each time, but usually that moment of peace was worth everything I endured. The only consequence that stopped the hiding behavior was when I did it to Jolly in August of 1999. I sipped my tea as I remembered that horrible day when I had run away from her.

Hearing her scream in agony when I left had been the ultimate consequence. She'd been at Broughton's house, her boyfriend at the time. I was there to take her home after he left for work. We lived about forty-five miles from him. He didn't want her to go to the school for gifted children down in Mobile and had changed Jolly's mind about wanting to go there. He and I exchanged some harsh words over it that day.

"There's no way you can claim you love Jolly and be so damn selfish," I told him. "Love is letting go, not tightening the noose."

"I do too love her," he said. "I can't live without her. She don't want to go there no more."

Jolly sat this one out. I understood that she agreed with him but didn't want to attack me.

"Right now," I said, "you two depend on Joe and me to bring her to your house since your mom won't let you drive on the highway. You're a fool to oppose us."

"Well, call me a fool, but I love your daughter. She deserves to be happy and not forced into going off to school to live on her own. You must want to get rid of her."

"She was fine until you came along and brainwashed her."

"Listen," he said, "I'm running late for work. You need to care for her and let her stay home."

"You're being a first-class redneck asshole."

His attitude made me furious. That school was the opportunity of a lifetime for Jolly. Joe and I were so worried she'd throw her life away for her puppy love that would be over within a year. The tension from telling her boyfriend off had carried over to when I attempted to talk some sense into her about it after he left. Normally, Jolly listened to her daddy and me. This time she was blinded by love.

"Listen to me," I said. "Don't throw your life away for that boy. You two can still see each other. I'll come get you every weekend so you can visit him."

"I've changed my mind, Mom. I don't want to go to school down there anymore. I don't want to have to study. I'm having fun now for the first time in my life. Please don't make me go." She tossed her hair defiantly, brushing the long strands out of her eyes to glare at me.

"Jo Lee Thames, stop that. You're being silly. You've wanted to go to a math and science school since you were seven years old. You've set your compass on that goal for the past eight years. You worked hard to be asked to attend and even harder to be one of only thirty sophomores chosen out of three hundred applicants."

I pointed my finger at her, cocked like a gun and aimed it at her face.

"It's too big of an honor to toss away. Your daddy and I are going to make you go even if it boils down to hogtying you and literally dragging you there. You are going and that's final!"

"No, I'm not! You can't make me. Even if I go, I won't study. I'll flunk out and they'll send me home!"

"If you keep talking like that, we'll never let you see Broughton again. Do you understand me?"

When she started crying and screaming at me, I lost it. I jumped into my F-150 pickup and started it up. I rolled down the window, yelling above the engine's roar.

"Stop that! Stop it right now. If you don't stop, I'm going to leave you here and never come back. You can make a decision. Who is more important in your life now? Do you want to become a part of this small town life over here—this rural, country hick redneck life he lives? Is this what you want? You make up your mind, because I'm not putting up with your mess anymore. I'm tired of dealing with it."

"Go ahead and leave!" she yelled. "I love Broughton, and you can't do this to me."

That one statement triggered a rage in me.

"Oh, yeah? Watch me!"

That's when I took off.

When it sank in that I was really going, Jolly started screaming. That helped me get a grip on myself. I loved her more than anything could ever upset me. At least for a while, that held true. I would not do anything to hurt her—that is, until I tried to kill myself. I made at least eight attempts. I had to be out of my mind not to realize what each one did to her.

"Don't leave me, Mom. Come back. Don't do this to me!"

Oh, yeah. I was mad and in the middle of a meltdown. About a mile up the road, the picture of her crying and begging me not to go—imploring me to come back—almost knocked me out. I did black out for a second—the emotions were that intense. I turned around and drove back, wondering how I could have left my child screaming in agony.

"God, I'm so sorry, Angel," I said when I got to her. "I don't know what came over me. I'm ashamed of what I did to you. Please forgive me and know that I'll never do that to you again, under any circumstances. I promise."

Jolly looked pale, defeated and scared—rare for her. "It's okay, Mom," she said. "I understand. You've had a bad day today. I know you were upset. You came back, that's the main thing."

"Thank you for forgiving me."

As I relived the story in the present, I understood she had been trying to be strong to protect me. Her face, drawn and tired, betrayed her noble words. She came through for me that day as she did in too many other cases. Recently, if it hadn't been for her, I'd literally be dead. Guilt gnawed at my soul, at least for Jolly's sake. I would never understand why God had blessed me with such a sweet and understanding child.

Whenever I ran away, Joe would worry and be upset. His calm demeanor kept it from registering with me how much it hurt. If he'd screamed or even cried, maybe I would have stopped doing it to him. Poor Jolly's guttural wail was the one thing I couldn't bear, and it had brought me back to an abrupt reality in which there was no longer a peace dividend for running out on intense emotions.

That day, I created a boundary that I'd never cross again. Somehow, in my uncontrollable mind, I developed a routing of that action to the boardroom up in my head where a vote took place and everyone voted against the voices telling me to go and do it. See, that had been my biggest problem in my life. Part of the time, I didn't have a boardroom. I didn't have a means to think of my actions in a cause and effect way. Sometimes I scared myself to death. Thank God, Jolly wasn't that way.

The present murder in my heart made me restless, walking from room to room. I walked through our den, noticing the primary colors of Jolly's ribbons hanging in the corner, won by showing first her Lipizzaner cross pony, then later her Lipizzaner cross horse. In 1984, I'd sold most of my purebred Lipizzan horses to pay off the twenty-thousand-dollar debt Joe had accumulated with his ex-wife, Regina. I'd given up my life's dream—my farm, Flying Horse Farm—for Joe. In 1992, to pay the down payment on our farm in Senora, I'd sold my very rare, bay-colored Lipizzan to make the dream of owning a farm possible. That was why Jolly rode Lipizzan crosses rather than the purebreds.

Jolly was the type of child who understood cause and effect at an early age, her chronological age and her mental age years apart. Rarely had I needed to spank her, and Joe never did. I was the disciplinarian of the family. My schoolteacher training made me authoritative rather than authoritarian. Joe was too soft. Jolly had him each time she did The Pout. He'd mimic her with his big protruding lips, breaking her into laughter. That had always ended Jolly's temper fits as a young child. Joe did look funny when he did it, since he could stick out his bottom lip nearly half an inch.

I remembered one time that hadn't worked—at a horse show.

Jolly had put me to the test while I registered her for the classes to show her black pony named Onyx. She kept up a barrage of annoying questions while I tried to concentrate on filling out the various forms. Asking then telling her to stop had no effect on her actions. I quietly excused myself, left my checkbook on the table with the paperwork, took her behind a building and spanked her, saving her the humiliation of being disciplined in front of her friends. I'd sworn a long time ago that I'd never do that to her.

I glanced up at our mantel in the den. To the right of a painting I'd done of a mountain scene was a tin hen that looked identical to our Miss Hen who'd raised many baby chicks for us. I remembered when we'd almost lost her because of a lie Jolly told me when she was eight.

"Jolly, I have to go to the store. I'll be back in a few minutes. I need you to water the chickens for me."

"Yes ma'am."

The temperature was over one hundred degrees that day, and the chickens were going through their water like tornadoes cutting through the Midwest. I left the house confident that they were in Jolly's capable hands.

When I returned home nearly an hour later, waylaid by a friend in the grocery store, I decided to check on the horses' water and fill up their trough. I had to pass by the chicken coop to get to the horse trough and was shocked to see the chickens didn't have a drop of water in all three of their water containers.

I could tell the chickens were in distress, and tears scratched behind my eyes as I watered them. I wanted to continue my innocent belief in Jolly's veracity, but I knew, as a parent, it was my duty to find out the truth.

"Jolly, come in the den for a minute. I need to talk to you."

"Yes ma'am." She walked in clutching her toy Bryers horse decked out in a blanket and shipping boots. She played with her horses in the toy wooden barn the way most girls played with dolls in a dollhouse.

"Jolly, did you water the chickens like I asked you to?"

"Yes ma'am."

"Are you sure? I checked on them, and there was no water in the coop."

"I don't know what happened. I watered them." Her eyes met mine in a guiltless stare.

She's lying to me. Is she going to turn out like her dad—look me straight in my eyes and lie without a conscience? I felt the blood rushing to my head as anger tried to control me. I had to remind myself she was only eight and more than likely didn't realize what she was doing. I knew I needed to remain calm.

"Tell me the truth, Jolly. I don't think you did. I think maybe you forgot because you were playing with your toy horses." I'd placed my hands on my hips and said this in a voice growing ever louder. My tone was not gentle anymore.

"Mommy, I'm sorry. I did forget. I'll go do it now."

At least she had admitted to the lie. Her dad never would. He'd lied more and more until he wouldn't know the truth if it ran him down. Maybe there was hope for her and she'd merely tested me.

I knew I needed to calm down and stay in control, although it proved to be difficult. I refused to act the same as my mother who would have handled the situation very differently. I whispered a benediction for my mauled beliefs—trust clawed from within my soul.

"That's okay," I said. "I've already done it. I want you to know I'm disappointed in you. If someone had asked me to lie down in the street in front of an eighteen-wheeler with my life being protected by your telling the truth all of the time, I would have done it in an instant. I believed you and believed in you. Now you've broken my trust." I sat down on the couch, and a tear slid down my cheek.

"Mommy, I'm so sorry. I didn't mean to tell a story."

There she goes again with another lie. Jolly knows not to make it worse by lying again.

I paced around the room, unable to speak for a moment. I wanted to slap her at this point, instead I counted backward from ten, nice and slow.

In a voice that squeaked with anger, I said, "That's where you're wrong. You did mean to tell me a story. That's another cover-up. You've really hurt my feelings and made me angry. I'm too upset to whip you right now. I'm afraid I might hurt you. Go to your room and get out of my sight for now."

"Mommy, please forgive me." Jolly's eyes were wide with fear. She knew she'd pushed my button. Then tears quickly filled her eyes.

"I forgive you, but you had something precious from me, Jolly—my trust. I still love you and always will."

By now, she was crying hard. Jolly was smart and realized what I'd said. I knew I didn't need to punish her. She understood the ramifications of what she'd done. To make sure that she did understand, I continued.

"I want you to think about what you've done, Jolly. If you didn't water the chickens, all you had to do was say so. Not only have you lost my trust, just think of the poor chickens had I not gone out there and found their water dishes dry. As hot as it is, they might have died. You have to be responsible, but more importantly, be honest about it if you're not. There is nothing you can do that will upset me enough that I won't appreciate your telling me the truth."

By now, she was bawling as she walked back to her room with her head down, ashamed of herself. I gave her a few minutes to stew in her thoughts, then I went to her bedroom. I knew our talk was punishment enough.

"Listen, I'm not mad with you," I said. "I'm not happy about what you did. Jolly, it doesn't mean I don't love you. I know in time you will earn my trust again, and we'll have that special relationship we had before. You learned an important lesson today, and I have no doubt you will always think hard before telling another story."

Now, I was sitting on the very same couch where I'd hurt my child to the core with such harsh words. Looking back at the incident now, a whipping might have been kinder.

I continued to look around the den and noticed the brass Buddha incense burner on the round end table next to the plaid platform rocker. The chair had been used to rock my sister then me, then my sister's two children, and, last, Jolly to sleep. Upholstered only once in its forty-year lifespan, it was threadbare and worn out. It rocked crookedly because of a broken spring.

The phone rang and made me jerk. Who would be calling me other than Jolly?

"Hello."

My neighbor Jessica said, "I'm really worried about you having the gun, Lee. Let me speak to your sister and make sure she's put it up. I'm getting a bad feeling about giving that gun back to you."

Of course, my sister wasn't there. I'd lied so Jessica would give me back my gun. I knew I had to stall her while I came up with an answer. My pulse quickened. This I hadn't planned.

"She's not in here with me right now," I said. "I think I heard the shower running earlier. Let me see if she can come to the phone. I'll be right back."

I put down the phone and purposely walked toward the bathroom and

33

into the guest bedroom to make sure the time frame would be accurate. I returned to the phone left on the table in the den. I cleared my throat and grabbed my neck. That damn tickling was driving me nuts! I picked up the phone and, in my most sincere voice, spoke to Jessica again.

"She's already gone to bed. She never has been one to stay up past seven, and she was tired after the long drive from Meridian." I monitored my voice to slow down as my lying heart sped up. "Crossing the entire state of Alabama is exhausting, you know. I'll get her to call you first thing tomorrow morning."

"Well . . ."

"Hey, thanks for caring, girl," I added quickly. "Everything is under control. I've taken my sleeping medication, and I'm fixing to head to bed myself. Margaret and I visited after I got back from the doctor, and all that talk tuckered me out. I'm not used to having anyone in the house with me now." I hoped I sounded convincing.

"Lee, promise me you won't do anything to harm yourself."

"I swear on Jolly's life that I am not going to use the gun on myself. So relax."

It satisfied her even though it was only a half-truth. I'd never mentioned anything to her about wanting to kill Joe. I assumed that's why she never thought of such a thing.

"Okay, remember to have your sister call me in the morning. I want to talk to her about the stained glass window in her bathroom. The Phillips commissioned me to do one, and I need to ask her about its size. Why don't the two of you plan on coming over for coffee tomorrow?"

"Sure, that sounds great. We'll see you then."

By the time tomorrow arrived, she would learn the truth. I hoped the fact that I'd lied to her would assuage some of her guilt. I hated doing it to her, but I hated Joe more.

"I'll make some of my homemade bread you like," she said. "See you around eight o'clock. Night, Lee."

The exchange shook me up because I truly hated lying. I decided to burn some incense to calm down. The taupe-colored stick matted with dust and animal hair begged lighting. I took out my Bic lighter, and the scent of sandalwood soon filled the room, reminding me of William, my first husband. That same incense burner had decorated our table back in the early eighties.

As I headed to the kitchen for another glass of tea, I heard the clock above the mantel with its rhythmic clicking as the secondhand trekked around the clock's face. It was an older clock with a pendulum, the time kept in ebony Roman numerals against a brass face. Hearing that clock chime was one of the rare pleasant memories from my childhood.

Tea in hand, I went back into the living room to sit in my recliner, wound up thinking about Joe coming home to my surprise. I looked over at the bookcase in the living room that held the many journals I had sporadically written in, including one I'd had since I was fifteen. It covered my life through college and both my marriages. To kill some time, I walked over, pulled it off the shelf and started reading one of my entries, a short story written when I was fifteen. Even then, I'd loved to write. I turned the pages and remembered when I'd literally almost gotten myself killed by my own father.

Chapter Five

God, I was an awful writer at age fifteen. I didn't do the simple "Dear Diary" the way all my friends would have done. I had written a story about the event.

I chuckled to myself as I remembered the tale of wildly sneaking out of my house to send a love letter to the drummer in a rock band, complete with sculpting my bed to look as if my friend Lisa and I were asleep in it. I turned to the page in my old journal and read about the incident.

> *I stuffed the arm of my pajama top with socks while Lisa rolled my long brunette fall with huge pink foam curlers. With the cunning of a thief, I pulled the arm out of the cover and bent its elbow to look like my hand was under the rolled up fall. It appeared as if my arm were under my head.*
>
> *"Hey, Lisa, look under the bed and hand me my slip, bra, and panties. Ball up my skirt too. I need to make it look like your body under the cover."*
>
> *"Lee Snowden, don't you make my butt too big!"*
>
> *"Oh, you always worry about your hiney. I wish I had one. I look like a boy. At least you have some curves. That's why boys asked you to dance tonight and didn't ask me."*
>
> *"Well, you danced, didn't you?"*
>
> *"Yeah, but only because I went up, grabbed them and drug them out on the floor."*

God, remembering how brassy I had been made me flush with embarrassment. I was loud, clumsy, and ugly as shit back then. I continued to read

> *"I shook my booty in front of Bobby. God, he was so cute!"*
> *"I adored the lead singer."*
> *"Bobby's shoulder length blond hair is such a turn on, and did*

you see those blue eyes? I swear they are the sexiest I've ever seen. I think I've found my true love."

"Lee, honey, he didn't notice you. Not with Stephanie shaking her Barbie doll figure in front of him."

"I thought I was going to drop my panties when he looked up from his drums while playing 'Wipe Out.'"

"You fool, he wasn't looking at your skinny little tail."

I closed the book and replayed the rest of the story in my mind. Lisa had a point about my skinny tail, because my measurements had been 31-28-30 back then. With baby fat around my waist, I stuffed my bra with Kleenex to have any bust at all. Coupled with zero butt, I was no Playboy Bunny for sure at five-four with probably half my height in the length of my skinny Olive Oyl legs. My upper half and bottom half didn't match. I was short-coupled and looked like a midget walking on stilts.

However, our bodies in my bed made from dirty clothes had perfect, rounded-out little bottoms. Being an artist, I sculpted our feet by stuffing the terrycloth bedroom shoes into upside-down heels sticking up near the foot of the bed. I had filled Lisa's sleeping cap with some of my ruined nylons to look as if the back of her head snuggled in a pillow. It was a perfect ruse. I pulled up the rest of the covers, inspected our little "happening art," and pronounced us ready for our adventure.

Earlier that night, we'd attended a dance at the local country club, and I fell madly in love with the drummer in the band. The sight of his long Beatle-shaggy hair in my crew-cut small town had flipped my fifteen-year-old crazy switch for sure. There were two things that made me go into heat, even before I knew anything about sex: long hair and a drummer.

That fateful night began my fall—when my brain's boardroom recessed for the first time. I lived only half a block from the country club, so at eleven o'clock, with lust in my groin and love in my heart, Lisa and I walked home to make my curfew. As if I'd been doing uppers—something I didn't know anything about back then—I felt high from the thrill of getting out from under my parents' iron fists for the night. I stayed grounded most of the time because I displeased them on a regular basis, so whenever my parents allowed me a little freedom, I made full use of it, which usually cost me more freedom in the end.

Going to the dance had been Heaven, but seeing the love of my life, who didn't even know I existed, made me certifiably nutty for sure. As soon as Lisa and I walked through the door and let Mark and Laura know that we'd obeyed my curfew, I concocted my plan to escape again.

I got out my cutest stationery and wrote Bobby a long love letter. I knew his name—at least his first name—the name of his band, and the city. I hoped the letter might find its way to him. On the million-to-one chance that it could or would, I'd cooked up a scheme that I knew would end my dance-going privileges for the rest of my life if Mama or Daddy discovered I had sneaked out of the house. True love was worth any sacrifice. Besides, I was going to outfox everyone. I knew I could fool my parents into believing I was in bed should they decide to get up and check my room. I had that part covered. What could be more natural than finding us in our rollers and nighties? The plan was idiot-proof.

Mailing the letter was the hardest part. We'd sneak out of the house, go to the post office and mail the letter, then sneak back home. Since Margaret's boyfriend was there visiting her, and it was cold outside, the plan called for recruiting him into giving us a ride to and from the post office that was a good three miles away. I had been so busy coming up with professing my passion for my drummer that I stayed in my pajamas and didn't even put on a coat. Neither did Lisa. We hid in the living room and waited for Turner to leave.

"Why do I always let you talk me into your schemes?" Lisa whispered.

"Because you'd lead a boring life if you didn't."

We giggled when we realized how true that was. Lisa's home life was just too "Leave It to Beaver" perfect. The crack in the living room door provided just enough light to make our setting strange. My mom was very progressive. Instead of the typical Victorian furniture in most southern living rooms, ours featured a dark green couch with tangerine carpet and pale orange walls. Two futuristic rocking chairs and a modernistic, low-slung walnut coffee table topped with plastic color-coordinated decoupage fruits and vegetables balancing each other on a set of scales ordered from Southern Living complemented the color scheme.

The oddest things in the room were the lamps made by my mother's brother—bamboo slices glued together to form a lantern effect on a wooden base, each with an orange light inside. Hand-carved musical instruments jutted out as contemporary sculptures from the room divider, set off with a fake orange tree. Everything had been very modern and avant-garde in its day. Every living room in our town looked identical, except ours. Orange and olive green, modern and monolithic, wild and abstract instead of claw feet, lace, and wingback chairs made me proud. However, that night all of its oddity stared back at me, as if to warn me that my own breaking with tradition was going to cost me in some horrible way.

We managed to catch Turner leaving and caught a ride to the post office. He thought it was cute and even brought us back home. Operation 007 was working great until we tried coming back through the living room door. Someone had locked it. Maybe I'd done it from habit when we left, as I had been instructed to do a zillion times. I also knew Margaret would have locked the kitchen door when Turner left. Sure enough, we were stuck outside. Most kids could have gone to their older sibling and asked to be let in, but not me. I think Margaret hated me. I don't know why she did. I knew better than to involve her.

The temperature dropped into the twenties and started to get really cold. Our pajamas weren't nearly enough protection against the sub-freezing temperature. We climbed into Mama's Impala, thinking that would do the trick. God, what an ugly car! It was the color of an avocado, with a long hood and huge trunk. It was a big ol' awkward box with tiny square taillights. Oh, it had all the works even though it looked like a little old lady's car.

Mama was only forty-one and didn't even look that old because she was trim. However, she acted as if she were a hundred. I hated her. Hers was the main car I'd practiced driving in and, unfortunately, she was my teacher. Unlike most fifteen-year-olds, I dreaded the lessons because my mama was such a bitch.

My dad was something else. When he took me out driving, we went in his special-order red Thunderbird. It was sleek, modern, sporty looking, and could go really fast. With every possible extra on it ever sold by Ford's special order division, it was a one-of-a-kind car. His radio boomed out quadraphonic sounds long before cars were equipped with such systems. Talk about listening to some music while driving! Sad to say, though, he kept the damn radio rigged so it only played on his radio station and not The Big Bam—the rock station out of Montgomery. I could push any button and old WLAX would come on with its soft and soothing music.

My sister drove the T-bird some, and she always left the radio on BAM and got into trouble, never the kind of trouble I'd get into with my parents. The worst she ever got was a lecture. They never grounded her. How could you ground a beauty queen, cheerleader, and member of all the social and civic clubs the high school offered?

I was an easy target because I was not a joiner. Mark and Laura forced me to go out for cheerleading, and I totally embarrassed myself. Later, they forced me into a beauty pageant where I nearly tripped walking down the steps. They wanted me to be the same as my sister, and I just couldn't live up to their expectations. I was the one main disappointment in their lives. Daddy at least gave me the benefit of doing things with me, such as riding horses or going out on the river together to spend the night on the houseboat. I adored him. I prayed it was reciprocal, but I never felt it was. He was my favorite parent, just as my sister was their favorite child.

I enjoyed my driving lessons with Daddy. He had more patience, and driving with him was fun. I hoped I'd get to take the T-bird out by myself when I was sixteen, lusting for the popularity I thought that car would bring me.

While Lisa and I shivered in my mother's ugly car, my thoughts of driving the T-bird someday were blasted by the cold I felt going up my spine. My teeth started chattering, and that caused Lisa to laugh at me. Skinny ol' me had no meat on my bones to keep me warm.

We giggled, laughed, and had a great time for about twenty minutes. The warmth in the car was relative to the cold outside. It felt warm compared to being out in the wind, yet it was probably freezing inside the car. We took turns pushing the cigarette lighter in and holding it to our fingertips or the tip of our noses for a millisecond of warm relief. We knew it was going to be a hell of a long night at this rate.

Then I spied our outdoor laundry room and remembered the clothes dryer. Praise God! What wonderful warmth. We raced from the car to the laundry room. It was a small one with the washer right across from it, crowded for two people to stand in it. I realized Edna, our maid, was large. This made me wonder if she had a tight fit whenever she did the laundry for us.

I turned on the machine, and the thump-thump of the drum turning was the sweetest sound in the world. I let it run a few minutes to get maximum heat in it. Then I opened the door so the wonderful heat would blast out and warm us up. Damn! It turned itself off whenever the door opened. We both tried to put our hands inside for the little heat left in it once the door opened and cold air replaced the warmer air rising to the top of the laundry room. Since it was outside and down three steps from the rest of the house, it had a high ceiling, so most of the heat escaped our use. After trying to warm up for about an hour, we gave up.

The car was warmer than the laundry room because we could sit next to each other and share our body heat to be halfway comfortable. This was back before cars had bucket seats, although Daddy's cool car had them, a new phenomenon at that time. We had gone back to using the cigarette lighter when I spied my Aunt Gigi's blue cracker-box Corvair parked over in the side yard. I'd forgotten we were keeping her car while she was visiting her daughter in California over the holidays.

"Yippee! Lisa, our troubles are over."

"What makes you so sure of that? Remind me to never believe anything you say or come up with again."

"Well, a Corvair cranks without a key. The switch juts out, and you can grab hold and turn it to start up the car. With the car running, we can use the heater."

I had sense enough to know that meant taking it for a spin rather than chancing anyone waking up to the constant hum of the car running. We got in and I cranked her up. That baby put out some heat immediately. I headed up the street toward the country club, figuring we could park up there. We'd let the car idle and warm us up. When my parents woke up, we'd knock on the door and act as if we'd just gone outside and gotten locked out of the house. Teens did stupid things like that all the time—especially me.

On the way up the hill to the street corner, I glanced in the rearview mirror and saw lights coming on at my house. First, my parents' bedroom light, then mine, then they went off and the outside lights came on, flooding the three lots that made up my parents' property.

"Holy cow, Lisa, we've been caught! What are we going to do? I'll be grounded until my senior year and never allowed to drive again. Should we make a run for it?"

"No, Lee, I've had enough getting in trouble with you. Take me back to your house. I want to call my parents to come and get me. You need to go 'fess up and get it over with."

She was right. The more I did, the more trouble I'd get into. Right now, sneaking out and taking my aunt's car for a spin around the Country Club wasn't a terrible offense, but joyriding in it would add to the crimes I'd committed that night. I was had. Time to go and face my maker, and I wasn't talking about God.

I turned the car around, and just as I pulled into the drive, my Daddy came out holding his shotgun. Talk about mad. Normally, he kept it loaded in his closet. As I drove by, he pointed the gun at me because as he saw it, the brazen car thief rode back by the house and was fair game. He fired and meant to kill. Lucky for me, the gun was empty.

I'd forgotten all about the little charade in my bedroom that made it look as if Lisa and I were safely tucked away and asleep. Since Dad believed we were in bed, he thought a crook was stealing my aunt's car. He started whipping me right there in front of Lisa. He was furious, but mainly he was upset that he'd come so close to shooting me.

Then my Mama came out and got into the action. Lisa's parents arrived shortly afterward because, once my mama realized it was us, she'd called them to come and get Lisa. We were restricted from seeing each other or talking on the phone, and, of course, my parents grounded me for an indefinite amount of time. Lisa's punishment: digging weeds in her mother's flowerbed out in the cold until the sun came up. Actually, of the two of us, her punishment was much harsher. I was so used to being grounded that it had zero effect on me. Staying out in the cold doing physical labor might have set me straight.

A ticking sound reminded me of a clock building up to the climax in an old B-movie thriller, except there was no ticking clock in my living room in Senora, Alabama. Neither my television nor my radio were playing. I was inside my bipolar head. The ticking was a combination of my heart along with my own memories building up to the climax of my life. My life had become unbearable, and the voices convinced me that tonight was the night to fix things, one way or another.

I closed my eyes and pondered my next action, trying to remember when Joe and I had been lovers. I looked around at the nearly empty house that had once been filled with so much happiness. Anger flushed my face as I remembered the day I had come home to tell him everything was going to be all right.

It was one thing for my husband to dupe me once and another thing for him to dupe me three times over the course of twenty years. In December 2002, Joe and I had separated temporarily in order to sort through some issues. I'd come home to visit him with the full intention of putting the past behind me because I thought I finally understood the role I had played in our marital problems. Three times my blind eyes had trusted him. That day, January 15, 2003, had been strike-three-I'm-out-of-there.

The day before, I found the love letter e-mail to another woman on his computer, and it had pushed me over the line—the one defining our marriage's ending or healing. Joe had promised he'd always cherish me, and because of my first marriage, his lie had enticed me into his trap. He'd devoured me much like a lure fish gobbled up the unsuspecting clownfish. That was me, a clown—a stupid, gullible, idealistic, trusting, madly in love idiot. Because Joe had been sweet and because I had wanted to believe him, he'd convinced me that he'd never hurt me. Each time, he'd thrown me off an emotional cliff.

While I waited to kill him, I remembered all the things I'd done in the name of loving Joe.

Chapter Six

Back in 1998, Joe had cheated on me. The fall of 2002, in an effort to keep him faithful, I'd sunk to swinging—"gifting" sex between friends, the swingers' lingo and code words for cooperators. Since the sex was out in the open, we were able to keep an eye on each other. Doing this had unleashed a monster: sexual addiction. It had also proven to be my biggest mistake. Swapping partners hadn't been good enough for Joe. Next, he wanted us to have an open marriage where we'd each go out and sleep around separately, just as my first husband and I had done twenty years earlier.

Joe constantly begged me about it. I finally admonished him that if he asked me to meet a guy one more time, I would leave him and make him sorry. I kept my word. Although a major player, he hadn't benefited from the mistakes that William Peterson and I had made. I warned him that if he cheated again, I'd make him pay—literally.

That January day in 2003 when I severed our matrimonial bonds, I cleaned out our checking account and two savings accounts. Fed up with Joe's manipulating me for sex by using his sweet and caring persona, I moved out permanently and had my lawyer draw up a legal separation. From day one, Joe had put the make on me. He'd realized how much I needed honesty and love and had used that against me.

As I drove quietly south to Mobile that day, the radio had played "Eye in the Sky," my courting song with Joe, and hearing it brought me to tears. I hadn't heard it played on the radio in a long time. It caught me off balance as it took me back to 1982 when Joe and I had been best friends, before we had become lovers.

I remembered sitting with him at our little gray table, taking a break from our jobs at the paper mill. Joe and I had loved to talk and share our dreams and goals back then. We had been candid with each other.

"You know, I think I killed a man." Joe said this as nonchalantly as one would mention leaving their car lights on. "I was part of a motorcycle gang while in the Navy, and we were involved in a shootout. One man died, and I never knew if it was my bullet or someone else's."

Lucky for me my mouth had been full of pimento cheese sandwich. I had been unable to say anything, which was good because, frankly, it had shocked me. When I didn't say anything, he continued.

"I'm pretty sure it was mine."

The sound of the paper mill hummed and rattled in the background. Our noses had long ago gotten used to the scent, so unappetizing smells didn't inhibit our appetites. Spider webs hung from the ceiling as sculptures from years of dust defining their shapes. Occasionally, some had feathered down on us while we ate or worked. The paper mill was not a place for the squeamish.

"There were at least six of us shooting at him," Joe said. "I was closest. I aimed and unloaded three bullets, all striking his chest. He died and we took off on our cycles."

This couldn't be the Joe I knew—the shy and serious, always-reading-a-book Joe. He'd been one of the few men at work who never made a pass at me and treated me as a team player. Very soft-spoken in his deep, southern drawl, he'd had a slight country twang to the pronunciation of some of his words, especially those with an "I" in them. How could that man, the one that was kind and considerate, ever have pulled a trigger?

"You didn't kill him," I said. "Don't worry about it."

"That's it—I'm not worried about it. Any guilt I feel is from the fact that I don't feel any at all. I'm a dog, aren't I?" Joe took a drag from his cigarette—his after-supper treat.

I could almost smell the cigarettes as I sat there remembering that revelation. I nodded my head, clearing the memory and the smell. Smoking used to be a big issue between Joe and me after we married.

Smoking was a habit I'd picked up from Joe. When I quit, I tried to get him to quit too. In fact, to be honest, I bullied Joe about his smoking, especially whenever I felt bossy. I became a control freak. In hiding his smoking from me and his parents, he literally inhaled them. When he smoked, about half of the cigarette burned bright red then paled into an inch-long gray ash. He'd finish a smoke in only three tokes. That was the deceptive Joe. Thinking about his deceit led me back to the Joe I had first met and how wrong I had been about him.

That Joe's personality had been so gentle that I couldn't imagine him in any kind of fight, much less a shootout definitely warped my perceptions of him. My mind focused on the fact that he had used a gun. My concern had been more for his safety rather than worrying about the poor soul they had killed.

I had really cared for Joe once, and he had appreciated my understanding everything he'd done in his life. He felt comfortable telling me the truth about himself. I appreciated his frankness. We could talk for hours about any-and-everything. In time, I learned it was far more complicated than I had imagined.

I paced through the house as I realized how my feelings could have changed so dramatically as I wandered back to 1982.

"No, you're not a dog," I said. "You are no worse than I am. You aren't feeling guilty because, deep down, you know you didn't kill anyone. Quit worrying."

My telling him to quit worrying brought me back into the present, because that was the only time I ever said that to him. Joe never worried about anything.

Something had attracted me to this image: a sweet man who obviously was a bad boy in reality. We were two of a kind. Neither of us were innocent people. We didn't judge each other for present or past mistakes, and that's what made us feel so incredibly close. It had been us against the rest of the uptight world. I'll never forget when I told him about my first husband and my open marriage.

"Joe, what would you say if I told you my husband allows me to date other men?"

"First, I'd say he was a fool. Next, I'd be first in line to date a woman like you. Damn, you are sexy. What's wrong with William that he'd do something like that?"

That memory brought a tear to my eyes. There had been a time when Joe did cherish me. William obviously never had. I started thinking about William—why I had ended up marrying a man in a wheelchair. Most women wouldn't have saddled themselves with the responsibilities I had, but I'd loved the man. He had grounded me. I was always a cloud dancer while he was practical. Besides, he was my first love.

A friendly fire bullet had clipped William Peterson in the Vietnam War back in 1970. It went through his neck, leaving him paralyzed. As impulsive teenagers, we had promised we'd marry as soon as he returned from 'Nam after William's birthday drew number three in the draft lottery, and we knew there was no way he was going to get out of the draft. Of course, we expected him to return home unchanged. When his mom received the news of his injury, it had never occurred to me not to marry him after he completed his rehabilitation. I had been loyal and kept my promises because, at age nineteen, I couldn't understand the consequences of marrying a paralyzed man. Although in a wheelchair, he had remained a complete person, something I felt I lacked.

William radiated such a positive can-do attitude that I often forgot he sat in a wheelchair. He was a dreamer, and I think that's what set him apart from other handicapped people. They viewed their life as limited, and he saw his as limitless. I'd often forget that his eye level wasn't the same as mine. I truly didn't think of him as being wheelchair bound.

I never really missed the so-called normal sex life. I loved him that much. Besides, we had oral sex. It wasn't as if he didn't satisfy me. Both happy and contented, our sex life proved to be everything I needed. However, in time, he had decided he needed to spice things up in our marriage for him to have sex mentally. He had also wanted to prove a theory he'd put forth in the book he was writing.

I'll never forget when I came in from work that spring day in March of 1981, tired and ready to relax. When William greeted me, his eyes kept darting past me.

"Would you enjoy having sex with some of those men you always talk about at the paper mill?" William cleared his throat.

Caught completely off guard, I didn't say anything at first.

"You say they're always hitting on you," he went on. "You've often spoken about times in the past when you turned down many men, including the boy who helped you with the horses."

I assumed it was a joke, except William wasn't the type who joked around. I noticed a pleading look in his eyes. I walked over to the cabinet, took out two cups, ran water into them and went over to our microwave to put on some instant coffee because he'd stashed the coffee pot into our sink, dirty. I was too tired to make fresh coffee, but we had always broached serious issues over a cup. Instant would have to suffice.

I remembered how I felt as I looked around at our crumbling dream. William had squandered the money for fixing up our horse farm on hiring an old man who charged by the hour rather than the job. Our house wasn't even half finished, and the farm didn't even have a barn. I'd had a dream of a horse farm since the age of seven. William's writing came above my dream.

We'd purchased an older Jim Walter Home and moved it to our sixteen-acre farm where we bred Lipizzaners, the white horses of the Spanish Riding School in Vienna, Austria. William had controlled all of our financial responsibilities. I merely brought home the paycheck.

Because William was a struggling writer, the character of the old man remodeling the place mattered more to William than keeping up with the cost. Still a great carpenter in his late seventies, old man. Adams out-worked men half his age. However, in an eight-hour day, he probably sat around for three hours or more, pouring stout-perked coffee from his beat-up thermos while talking with William, who kept a running log of everything the old man said.

The noticeable fact that the money we'd borrowed to remodel the place was gone had gnawed at my thoughts. The outside looked great, but the pinto-colored walls with green and white patches of plaster disgusted me. Each time I faced those walls, a queasy feeling churned in my stomach as I thought about all the money that went into a character study for my author-to-be husband while I sweated away in the one-hundred-plus-degree heat out at the paper mill.

"Remember the time Ronnie and you slept outside the barn waiting on Capriola to foal?" William said as he finally looked up into my eyes. "You came home and told me you were turned on."

William sat at our round oak table in the kitchen, an empty coffee cup in front of him. I knew he normally didn't come out of his office and sit at this table alone. He'd always waited for me to get home from work, then we'd share a cup and catch up on the day.

"What's going on?" I asked, a hint of anger rising in my voice.

"I've been thinking about that night between Ronnie and you. It inspired my latest book. I have a theory about married people. The fact that you were sexually attracted to him turned me on."

"Yeah, what about it? Nothing happened, remember?" Fear crept in when I figured he was trying to trick me into some sort of backdoor confession about something I hadn't even done.

"You said he reached across you in your sleep and started rubbing your stomach. You became turned on, but the two of you pretended that you slept through it."

The microwave dinged. I took out the two cups and made my coffee sissy style with Cremora and Sweet 'N' Low. I left his the hue of night. I smiled bitterly, thinking that something about the conversation reminded me of his dark coffee, even though I couldn't put my finger on it.

I heard a familiar scratch on the door and walked over to let our two Dobermans inside. I knelt down and petted them.

"How are my good dogs doing today?"

I talked to them as if they were my children. Both had answered with wagging nubs. I returned to our oak table and took a quick sip of my coffee, burning my tongue.

"Damn, I over-heated the coffee. Be careful, it's lethal."

Alice, the black-and-tan, walked up to William and gave his hand a lick, while Red sniffed out a cool spot under the table to catch a nap.

The day had been an unbearably hot spring day. The heat tormented all the animals that hadn't shed their winter coats. The familiar whine of the AC cranking up surprised me. Of course, our thermostat incurred the full brunt of the western sun in the evenings. William's curled hand glided over Alice's smooth slick coat. As soon as our AC kicked on, the now-familiar scent of cat urine filled our kitchen. Our retarded Siamese cat, Ming, had used the vent once, and I was never able to remove the smell. I lit the Buddha incense burner, our table's centerpiece. As a carryover from the sixties, it blasted our home with the scent of sandalwood.

"I know you have a normal sexual appetite," William said. "You always claimed that doing your art and finishing a painting gave you the satisfaction that other people experienced sexually. I appreciate your loyalty, but maybe it's time after all these years that you tried it."

Alice moved away, and William leaned over the table to reach for something. I glanced over to see him brushing leftover biscuit crumbs off the table for Red.

"I really do get off on my art," I said. "I'm as happy, satisfied and fulfilled as someone who screws all the time. Besides, I tried it with Donny right after I turned eighteen and found it so awful that I knew I didn't need sex. He used me and didn't even attempt to make it enjoyable for me."

I paused to catch my breath. I blew on my coffee to cool it, then I started in again.

"And I tried it again with Lisa's lover after Dr. Wilcox suggested we have an open marriage. Except for it being a threesome, it was worse than Donny. In fact, overall, normal sex left me wondering why everyone thought it was such a big deal. At least, that's how I think I feel. I don't want to find out if I'm wrong."

By that time, I was twirling my hair with my index finger.

"Right now, I'm happy with my life. I don't need sex to make me feel complete. What's going on here?"

William seemed perfectly calm at this point and perfectly earnest. He was in control as he stared at me with eyes that expressed no malice, slowly sipping his coffee. He held the cup by hooking his chronically bent thumb through the handle, balancing it more than holding it as he intoned his thoughts.

"Well, I also think I'd enjoy hearing about the sexual things you could do with other men. After you confided in me about that night with Ronnie, I found myself turned on, although nothing happened."

Almost as if to highlight his feelings, his left leg started jumping, which forced him to take his right elbow and hook it around the back of the chair to keep from throwing him out of the chair from the spasm that suddenly erupted. This happened whenever he was stimulated in some sort of way. Watching his struggle interrupted my thoughts, but he never missed a beat.

"To be truthful," he said, "your honesty and the fact that you came home and never concealed it from me made me start thinking of an idea for my book. You and I have a special love. I think you could have sex with other men and continue to love me."

I looked over at William. A full beard and mustache encircled his face. Ten years of living in a wheelchair had aged him much faster than life had aged me. Strands of gray and dirty blond stippled his thinning hair. His face didn't betray his age, but his body mimicked a recently broken down box leaning at strange angles. From lack of use, his limbs were like twigs—skin over bones. His hands stayed somewhere between a balled-up fist and open loosely. This prevented him from gripping things the normal way. Rehabilitation had taught him that turning his wrist caused an involuntary closure of the fingers toward the palm of the hand, which helped him to hold a coffee cup, fork and other necessities.

I was drawn back to the present from the memory when I heard my wind chimes, made up of glass balls the size of large marbles, clinking together outside. I listened to the gentle tinkling sound and again closed my eyes. Those glass balls reminded me of my favorite thing about William. His most striking features had always been his eyes and his mind.

He was charismatically brilliant, the leader of a young cult that looked up to him as a great guru because he remained positive about life in spite of his paralysis. He was goal-oriented, with an infectious laugh and a great sense of humor. A champion chess player, he was wise, analytical, maddeningly methodical, and slow at problem solving because, unlike me, he pondered every single possibility before making a decision, proving that opposites did attract. I could make up my mind in seconds on any matter. I called it by either thinking fast or by not thinking at all. Most of the time, it served me well enough.

Everyone had respected William's abilities and ceased to see any disabilities. I, too, had been impressed with him and his attitude about life. However, that positive attitude hadn't been enough to keep me moored to him. I mentally trekked back to that day in 1981 when William had suggested that I quit being monogamous.

We had both finished our coffee, so I said, "Another cup?"

"No, I had some before you drove up." He tilted his head toward the dirty coffee pot. "I emptied the pot."

That prompted me to clean the pot and fire it up for later. The aroma of the brewing coffee filled the room, temporarily masking Ming's odor. While the coffee perked, I walked back to the bedroom and changed out of my work clothes. I figured William would return to his office, but he didn't. I knew then he was serious about what he'd asked me to do.

I poured myself another cup of coffee. For some reason, caffeine calmed me. I knew I needed to prop myself up for this life-changing proposition. As I fixed my coffee, I looked over at William and stared into his blue eyes that reminded me of the giant, prize-winning cat's-eye marbles we had lusted for when we played back in the fifties. The most serene lenses ever to gaze back at a person telegraphed his sincerity.

"I could never do what you asked me to do, William. Sure, I'm a woman. When my favorite Lipizzaner mare was due to foal, it jazzed me up. When a man rolled over and rubbed my stomach, of course my adrenalin pumped me up that night. Since it was cold and we were on the ground, we sought out each other's body heat because we knew it was going to be a long night. Of course my heart speeded up!"

As I said those words, the memories of that night rushed back. Thinking about it made my heart do a little flutter. It shocked me that the memory could still cause that kind of reaction.

"I'd never want to have sex with another man," I said. "I love you, William. I've been faithful all these years and totally happy."

Uncomfortable with what I knew was a lie, I aimlessly ran my finger around the rim of the coffee cup as my mind spoke one set of words while a flashback disturbed me. Maybe William was right. Maybe I did need something more in my life. Maybe I had missed out on one of life's greatest gifts.

"Lee, I really think if two people love each other, sex with someone else isn't important. It's physical. It has nothing at all to do with love. So go ahead. Start flirting back. Enjoy yourself." William broke a smile as he said that to me.

All my present problems stemmed from a misdiagnosis by a doctor back in 1980. How could Dr. Wilcox have been wrong? I'd felt funny about the issue of sex outside of marriage, but once I'd gotten involved, I had overdone it as I tended to overdo anything I endeavored.

After Dr. Wilcox's pronouncement that I was sexually frustrated, we had ended up having an open marriage from 1980 through 1982. William had savored the sex in his mind whenever I told him about my sexual fantasies or exploits, whether real or imagined. It worked to a degree. I could have sex and keep my emotions separated from the way I felt about William. Shot while he was still a virgin teen, William had never experimented with intercourse, so doing without it hadn't been too difficult for him. Married for eleven years, I wanted to please him. Deep down it had hurt me that he was willing to share me.

All that thinking and remembering made me hungry. It was seven twenty-five, and I hadn't eaten anything all day, so I went to the refrigerator and pulled out a container of pimento cheese to make myself a sandwich. I wasn't finished with all my remembering, because even that made me wander back to the time when Joe and I had worked together at the paper mill and had shared a pimento cheese sandwich out of the snack machine daily. I laughed softly as I remembered the time that Joe had met William.

Chapter Seven

That September day in 1982, I walked outside the paper mill and felt my skin plump with goose bumps, a reaction to the intense heat inside the mill that never ceased to amaze me. Although that fall produced a record heat wave, the ninety-two degrees outside felt cool and made me shiver. After coming off the test floor where temperatures exceeded one hundred five degrees, Alabama's nighttime nineties felt downright pleasant. For a while at least.

Joe and I headed toward the gate with our black Bobbsey Twins lunch boxes cluttered with half-eaten sandwiches, instant coffee, cigarettes and change for sugar cookies from the snack machine. The stench of the settling ponds smelled like a cocktail of rotten eggs topped with burnt oils. The mist falling from the recovery stacks showered our shirts with a powdery white coating dust. I tended to walk faster than Joe's ambling gait. While I waited for his familiar shuffle behind me, I looked up and watched the twin stacks fart pollution high into the nighttime sky.

"Are you sure William won't mind me dating you?" The paint-can-shaker sound made by the pumps and drive shafts of the paper machine drowned out Joe's yelling.

"What did you say?" I yelled back.

"I can't imagine William letting another man date you. If you were my wife, I'd cherish you. You're beautiful and kind."

In spite of the noise, my heart heard that part. Joe opened his lunchbox and took out two cigarettes, lighting them both and handing me one. I thought Joe Thames looked sexy when he did that—put two cigarettes in his mouth and lit them both, silver screen style.

"Is William nuts or something?"

"No, he's writing a book," I said. "He thinks he's discovered something and wants to see if it works or not. He's using me as his guinea pig."

"How do you mean?"

"In 1979, I owned a frame shop and made my living as an artist. When I lost it, I broke down and became depressed because I no longer had my studio where I could paint. My doctor diagnosed me as being sexually frustrated. The perverted quack convinced William that I needed to have sex outside of the marriage. William thinks he's cooked up the old-but-new-for-us construct that husbands and wives who love each other won't get jealous if everything stays out in the open."

"Damn, you use big words. You are one smart woman. William is a fool."

"No, I'm retarded compared to William. But thanks anyway."

"I'd never share Regina with another man. We don't get along, but it would bother me for another man to touch her. I guess that makes me somewhat of a hypocrite."

"At least you're honest about it and care enough for your wife that you consider her yours and yours alone. I think she's pretty lucky."

I stopped in front of my truck and studied myself in the side mirror. It was a habit I'd recently developed since working at the mill—I couldn't pass a mirror without appraising my appearance, because my being one of only four women among five hundred men made me feel attractive. The other three women each weighed over two hundred pounds. I was trim and slim.

The image in my mirror was not flattering. Not only did the coating dust cover my shirt, plaster-white freckles dotted my nose and cheeks while my bangs stood up, tipped with coating. That night I had trained on the L3 job, picking up samples. The sample cup was a long-stemmed dipper. The coating, a thick, chalky blend of clay and latex, poured out of a pipe into a vat designed to deliver it to the paper machine's coaters. While reaching across the vat at an odd angle due to my short arms, I'd caused the cup to slant, spilling it. Some of the coating hit the side of the cup and splattered all over me.

"William feels secure in our love," I told Joe. "Listen, I don't want to drink and drive because I can't hold my booze too well. Can you pick me up tonight to take me to The Studio?" I tried my best to sound sexy despite the hilarity of my nasty appearance.

"You mean, me come to your house and meet William?" Joe's Bogart toughness slipped away for a second as I watched his hand shake when he reached back into his lunch box for another cigarette to light.

"Yes, he won't mind. I promise you."

"I don't know. How can I look him in the eye with him in a wheelchair? I feel like I'm cheating on him. But I'll do it if you insist."

I noticed Joe couldn't look me in the eye as he said that. He turned his head at an angle and blew smoke out of his mouth sideways.

"I insist," I said. "I can't drive after I drink a single glass of wine. I'm a cheap drunk for a date." With that, I winked at him. He knew what that meant.

Apprehension had flirted with me before our date that fall. Joe was married. I believed that his wife knew about us and didn't mind that we were seeing each other. I couldn't imagine that Joe might be lying to me. Looking back on it now, I feel like a fool for not seeing the obvious.

Back in the present, my mind raced and the slow ticking of the clock was an irritation.

I remembered how I had stood in the bathroom that evening getting ready. I heard the timid knock on our kitchen door and wondered if Joe understood my marriage with William. I recognized that it would make him uneasy and self-conscious to engage in small talk with my husband while I dressed. I heard the familiar squeak of one of William's wheels and knew he had rolled over to open the door, something that could be difficult for him because he didn't have the use of his fingers.

He leaned over precariously to open the door, then he backed his chair out of the way. Joe's good manners allowed William to invite him into the house. A clear view of them as I continued to get dressed aroused my curiosity. I kept glancing at them, studying their faces for signs of trouble. Our bathroom was a straight shot view into the dining room with the door opened.

"Come in, Joe," William said. "Can I get you something, perhaps a cup of coffee while you wait? Lee is never on time for anything, and we'll probably be here for a while."

"Nuh-nuh-no," Joe stuttered. "I'm fine."

"How did work go tonight? Lee said there wasn't a hay party." William stared boldly into Joe's eyes.

"We ran pretty good and didn't hay out once. You know . . . I mean . . . the machine didn't lose its sheet and dump a huge load into the basement."

Joe looked over William's head rather than at his face, which made me feel uneasy for some reason. I winced as I realized Joe had messed up— explaining something to William that didn't need an explanation. The situation was already awkward, but I could tell William knew Joe was nervous and was trying to make him feel comfortable.

"That's good I guess. Lee always said that whenever it hayed out, the lab took a break from all of the testing of the paper."

There was a pause before Joe answered. "Well, yeah, that's right. I guess it was a good night because we had some time in between the reels."

I listened to the relaxation in Joe's voice as he seemed to understand that William honestly did not mind that I was going out with him that night. Knowing that William knew we would end up having sex appeared to no longer bother him.

"Joe, my only rule is that you have to tell your wife," William said. "I don't believe in cheating. Lee says you have done this. Is that true?"

"Yes, we went to marriage counseling. Dr. Wilcox told me to start having sex outside of the marriage 'cause Regina don't want to have sex with me no more. She agreed to it as long as I brought my pay check home and gave it to her."

Finally, I watched Joe look William straight in the eyes as he said this. That gesture made me believe he was telling the truth.

"That's not what I asked you. You seem to be avoiding the question. Is there a reason why?" Obviously, William was trying to catch Joe in a lie. "Does she know you are going out with Lee?" William cleared his throat as if he were the nervous one. He often did this when something bothered him.

"Yes, I told her," Joe said, cracking his knuckles as he said it. "She was fine with it."

Standing in our bathroom, I watched Joe fidget with his hand and tilt his head to the side, not looking William in the eyes. He gazed at me with a pleading look to hurry up.

"Well, in that case," William said, "you wouldn't mind my having her name and a way for me to talk to her?"

By now, I thought William was acting strangely. He was going to ruin the night. I was almost ready, and I rushed to finish.

"Uh, they won't let her have . . . you know, calls at work, and our phone is an unlisted number. I'll have to ask her before I can give it out."

It was news to me that their number was unlisted.

"I'll ask her about it," Joe said, "and if she agrees, I'll give it to Lee to give to you."

Thinking about his lies that night brought me out of my reverie. How stupid I'd been. I'd caught him lying yet ignored all the red flags warning me to stay away from him. Of course, he never did give me the number. I overlooked that, as I tended to overlook everything that was bad about him.

What William said next should have made me run from Joe.

"Regina and I have already talked on the phone."

Joe's eyes widened when William said her name. All sense of calm departed his face.

"She called me," William said. "Gossip had reached her place of employment. She called to warn me that Lee was cheating on me—with you. I told her I knew about everything and that I was fine with it. However, you lied to me. Why?"

"Ahem," Joe coughed." To be honest, I'd forgotten that I didn't mention Lee's name. I figured after the doctor's visit, she'd know I was seeing someone else. I didn't think it would really matter who it was. Besides, I never get a woman in trouble. That's wrong in my book."

"I would prefer that you tell her the truth. She deserves that much. Don't you agree?"

"I'll tell her, I promise you. It's strange for me to be this open. I'm not used to it." Joe shuffled from one foot to the other, looking above William's head, not bothering to look down. Again, he gave me a pleading look, and I couldn't help feeling sorry for him.

A glance in the mirror reflected that I was dazzling, so I hurried into the kitchen to rescue Joe from William's grilling. I wore a backless wraparound red dress that showed I wasn't wearing a bra and didn't need one. Paisley shades of red accented my eyes, making them look sapphire blue. My dark hair hugged my face in soft, dark brown curls that framed my high cheekbones. Lips like a flame beckoned a passionate kiss.

"Isn't she beautiful, Joe?" William said. "I know you two will have a great time tonight." Then he added sadly, "Have fun."

William turned around and rolled back toward his office in the rear of the house as Joe and I left. We got into his car feeling the magic and chemistry between us. We both knew how this night would end.

Thinking about that night most definitely mellowed me out—for a while. Then the dirty truth of that memory no longer holding its sacred place in either my heart or Joe's infuriated me. How dare he ruin my life! I felt my blood pressure rising and started getting dizzy. True to form, the only thing that tended to calm me down in a crisis was a good cup of coffee.

My anger turned to sadness when I looked at my black coffeemaker sitting alone on the counter. I'd long ago given up caffeine and only drank decaffeinated or the light blend. Joe had a white pot where he made his strong caffeinated coffee, and the black pot was where he made my light blend in the mornings or my decaf in the evenings. God, how I missed those little things.

The sadness brought my blood pressure down and made my emotions plummet into a depression. As I took out the coffee filter and started making my coffee, the tears flowed freely. Why was love so damn painful? As I thought about how sweet Joe had always treated me, it took me back to the night of our first date and what a gentleman he had been. I didn't want any other woman to have him. By God, if he were no longer mine, he'd belong to no one! In perfect bipolar irony, even thinking about how much I still loved him fired up my drive to kill him.

The mantel clock chimed eight o'clock. I poured myself a cup of coffee, drowning it in Cremora and adding half a package of Sweet'N'Low. A full one made my coffee taste too sweet now. I was trying to cut down on sugar or sugar substitutes in my life. With all of my medications working on my brain, I didn't need to do any extra damage to it by adding bad stuff to my coffee. That was the reason I'd switched to sweet tea, preferring the sugar to the chemicals in the sugar substitutes.

I was finally beginning to put my weight back on. Now at least that red dress wouldn't look as if it hung on a skeleton. I didn't look as good as I had the night of the date, but at least I could still get into that dress at my age. I'd always tried to stay thin and sexy for Joe. That had been one of his biggest gripes about Regina—her getting fat.

I carried my coffee and pimento cheese sandwich to the kitchen table, smiling as I remembered the first time Joe saw me nude. I'd been thirty-three but looked twenty-one. I was five years older than his wife, and he had nearly

55

swooned when he saw how firm my breasts were, how flat my stomach was, and how smooth my skin felt to him. That had been a magical night for us.

Chapter Eight

The third time Joe and I met for drinks had been our first official date. When we got into his car that night, the air was full of sensuous electricity. Seeing him out of his work clothes with his clean, shiny hair made me notice him and consider him in a different light—enchantment had definitely been in the air. I knew in my gut that night promised to be different.

When he told me he'd borrowed his wife's car, a 1966 red Mustang, and I saw his kids' toys in the front floorboard, I knew I'd lost my soul. There I was a married woman dating a married man, sent off with my husband's blessings while I was still pining over another married man—James, an electrician I'd met at the plant. My heart was still recovering from the waning affair with James, who actually had gotten me pregnant. I'd miscarried at work one night to his great relief. Having sex with a third man whom I couldn't stand and had pursued me, I'd been a trashy slut that summer. Not seeing James for the past two weeks had made me horny as hell.

Joe and I had only been best friends until September 1982, because I understood what he was going through. He wasn't getting any love at home, and I knew what that was like because of the time William had stopped having sex with me. He had struggled to be a writer all of our married life, and I guess I always competed with him in that. He told me straight up that I'd never complete a book because I didn't have the staying power it took for all the many rewrites.

He had been partially right, because I did underestimate the dedication it took to be a writer. Printed out copies of chapters were now scattered all around my house, but I wouldn't have given up sex to be a writer the way William had done in the summer of 1980.

William had vowed chastity until he published his book. Well, at least he meant no sex with me. I'd been chaste—except for one short-lived fling with Barry back in late fall of 1980. It had been a revenge affair after William betrayed me with nineteen-year-old named Rachelle who had lived with us for a couple of months. High and dry sexually, I was ripe for a promiscuous summer. However, I had remained faithful to William for almost a year, even during the open marriage.

Then the crazy summer of 1982 hit me, and I combusted into a heat. I must have gotten high or nutty from adrenalin overload that caused me to be energetic as well as promiscuous with many lovers. I juggled men around similar to the person riding the unicycle on the Ed Sullivan show tossing those ugly cones up in the air.

I chewed my sandwich thoughtfully and drifted back to the night Joe and I had our first date. Normally, I wolfed my food, but I guess the serenity of contemplation slowed me down. Pimento cheese always reminded me of Joe.

Joe and I were supposed to have a strictly friendly sexual relationship, or so I thought, as he opened my door and I settled in for our first real date that September night. I remembered the first time Joe had paid attention to me as a woman a month earlier.

In August, we'd met with the rest of our crew for drinks on a Thursday night when working off a three to eleven shift. Having an off day the next day had accommodated the hangovers we were all guaranteed to take home with us. We'd worked hard and, after that last one shift, we partied even harder. I was the only female on our crew. Most of the time, I went out in my work clothes as did everyone else.

That night, I'd gone home to change clothes because I had been so nasty with coating. Joe noticed that I definitely was female—or led me to believe that he hadn't noticed until that night. I walked in with my no-panties-buttock-revealing white shorts, a tube-top, wearing makeup with my hair cleaned and styled. Joe's eyes had steeled with a lusty stare—his pupils the size of dimes. Painted red toenails and fingernails along with a feather in my curly hair emphasized the cerulean blue of my eyes. Sure enough, Joe paid more attention to me than anyone else did, which was a first. Normally, Joe treated me more like a sister than a woman.

That night at the bar, I felt akin to a queen rather than one of the boys. I understood the power I had over them all. At work, I was "low man on the totem pole," but at the Studio, I was at the top of my game, especially when I dressed sexy and showed off my tanned, muscular body. I must have been insane as shit to run at least a mile a day at high noon in triple digit temperatures. I'd barely break into a sweat much less tire myself out—more proof that I was in an abnormally high state.

Since I was so manic at the time, I exuded sensuous self-confidence, and poor Joe was falling all over himself. We played Foos-ball and laughed until we cried because I was such a klutz.

"It's good to hear you laugh," he said. "I love your voice. Regina would have been embarrassed and never laughed at herself. I could sit and watch you all night and never tire or get bored. You're fun to be with."

"I don't think I've ever had this much fun. I've been missing out a lot on life."

As soon as I said that, my mood changed to sadness as I remembered my recent miscarriage. Joe immediately noticed and spoke in a gentle voice.

"What is it, Lee?"

"Do you remember that night I had to leave work during our last graveyard shift?"

"Yes, I could tell you were in a great deal of pain. I wished there had been something I could've did to help you."

"Nobody but God could have helped me that night. I lost my baby."

"Lee, I'm so sorry. I know that broke your heart. I don't know what I'd do without my kids. Regina was her most beautiful when she was pregnant."

"William was angry with me for being careless, and the baby's father was relieved. I had to suffer through it all alone."

"How awful! Honey, I wish you'd told me. I would've helped you in any way I could. I know it was hard on you."

"Thanks, Joe. You're the only human being out there who understands that I wanted that baby. It left a hole in my life that I'll never patch up with good intentions. William finally started acting concerned when I kept moping around. I guess he felt sorry for me. He couldn't understand that my empty womb left my purpose for living empty for about two weeks."

Thinking about my empty womb reminded me of my now nearly empty house. I continued to eat my sandwich. Thinking about that side of Joe softened me up as I remembered the good Joe.

He'd been a gentleman and hadn't asked me who the father was. He did reach over and hug me in a brotherly kind of way. That set the stage for what was going to happen between the two of us.

Chapter Nine

I hadn't expected to fall in love with Joe. To be honest, except for his slim build and his long silky hair, he wasn't the type of man that turned me on. William had been more of my primal map of what turned me on sexually. I'd had to acquire a taste for Joe's appearance. That night in September of '82, my primal image went from blond and blue-eyed to the likes of Joe Thames.

All my life I had lusted for blue-eyed men, preferably with blond hair. All my high school boyfriends had those features. Wait, who am I kidding? I didn't have any boyfriends. The one boy with long blond hair and blue eyes had only dated me once when I asked him out back in the sixties. Otherwise, he never gave me a glance. Who wanted a girl with long lanky legs without any tits or ass?

William had dirty-blond hair that bleached out in the summer because he worked outside. Although he was blue-eyed, he hadn't been my first choice. My infatuation with blond-haired males really started at age fifteen. John England, with his Beatles hair, had melted my heart. But when William asked me out for the next-to-the-last of our senior parties, I said yes and we started dating. I fell in love with him by the end of our senior year. I guess my attraction changed with his surrogate sun-bleached hair satisfying what I longed for.

William's body was hot back in the sixties when we dated, because he worked outside on the farm and had a terrific tan to boot. William's dad made him keep his hair Marion Military Institute short when we dated. Now, poor William's hair was almost gone. He made up for lack of head hair by a full curly beard and a mustache. What hair he had on his head, he still kept extremely short, so I'd given up on the long-haired vision of my dream male—until Joe came into my life.

Joe's hair was longish and light brown. He had faded freckles that matched his hazel eyes. His lips were big, followed by even bigger teeth with a gap between the two front ones, which were slightly bucked. Growing up, we'd always called those "rabbit teeth." It wasn't a complimentary term. His teeth were also coffee and cigarette stained to a pale yellow, which turned me off. I checked those kinds of things. He had a cleft in his chin that was weak rather than a strong jaw line. In the beginning, nothing about Joe's physical appearance drew me to him in any exciting or sexual way.

In fact, I had originally planned to have sex with him that night because I felt sorry for him. He complained about how horny he was, and I liked him as a friend. I was going to gift him with the power between my legs. Since we were close, he talked openly to me about how horny he stayed. I mean, what were friends for if not to help each other?

Our "friends with benefits" relationship changed one rainy day in October. Not only can I pinpoint the exact date I fell in love with Joe— October 21, 1982—I can actually pinpoint the exact moment.

I'd ridden with Joe to LaGrange, Georgia to pick up the Christmas layaway for his kids. It was pouring rain. We drove up to Big K, and Joe took me to the entrance under an overhang to keep me dry.

"Hey, go on and get out," he said. "I'll go park the car. Just wait for me inside the door. Honey, you'll never have to get wet again as long as I have anything to do with it."

Joe knew that I always got William out and into a store. It was always me who got drenched while William stayed dry. I was shocked at his thoughtfulness. Nothing he had ever told me in terms of things he did had ever fazed me, but this I totally hadn't expected. No one had ever done anything like that for me. All I could do was look at him. He'd won me away from the baby's father. I was Joe's—not William's, not James's, not anyone else's ever again, not even mine. As I handed Joe the power over my heart that day, I became a changed woman.

After parking the car, he was soaked by the time he made it into the store. In that moment, I realized I needed someone. Until then, I'd been this independent women's libber, standoffish, I-don't-need-anyone kind of person. I'd had relations because I wanted to, not because I needed anyone—or so I thought.

In that one moment with Joe, from his simple gesture of being considerate of me and my needs, I fell madly, deeply, passionately in love with him. We hid nothing from each other. That's why I trusted him even though I knew he was a dog.

I looked at my sleeping Pomeranian and felt guilty for comparing Joe's negative traits to dogs. I also chortled as I thought about how much I had trusted Joe. I felt as if he and I could talk about any and everything. Nothing we said to each other ever made us feel guilty.

Working at the paper mill was one of the happiest times in my life, next to having Jolly. I felt loved by many for the first time in my life. That sensation was exhilarating and caused me to churn out Dopamine—making me feel euphoric. I felt proud that I could do a man's job. Of course, the association the mill had for me of falling in love with Joe always gave me fond memories of the place.

After catching up on our work one night in August of 1982, Joe and I sat at the little gray table next to the log sheets, eating our sandwiches for supper. He was the L3 who tested the coating for the board, and I was the L5. My job was to test for effluent problems. I could potentially find a problem that threatened the environment and shut down the mill, so I took my job seriously. If I messed up, it would bring down the EPA on the mill and my back.

Joe bit his sandwich and chewed it slowly. He always took his time eating as he did everything else. He was methodical, able to run all of the tests easily since he was ambidextrous and could use both hands equally well. I was wolfing down my food so I could be ready when my timer went off. I wasn't coordinated, and it took me more time to run the tests. I had to slow down to do them properly. I had a hard time staying caught up.

Joe was always finished and taking breaks in-between rounds. I, on the other hand, had to work wide open to finish, save the one time that I had a short round and was able to eat. I never stopped gulping down my food to react to any of our conversations, no matter how unsettling our topic. This was the night he'd mentioned his lack of guilt for killing a man.

"There's nothing wrong with you," I said. "You're a kind and good man."

I mumbled that with food in my mouth, desperately trying to finish my pimento cheese sandwich in the next few seconds before the timer went off to tell me I had to finish titrating the settling pond sample I'd picked up.

"You always make me feel good," he said. "No one has ever made me feel like you do. Regina don't even know about this. She'd be yelling and raising hell with me if she ever knew about it. You know what I did the first week we were married?"

"What?"

"I picked up a WAVE and brought her home to our apartment."

Of course Regina would be raising hell with you for bringing home a Navy woman! Duh!

He met my gaze, obviously studying my face for a reaction. The contortions of chewing a thick wad of pimento cheese sandwich saved me from any expression other than trying hard not to choke.

Joe went on. "I was unlocking our apartment door when I remembered that I was married and my wife was asleep in the bedroom. We were drunk. I was a jet mechanic, and picking up WAVEs was easy the whole time I was in the Navy. I cheated on Regina all the time. I never did serve on a ship or leave Norfolk. I stayed stateside working in a hangar or being a cabin boy for some of the big brass on their helicopters. I was able to impress the women because I had a cushiony job whenever I flew."

For once, I was speechless. To be honest, hearing him talk about cheating on her when they were first married did bother me. I'm sure my eyes finally widened in shock.

Buzzzzzzz! The timer told me my sample was ready. I jumped up to run to my station and finish my testing. This wasn't unusual, as I always rushed, but I think he noticed I hadn't said anything negative or judgmental about his revelations. I guess he took that as approval, and since I hadn't been judgmental, that drew him even closer to me. Who was I to say a word? I was as bad if not worse. We were two despicable dogs running in the same pack, taking down innocent people.

I wandered around the house, pacing with anxiety at having been such a complete fool. Now, that was the real Joe. Stupid me, I'd thought my love would be enough—that he'd change. He swore that he'd never cheat on me. I had to have been crazy that summer our relationship became sexual not to recognize the trouble I was getting myself set up for later on in life.

I checked my watch and couldn't believe it was only eight thirty-five. This was going to be a long night. I figured I needed to find something to do, so I started cleaning up the kitchen. Normally, I hated housework, but maybe it would get my mind off things. Being bipolar, I multi-tasked easily and cleaned as I continued to think about my life.

That summer of 1982, I had been crazy but never realized it. First, I had to be a fruit loop to work at that paper mill—pulling sometimes eighty-hour weeks, carrying heavy things as well as opening and closing huge valves, my adrenalin staying pumped up as it surged through my system. Not understanding that I was mentally ill, I didn't realize I needed to avoid stressful and demanding situations that produced adrenalin and led to my downfall.

I was in a constant high and never thought anything about it. I was the only person on the crew who never tired. It should have been a clue when I had more energy than all the other men on the crew combined. I guess I thought I was superwoman, which was part of the arrogance of my mind's state. Because I was in the white mania, which was productive and kept me feeling good rather than irritable and angry, my illness went undetected. Had I slipped into black mania, the secret would have been out, and I probably would have ended up in a mental hospital. Work kept me stimulated and challenged, and I fed off it.

Having the men make me out to be a goddess only exacerbated the problem. It gave me a sense of power the summer I discovered the secret all women carried. What's between our legs controls the world when we are smart enough to realize it and use it to our own advantage. I didn't know about this until I was thirty-three, but once I understood it, I was a master at using my sensual nature to get pretty much anything I wanted.

Joe, too, had mastered the power of being attentive. There we were—me oozing the sexuality that drove him crazy, and Joe showering me with caring and attention that drove me crazy. Our stars were destined to cross, collide, and create an explosion.

I unloaded the dishwasher and pulled out the iris mug Joe had given me the previous Christmas. Our house had been filled with our iris collection. When we renewed our commitment to our marriage, we'd been at an art gallery and purchased an iris painting. That became the symbol of our eternal love.

I knew better now. As they say: once a cheater, always a cheater. Joe cheated throughout all of his first marriage, and I knew he'd cheated at least three times in ours. Why hadn't I recognized the destructive nature of our relationship? I guess it was because I was sick and didn't have good judgment that summer of 1982.

I drifted back to the night he confessed about another of his affairs on poor Regina. He told me he was also seeing his wife's best friend, a woman named Abbey who got off on being tied up and having oral sex performed on her, because her dud of a husband wouldn't do it.

"Regina is so dumb, but she almost caught me one time. I tied Abbey up twice at our house I'm building. Abbey was spread-eagled in an unfinished door frame with me going down on her when I glanced up and saw Regina coming across the side yard."

"Oh, my God! What did you do?"

"Abbey don't like me to undress whenever I do her. She fantasizes that I'm raping her. Lucky for me, I had all of my clothes on when I noticed Regina through the window." Joe's expression was wanton, as he seemed to be bragging on his ability to outfox poor Regina. "I grabbed a hammer and hurried to the kitchen. I told her I was hankering for some fried chicken and asked her if she'd go pick us up some at the Seven Eleven store. I smelled like Abbey, but Regina don't ever notice nothing about me."

"Did she go for it?"

"Yeah, shaved seven inches off my dick as it went south. I learned never to bring Abbey back to the house again. Heck, only thirty minutes earlier we'd been in the living room with me eating her after I tied her up on my weight bench. Regina would have seen that when she walked through the kitchen door. Actually, if she'd taken three steps more, she could have looked through the section I hadn't sheet rocked yet and seen her tied up in our bedroom doorway."

"Damn, Joe. That was stupid and way too risky. What do you think she would have done? Divorced you?"

"Hell, she'd already given me an ultimatum three years ago to build her a new house, buy her a car, or grant her a divorce. I always wished I'd chosen number three instead of number one. I couldn't be lucky enough to get her out of my life. We can't stand each other. If it weren't for Jeff and Rose, I'd have left her a long time ago. They're the only reason I stayed to build her the house. Everyone at work says I'll never sleep a night in it because she'll kick me out once I finish."

"You poor baby. I can't imagine anyone mistreating you."

God, what a sucker I'd been. He had brought about all the mistreatment he received and deserved more than he got. I slammed the dishwasher shut in anger thinking about it. Joe was a champ at gaining sympathy and getting himself out of bad situations. I could attest to that.

I smiled as I thought about what Regina would have done had Joe not seen her and she'd walked in on that scene. All these years she'd thought he'd only cheated with me, that I was the wild bitch who had tempted and stolen her faithful man. She had been fooled by him even worse than I was.

At the time, I had been cooling off my affair with James and scrumping Dan, an older man who had the hots for me. I was whoring with him so he'd bring in dump trucks of topsoil and heavy equipment to level out a couple of bad gullies on the farm William and I owned. Yup, you might say I let him plow my gully to smooth out our ravines. At least I knew I was an expensive tart. Dan had probably hauled in six or more dump truck loads of dirt then used a road scraper to level it off and planted some grass. None of this bothered me as long as it didn't bother William, and it hadn't, so I hadn't felt as if I were doing anything wrong. I never considered the wives of the other men.

I decided to be productive and put on a load of clothes to wash. Lately, I'd been very lazy and selfish and felt free to clean and wash only when I wanted to, not because I had to do it to keep Joe happy. It reminded me of the selfish bitch I had been back in 1982. While caught up in my selfish world and working such long hours, whenever I'd had a moment for some fun, I had totally justified it in my mind.

Joe and I were twins when it came to that. These were classic symptoms of sexual addiction, though neither of us had even heard of that illness back then. Neither of us had a conscience due to my bipolar mania and his sexual addiction, as well as my co-addiction to him. Sadly, we felt great all summer long as we were destroying many people's lives. I look back now with my informed hindsight, and I'm ashamed of the person I was that summer.

What attracted me the most to Joe was that he never made any sexual innuendo. He treated me as asexual. That was his MO, of course I didn't know it at the time. Practically every man at the mill had his tongue dragging and drooling to have a piece of me. Joe seemed platonically indifferent. I guess that's why I made the play for him that night by asking him to pick me up. I felt as though I had lost my touch or something. If I dressed up sexy and Joe didn't respond to me that night, except for all of his tales of all the women he had, I would have sworn the man was gay.

I had been pulling out all my feminine charm, and my pulsating sexuality had been aimed at making a complete circuit to light up Joe Thames that night—not because I really wanted him sexually or emotionally, but simply because I could. By the time we got to The Studio, his charm had turned me on. I'd made the circuit. He ignited something inside me that I'd never experienced before.

Chapter Ten

When Joe shut the car door, even with the kids' toys plainly in sight, I managed to step on a whoopee cushion, making an embarrassing noise. Not exactly a sexy beginning for me in spite of how hard I was trying to be seductive. Joe never missed a beat.

"You shouldn't have eaten that banana I gave you," he said with a smile.

We both howled with laughter. I never knew Joe could be witty. He'd always had his head in a book and seemed quiet and serious. Slowly, Joe sucked me into his snare.

"You are the most beautiful woman I've ever seen in my life," he said. "William is an idiot. I can't understand how a man who has a wife like you— sexy, smart, hard-working, beautiful—can share you the way he does. God, if you were my wife, I'd keep you under lock and key because I'd be so afraid of losing you."

I can't believe I bought that line for a penny, completely shutting down my bullshitometer. Even today, he manages to dupe me repeatedly. Back then, I fell for him and fell hard.

I hadn't expected to hear those words that night, and I guess they caught me off guard. They also played inside my head something I'd been denying for the past two years—I wanted a man to keep me under lock and key. I wanted a man to cherish me. I was having a great time and had no sense of right or wrong, but I felt a great disappointment in love. I wanted someone to love, admire, respect, and—most of all—desire me with a jealous heart. I wanted a normal marriage. Being married to William was no longer something that satisfied me. I'd kept that thought hidden in the recesses of my being, and only after Joe spoke those words did that thought surface and reveal the reality of how unhappy and dissatisfied I was in my marriage.

Joe's words changed my life. They opened a Pandora's Box, and I decided that night that I'd never go back to being William Peterson's happy little whore, helping him have sex vicariously through my lovers and me.

Besides, William had a lover too—Erin Wainwright, a young girl of twenty. I didn't know what they did and, by that time, I didn't care. I wasn't jealous because, that night with Joe, it hit me that the love I'd once had for William was gone. At first, I fought that thought with everything in me. Then I glanced at Joe and warmth entered my body. He looked over and winked at me, and in that one movement, with one gesture, my life changed.

"If you only knew how much I wished William felt that way."

I was trying to convince myself that I desired William's love. Joe had shed a light on my emptiness. I still had enough of my Alabama upbringing that I truly wanted it rekindled with William somehow. However, Joe was sending out karma that my body could not reject. My stomach had butterflies, my clit was alive with pulsating feelings, and my heart suddenly knew how empty it was. Tonight, when I had sex with Joe, it wasn't going to be some empty, casual thing after all. We both felt it, and the energy between us was active and building.

I looked over at his profile and, for the first time, my primal longing had a match. There he was, my perfect man—his height, his weight, his profile, even those washed-out hazel eyes. He looked over, and with that wink, he suddenly had the most romantic, sexy eyes I'd ever seen in my life. His big mouth was now a god's sculpted lips begging me to kiss and suck on them with sensuous savoring. Everything about Joe drew me to him. I fought it still, trying to change my thoughts, but it was as if I were playing a game of Password: everything I thought only led to another word that led me back to Joe. The worst thing of all was that I compared him to William, and William definitely came out a huge loser.

After obliterating as much time as I could with my cleaning, I sat at my kitchen table listening to the sound of the washing machine. It hadn't been fair to compare William to Joe. That had been the origin of our finish as a couple for William and me, but I didn't know it then. I never expected him to toss me out, because I thought he had unconditional love for me. I thought I was doing what he wanted me to do—it was my delusion. Boy was I ever wrong. Everyone has a breaking point, and William had reached his by that November.

Joe and I continued to see each other daily. We'd work days and go out somewhere at night. We'd work graveyard then go to the lake on my farm, making love for hours. One weekend, Joe spent the night at our house in the guest bedroom—all with William's sick approval. We'd cruelly subjected William to our moans and screams of ecstasy all night long. Joe and I hadn't slept.

I never worried about Regina. I was under the impression she was as cool with our love affair as William was. It never dawned on me that Joe was cheating on her, because William had made him promise he would tell her. I wanted everything out in the open. I did not believe in cheating. I felt too guilty about Barry then later James's ex-wife not knowing about us. If both parties agreed to sex outside of the marriage, I was fine with it. The way Joe described things between them, Regina wouldn't care because she hated having sex with him and didn't love him anymore.

William realized the thing between Joe and me had gotten out of hand and the supposition in his book was failing because love was entering the picture and messing up all his theories. My love for Joe drove my life to the extent that I never noticed William was starting to treat me differently.

That November night when everything changed, Joe was going to take me to Montgomery for an overnight trip as we worked off a three to eleven. William tested my loyalty by giving me an odd demand. By then, Regina, jaded by Joe's mess, had kicked his butt out. He was never home anymore. Once she knew he was seeing me, she went to her lawyer. She threw Joe out, which is exactly what he manipulated her into doing. With his own bachelor's shack across the river, he was free to do whatever he wanted without any sense of guilt. Not that Joe ever had any guilt.

On that afternoon, William rolled out of his office. I'll never forget it because it was Thursday, November 12, 1982, making the next day Friday the thirteenth. Since my first baby horse had been foaled on a Friday the thirteenth, I'd always felt it was my lucky day and number. Maybe in some ways it was, even though I didn't feel so damn lucky at the time.

I rushed around packing a suitcase while getting dressed for work. A strange look in William's sparkling blue eyes caught my attention. I noticed the lacy black teddy draped across his claw-like fist, balancing it.

"I want you to wear this tonight when you go out with Joe. Think about me and remember me by wearing this teddy. Do you remember the day you wore it and sat in my lap while Erin took pictures of us?" William grinned as he spoke. "You were so sexy in it. I want you to come home to change clothes tonight after work. I'll be up waiting on you."

Now, I thought this strange, because William had never put any stipulations on my going out with Joe or anyone else.

"Okay, William. I'll drive straight home and put on the teddy."

In reality, I didn't want to do that. I rummaged through our closet looking for a sexy dress to wear. I wanted to wear the red one that was backless, impossible if I wore the teddy.

Back in the present, the clock chimed nine o'clock. I decided to wipe off the kitchen table and get rid of the flowers—creek irises. While married to William, I couldn't grow any flowers, as if I'd had two black thumbs of death. I remembered a time that I'd tried growing some wildflowers at our farm. They never germinated. I think mainly because I didn't have time to water and baby them, and William couldn't.

William spent hours in his office typing away on a Smith-Corona typewriter. Paralysis had left him unable to use his fingers, but he'd designed a set of special splints that buckled onto his hands. They had wrist posts on them he used with his drawn up palms to type one character at a time. I had to hand it to him. He was one of the most determined people I'd ever known. I would have been bitter about the accident that had paralyzed him from the shoulders down.

It's strange that I'd married a man in a wheelchair, but I fell in love with him because he was inspiring and intelligent. He'd always made it plain to me that I would be second in his life after his writing. I accepted that just fine. That night in November, though, I couldn't accept much of anything William asked of me. I resented his interfering in my plans.

I pondered why I felt that way. Long before that summer, my feelings for him had changed. He never knew why. Actually, it had nothing to do with another man. Two years earlier, when he'd asked me to start having sex outside of our marriage, I caught him hiding an affair from me.

I was hurt that he wanted to share me sexually. I did experiment with the open marriage in the spring of 1980 and wasn't impressed. I wasn't innocent—especially when the first encounter was a threesome. No one made me do it. My best friend Lisa's lover screwed me while getting her off orally. He totally ignored me, only his dick in me meant anything to him. It was demeaning. I never wanted to have sex with anyone outside my marriage ever again—until I found out about what William had done to me. Jealousy makes us do strange things.

Thinking about William's affair inflamed my anger again. I played the "what if" game—what if William had never tried seducing Rachelle? Would I have gone outside the marriage for attention, romance, and comfort? How unfair of me to pin all this on poor William and still be angry with him, especially after all that Joe and I had done to him! He'd been out of the picture for over twenty years.

Actually, William and I had remained friends. In fact, hanging in my hall was a photo of William holding Jolly as a baby. Well, it used to hang there until I totally wigged out once and threw all my hall photos at Joe, trying hard to kill him that day. Both William and his mother Gretchen treated Jolly as though she were a member of their family. They always remembered her on big occasions. He had even sent Jolly a puzzle with a hundred dollar bill in it back in 2002 for her graduation gift.

Thinking of how sweet and forgiving William had been toward me calmed the anger and helped center me again, then my bipolar mind nagged me into remembering when William had kept a secret from me. Dee Dee, of course, chimed in with her rant about what an idiot I was, always allowing men to use me and abuse me.

By now, I was able to recognize Dee Dee's and Nancy's voices from my bipolar mind's voices. Tonight they were calm and didn't sound similar to a room full of radios all tuned to different stations. I was positive the murderous voice belonged to Dee Dee. She hated Joe. She'd love nothing better than permanently removing him from my life and having the pleasure of watching him die. She hoped it was a slow, agonizing death. Me, I wanted it quick and clean and over with. Dee Dee also reminded me of the dirty deal William had done to me. She kept score and never forgot or forgave anyone.

I heard the washer go into a spin cycle, reminding me of my life spinning out of control. I decided to go and double-check on the gun. I was obsessed with keeping it hidden yet having it handy enough to grab in a hurry. On the way back to the bedroom, the painting I'd done of the abstracted face with tears of blood streaming down in its candy-cane-colored red frame reminded me of the first time I'd lost control over my actions. I took the painting off the wall and dusted it with the tail of my shirt. God, how had I let my house get this nasty?

I studied the painting. Two black abstracted eyes, a hint of nostrils, and a black mouth with rivulets of red tears from each corner of my eyes converging on the negative space contouring my cheekbones. Then the tears made a straight line down the negative space to the jaw and proceeded to drip into a puddle at the bottom of the picture plane.

What had caused me to paint such a grisly scene? I had obviously been in deep emotional pain. Dr. Wilcox had hospitalized me, given me sedatives to knock me out for three days, yet somehow he had totally missed my diagnosis of mental illness.

I replaced the artwork onto my dingy wall, sniffing the layers of dust caught in the orifices of the paneling. The dust reminded me of the odor in the warehouse where my art studio had been located back in 1979—a sinking business that had taken me into a hole of despair so deep that I hadn't been able to return to work ever again. I had given up my painting due to that memory for nearly ten years. I'd lost my business, and I'm a sore loser.

I walked back to the bedroom to check on the gun then returned to the living room. Plotting to kill is an upper that creates a rush like no drug I'd ever taken. I bet my metabolism torched some mega calories that evening. As I sat down in the living room to wait for more time to pass, I recalled the day I had done the painting of the bloody tears.

Chapter Eleven

Back in the fall of 1979, Dr. Wilcox had been all wrong. Instead of being sexually frustrated as he thought I was, I had been depressed from losing my business due to the recession. The depression made my bipolar kick up for the first time, but it had gone undiagnosed. I don't know how the doctor missed the diagnosis when he put me in the regular hospital and knocked me out for three days with sedatives. My dad, Mark, was a manic-depressive, and it's a genetic disease. Anyone with a thimbleful of psychological training should have recognized that I was in a bipolar downswing.

I had been going to see Dr. Wilcox for a couple of months. Actually, an obvious mania took me to him in the first place. I was meeting myself coming out the door. Saying I was an overachiever and pushing myself beyond normal limits would be an apt description of me that fall of 1979. I ran my own business that consisted of a framing shop, an art gallery, art supply store, art school, and my own personal studio. I taught classes every day except on weekends. Twice a week, I drove thirty-five miles to a junior college to teach art at night.

One night I drove over there, and all at once realized I didn't know where I was. I'd blacked out and driven past the town, ending up on a strange road. At least I did know to turn around. Of course, it had been eerie to find myself a minimum of thirty minutes or more away from my last conscious thought. I hadn't had that brief road hypnosis that everyone has. No, this was a case where "someone" had driven that car for at least forty miles or more. But since I thought it was a fluke, I didn't do anything about it. Much later, I discovered it had been Nancy—who saw life as drudgery—in control of my life.

Back then, I was under a lot of stress. Staying up until three in the morning to do the commissioned pieces took a toll on my mental state. Add to that the fact that my business eventually tanked proved to be more than I could endure. Entrepreneur I wasn't. I wanted to promote art and help artists in the area. Of course, I would frame all their work for a show with the agreement that they would pay me when they sold their art. Most of the art hung on the walls and didn't sell. My bills had to be paid, and my creditors weren't nearly as generous.

I'd give the artists a show in my gallery and make a huge big social deal out of attending my openings. The first one had been for select "social lights" of our community, invited by invitation only. The gallery would be open to the public for a grand opening the next day. It pissed people off when they didn't receive an invitation. Naturally, when I had my next opening and started including more people, they wanted to be among the Who's Who of Opelika, Alabama.

After a while, I had a large crowd coming to these openings. I did it up right too. Wine, cheese, soft music, and genteel conversation cultivated an aura of sophistication for such a small rural town. This culturally deprived area thought that label meant the welfare people in the community, while it actually referred to the upper class. Previously, they had been purchasing prints for hundreds of dollars that were machine produced and signed by the artist. They thought they'd been buying original art, so my job was to show them what original art really was.

In addition to the local talent, including myself, I had some excellent budding international artists like Greg Cartmell and Jessie LaVon. However, most people came to my gallery mainly to buy my art. I stayed sold out as fast as I finished pieces. Still, my business didn't survive the recession.

Finally, after I had a second blackout spell, I decided I needed to see a doctor. I knew stress was making me do strange stuff. My therapist, Dr. Wilcox, found me exciting. However, he was a dirty old man and saw my marital situation as a prime opportunity to bring up my sex life. At the time, there was nothing to discuss. Occasionally, William performed oral sex on me and brought me to orgasm, but I didn't have an overriding need for that because I stayed busy. My life and art kept me fulfilled. Dr. Wilcox figured I was too young and attractive not to be the horniest female alive, though I actually wasn't interested then.

During our sessions, I wanted to talk about horses or art. My good friend Lisa Wing—recently divorced—posed nude for me. I rendered some drawings of her. Well, Dr. Wilcox practically salivated when I brought one in for him to see. In fact, he purchased that one from me. Now, let me tell you something about being bipolar. When anything like that happens while I am a little "up," I extrapolate it into being rich and famous in no time at all. The delusions would make me think more and more, and the more I thought, the higher I'd get. Soon, there would be no fine line between thinking about something and its being a reality.

In spite of seeing this phenomenon unfold before his eyes as I talked in speedy sentences, Dr. Wilcox didn't get it. His own preoccupation with sex colored his perceptions. The bad thing about that wonderful, delusional high when I actually believed I was the alpha mare in my herd was when I finally did grasp reality. It would send me spinning in a downward spiral.

Eventually, something would always burst my bubble and bring me back down to sanity again, but I wouldn't stop there. I'd keep on going down. One day I would be sky high and world famous, and the next I thought of myself as a worthless piece of shit.

Dr. Wilcox saw this change in me as I switched my brain speed from mega-thoughts to barely any conscious thought at all. He never told me I was depressed. Maybe I didn't show it around him because, whenever I had an appointment, we talked about horses, and that always brought me up. I sold him a Lipizzaner filly, and I was constantly asking him how Bella was doing. To tell the truth, maybe I wasn't as forlorn around him as I was when I was with William.

The Petersons didn't believe in mental problems. When William saw me acting strange, he ignored it. Their whole philosophy was that if you didn't talk about something, it wouldn't be a problem. I guess no one foresaw what was going to happen next.

That fall day of 1979 started on a strange note to begin with. The sky outside looked as if it were pure water. We were going to get one of those Alabama pre-winter floods for sure. As I drove to work, my soul felt as dark and black as those clouds pluming above me. It was a day that was neither comfortable nor cold. It felt as if it were going to enter your flesh and saturate you. The quiet of the street enhanced that feeling of being alone.

Everyone was staying in because this was going to be a terrible storm. I should have called off my classes. I really didn't expect anyone to come that day. I unlocked the door and found the mail I hadn't opened the day before. The air in the art supply store saturated me with an odor of oil paints and dust. The moisture in the air pressed the aromas down into my pores. My business was in an old cotton warehouse. I couldn't seem to win the war against perpetual dust and Grumbacher-colored rat pills, the result of their chewing into the tubes of paint scattered all around the studio.

There was electrical energy in the air. I could feel my hair tickling my scalp as positive and negative charges made it dance in a frizzed style. That energy was so strong I could smell it. I looked out the dusty front window, and the sky looked almost like there was a solar eclipse. Street lamps came on at nine in the morning.

When I opened the mail, my heart began to despair as soon as I saw the letter from the IRS. I had paid Social Security taxes for my helper who came in after school to do the framing, but I hadn't paid any on myself because I never paid myself a salary out of the business. Heck, without the money from the sale of my art and tuition from my art classes, the place would have closed long ago. William didn't qualify for Social Security disability. Of course, he was too proud to have accepted it anyway, but I worried about others in his condition who needed it that the Social Security Administration had turned down. There he was a quadriplegic living on his own and trying to take care of us, yet they wouldn't give it to him. Believe it or not, had he lived with his parents and not needed it to pay bills, he could have drawn from his dad's Social Security check. Friendly fire had left him disabled, however a typo left him unable to collect his military disability.

It looked as though the government was fixing to pay me a visit and demand that I pay all the back Social Security taxes I owed plus some fines. That was it. That pulled all the remnants of hanging on completely out of me. As my spirits sank into a deep, immobilizing depression, the sky seemed to validate it by pouring out its heart too. Soon there were sheets of rain falling that resembled pieces of Saran wrap blowing in the wind as the clouds let loose their payload. I went over to the front door and locked it. I got out my watercolors and a sketchbook. Sitting at my drawing table in the front room, I drew an abstracted face crying tears of blood with my brush. While I did this, my students and customers began arriving outside. They wanted me to let them in where it was dry.

"Lee, unlock the door and let us in. It's time for class. What are you doing?"

They banged on the window, but I never looked up or stopped painting. The phone rang, and they watched me ignore it too. I only stopped when I finished the watercolor, and at that point in time, my memory bled dry. I woke up in the hospital three days later.

Anyone could have deduced that I'd had a bipolar crash. Not Dr. Wilcox, no way. He told William and me that I was sexually frustrated and that William needed to let me start having sex outside of the marriage. William didn't know enough about my illness to question the prescribed treatment, because the doctor never diagnosed the problem. William didn't know if it was the right solution to my depression or not. Dr. Wilcox set me up to start doing things I shouldn't have been doing. But by the spring of 1980, my feelings for William just weren't the same.

Chapter Twelve

The first thing that changed the way I felt about William was when he wanted me to test the theory for his book. I truly didn't want to do it. However, he and Lisa had been pretty convincing that I didn't know what was best for me. Lisa's heart was full of compassion that I'd missed something important to her. I thought the same was true of William. Later I'd found out he had tried to seduce the nineteen-year-old girl who lived with us.

Rachelle stayed with us because her family had moved to Florida and she wanted to graduate from her home high school. Since she and I worked horses together, William and I volunteered our extra bedroom so she'd have a place to stay. God, her parents would have killed him if they'd known the truth about his lusting after her.

I found out one day while cleaning up his office. I didn't care that he wanted to do anything with her—we were trying an open marriage at that point with the understanding that being open and honest with each other laid the foundation for that kind of thing. What upset me was that he never told me that he wanted to be with her. As far as I was concerned, he had betrayed my trust.

I'd gone off that previous weekend to have sex with Lisa Smith Wing's boyfriend, John. It had been with William's knowledge and blessing. Now that I think about it, he had orchestrated the whole thing to get me out of the house that weekend. Oh, it had been Lisa's idea, but William had put the final touches on it. I simply went along, thinking that everyone else knew what was best for me. Because I'd gone crazy and had a horrible crisis, I doubted my own abilities. I could not discern right from wrong.

When I encountered my first extramarital sexual partner with William's blessing, he had expected me to come in and tell him every single detail of my exploits. William had been living vicariously through my sexcapades, or so I thought. The truth of the matter was that my first sexual encounter outside of our marriage left me feeling flat. It was as bad as my first experience as a teenager. Both left me wondering why everyone got excited about sex.

I never suspected anything between William and Rachelle. Two weeks after I returned from Lisa's house, while cleaning William's desk in his office, I unexpectedly discovered some of his writing. He'd not only written about his plans but had detailed the actual seduction. He rambled on for nearly six pages, babbling about wine, romancing, and things he hadn't offered to do for me in nearly eleven years. It infuriated me. I'm sensitive to someone lying to me, by either commission or omission.

I only talked to Rachelle to find out if it was fantasy or if it really happened. She confirmed that she'd come in from feeding the horses to candles, flowers, wine, and definite sexual overtures that evening. It still bothered me that he had romanced her. I remember being very jealous. I felt I could never trust him again, and not because they had made out and petted. The definition of an affair, as far as I was concerned, was doing anything with another person other than your spouse and hiding it from your spouse. William and Rachelle were having an affair right before my very blind eyes!

William pushed me away, and I began to withdraw from him.

The washing machine interrupted my memories with its loud ding. It had taken me a while to understand what I had done to William, but now I could relate to him because Joe had made me feel the same way. I never withheld sex from Joe the way William did with me over a period of many months.

Later that summer, William took his vow of chastity—making things even riskier between us. He stayed locked up in his office and wouldn't let me in. I'd always had a thing about locked doors. One day when Mama had locked me out, I encountered a snake, and it petrified me. Of course, I had wanted in and to be comforted. She'd given me neither. To this day, I have both a snake phobia and a neurosis about locked doors.

What had made things worse between William and me was his controlling everything about Flying Horse Farm, our Lipizzan farm. Breeding those horses had been my dream since the age of seven, yet I had absolutely no say in the running of the farm. For instance, we argued about the type of barn we'd build. I wanted to go with a cheaper one to have a place to feed my mares individually. He wanted to build the fancy one, although we were out of money, thanks to paying too much for remodeling our small house.

Although I was the one working at the mill every day and bringing home the paycheck, I didn't get to make the decisions about the farm. My work was even more demanding since I did swing shifts. I worked harder than any of the men simply because of my smaller size and lighter weight. Doing manual labor in the sometimes one hundred ten degrees or more heat on the machine floor in the mill demanded too much from me. Often I had to pull double shifts where I worked for sixteen hours. I really started resenting William and was ripe for a real affair.

I had one six months later in October of 1980. I felt so guilty that Barry and I only saw each other three times, because the lies and deceit it took for me to meet him finally took their toll on me and made me stop. I thought I didn't have it in me to cheat—though of course I did. Nevertheless, I didn't consider the gain worth the risk of William's pain.

I debated whether to tell him about the affair. After all, we did have an open marriage, thus my having sex with Barry shouldn't have been a big deal. I rationalized that to go and confess to William now would only hurt him the way he had hurt me when he did something behind my back. Since I had ended it, I thought I'd carry that secret to my grave—but I didn't.

Two years later, in the summer of 1982, I let my secret out. By then, William was courting Erin, a college student who was intrigued with him. He radiated charisma in terms of attracting people to him.

The three of us were sitting around the kitchen table having coffee, about an hour before I had to go to work. William was out of his office, though I'm sure it was because Erin was there. I wasn't fooling myself. I lit the incense burner, and rosewood scent softly tickled my nose. I looked across the table at Erin. She was beautiful. To me, pretty women had perfectly balanced features, but a beautiful woman illustrated a one-of-a-kind look with asymmetrical features. Erin had glossy black hair with natural waves, gorgeous blue eyes and a square, determined jaw. Her lips were big and full on a mouth almost too big for her face. All the features put together made a face one would never forget. I couldn't have handpicked a more intelligent mistress for William.

I studied William who was sitting across from me, never once looking in my direction. When had it all changed for him? He loved Erin, not me. I could see it in his eyes. It hurt some, but not nearly as much as I had expected it to hurt. I knew William and I didn't have what we'd once had. In some ways, that was a compliment to him. Despite the change in our relationship, I could still relate or not relate to him as any normal husband and wife would do.

Erin sipped her coffee and must have sensed the tension between us, because she started talking. "My doctor prescribed new birth control pills today. I hope these won't make me sick like my others did."

I nodded. "You know, I had that same problem. I got really nauseated and stopped taking them."

Back in 1980, I'd hidden the fact that I was on birth control from William because that was when I was having the revenge affair with Barry. I didn't tell William I'd gone to the doctor and he'd put me on the pill.

William glared at me and choked up. "When were you on birth control pills? We can't have any children. You used them when you were having your affair, right?"

William looked about as defeated as I had ever seen him in his life. He had survived a horrible war accident and made the best of his paralysis, but, in an instant, I had yanked him down to such despair that Mr. Stoic couldn't hide his feelings. William usually wore an emotional mask as one of his coping techniques. On that day, his face showed deep pain, and it broke my heart. For the first time in our marriage, I saw him cry. He hadn't cried when his father died or when we lost our Doberman who was like our child, and I'd heard tales that he never cried when he found out he wouldn't walk. What I'd done to him had brought him to unabashed tears.

"How did you find out?" I asked. "Who told you?"

William wouldn't look at me. He never said another word. I think the shock of realizing how much I'd hurt him created my confusion.

"Come on now," I said. "Tell me who told you."

The soft rattle of his wheelchair broke the silence between us as his muscles twitched involuntarily, causing his footrests to bounce and squeak. He twisted around to grab onto the back with his bent elbow to keep himself from falling out. He stared at his lap. I bowed my head with the most shame I'd ever felt in my life.

"I think I'd better be going," Erin said as she stood up to put her coffee cup in the sink filled with dirty dishes. I was a lousy housekeeper simply because I didn't have time.

"It's okay," I said. "I'll be gone in a minute. I know William wants to spend more time with you."

My eyes met hers with that woman-to-woman pleading expression of "help me by helping him." Instead of putting her coffee cup in the sink, she poured herself a refill. While she was busy with the cream and sugar, I resumed talking to William. Rather, I tried talking to William.

"Please talk to me," I said. "Tell me who told you. God, I'm so sorry."

When William ignored my question for the third time, my brain finally grasped what had happened.

"I told you, didn't I? I let it out. Didn't I?"

"Do me one favor," he said. "Tell me everything. Tell me who, when, where, and why."

The pain in my bowels from that memory brought me back into the present. At nine fifteen, I got up and put the clothes in the dryer. I took several deep breaths as I handled the damp materials, feeling the gut-wrenching pain finally dissipate. I couldn't help wandering back into remembering that I was no innocent.

I'd managed to tell William that the affair had been with Barry. I admitted that I'd used trips to go take pictures for my art as the excuse to get away and meet him. I let William know that I'd slept with Barry in the fall of 1980, right after our Doberman pinscher had died. All these answers satisfied him, but I'd left off the answer to the most important of his questions—why?

That had been the turning point for William and me. Neither of us trusted each other after that. We both felt betrayed by the other. Yes, what I had done was much worse, however the shock of finding out your mate has hidden something from you wasn't any different. Both actions killed what had once been Agape love between us. We started fighting and getting on each other's nerves.

When the summer of '82 rolled around, I had no problem having sex outside the marriage. Until Joe, it had only been sex with some infatuation. William told me that was fine as long as I was honest and told him about it. There again, he was being a hypocrite because he would never tell me anything about Erin and him. His famous quote of "A gentleman never tells" pissed me off, and I showed it. Why expect me to tell each naughty little detail in my escapades? In time, I grew to resent that. William was driving me crazy, or at least at the time I thought it was because of him. I didn't know I'd lived in the land of lunacy long before he entered my life.

Trembling at the thought, I focused on the television set I had turned on earlier while trying to kill some time. The TV distracted me as adrenalin pumped rapidly through my system. Anger came easily and made me as happy as a tick on a hound dog. I got up and turned off the television, but voices still plagued me. Fortunately, the memory voice was the loudest of them all. I listened carefully and recognized that the voice sounded like mine. Thoughts of William and Joe swirled around me.

Dee Dee reminded me of the similarity between my cheating on William and Joe's cheating on me. Oh my Lord, remembering those photography trips induced an uneasy feeling in my gut, bringing on a moment of déjà vu, because twenty years later Joe had used his own photography hobby to cheat on me. What goes around comes around. I'd brought this on myself.

"Shut up!"

I grabbed my ears as if that would drown out the noise inside my head, and it worked. Soon, there was only my regular thought voice thinking about William.

Chapter Thirteen

William had agreed to let other men have a turn with me because he knew I'd been faithful to him for the past ten years, even when we couldn't have normal sex. He'd also understood there had been many men who assumed I needed "a good fuck" as they would call it. He realized I'd never taken any of them up on the offer and appreciated that fact. Never breaking his trust, I'd always told him about each one who made a play for me, until my illness led me to being promiscuous by the summer of 1982.

The speed-like high of mania produced super-sexual stamina and energy. I was seeing two men while pulling double shifts at the mill. My other lover, James, an electrician at the mill, sizzled when Joe came along. I meandered in my mind to the day after my date with Joe when I'd made a confession to him.

"I have another lover, and you're going to have to share me. Are you willing to do that?"

As usual, we sat there on break having our pimento cheese sandwiches and sugar cookies for brunch—our daily ritual.

"You amaze me," he said. "I wouldn't like sharing you, but to have you in my life, I'd be willing to do anything. I'll prove to you that I'm the man you need. We Thames men are stubborn and don't give up. I'll win you in the end. For now, yes, I'll share you."

I studied his face. He had a mighty determined look on it. I thought I also detected some doubt. Remembering the performance anxiety he'd had the night before, I thought he might need some reassurance.

"Last night was really wonderful," I said, "and although you did have some problems, there is going to be another time. Don't feel bad or worry about it. You more than satisfied me. In fact, I've never experienced what you gave me. I'm awed at your lack of inhibition and your ability to do whatever it takes to satisfy a woman. You're the first man to bring me to orgasm in a long, long time."

I snickered to myself remembering that. It had been true, because I hadn't experienced any oral sex since the summer of 1980. All my other lovers had been too uptight. Maybe that doctor had a point. William's no-sex-at-all had been beginning to tell on me. Once I'd let loose, I went crazy. I was one hot chick. Only one of the men had accidentally brought me to orgasm once that whole summer. Then Joe came along and brought me to orgasm every single time. In fact, he taught me how to have multiple orgasms.

That first time in September of 1982, Joe had real problems. He couldn't get it up and keep his erection.

"Joe, it's going to be all right," I said. "I'm not the least bit upset about this. I know there will be another chance to show me what you can do."

I rubbed his nude muscular back as I said that. He had been working out with weights and had a wonderful physique that turned me on. William's body had atrophied, and none of my other lovers worked out.

After I reassured Joe, he pulled me back into his arms and kissed me again. Then his mouth trailed all the way down my neck until he found the places that drove me wild. Unlike William, who could do me orally but not move around on me, Joe used everything he had, including his long hair trailing over every inch of my body to stimulate me to the max. He definitely knew what he was doing and, damn, he was good at it too.

"You are one hell of a man," I told him afterward. "God, I've never had anything like that in my life. Where did you learn how to do that?"

"When I was fifteen, I had a thirty-two-year-old woman teach me how to be a good lover."

I shook off the memories for a moment and looked down at the shirt I was toying with in my hand. Heaving a sigh, I began to idly fold the clothes while my mind traversed time—the present warring with past, reminding me of the reason for my anger.

Back then, I had been thankful for the teacher Joe had spoken about so fondly. Later, I realized it had been that molestation—the stealing of his innocence in one fell swoop—that had created the monster of sexual addiction. He'd never learned to couple love with sex, yet he'd always thought sex was the only way a woman showed her love. He thought he loved every woman he had sex with, confusing love with infatuation and not realizing that he was incapable of truly loving anyone. That woman had messed him up good.

Back in 1982, Joe felt sure of his sexual abilities, especially that day of our discussion when I complimented him. He knew I'd want him to make love to me and would be impatient for the day that he could. He was right about that.

"Honey, you are such a woman," he said. "I've never felt this way about anyone. The way I feel about you, I can't put into words. I've never experienced love before you. Now I know how it feels. You are beautiful. Listen to the words of 'Be My Lady' by Jefferson Airplane. Maybe that can explain how I feel. I believe it says 'I'd gladly burn to ashes for you, be my lady.' You are all that I think about now."

Those words had awakened something inside me that had been dormant for a long, long time. By the time Joe courted me, I had become aware that I was indeed missing something in my life: the connection between emotions and sex. It was powerful, and it intoxicated me. However, I had never felt that way about intercourse until Joe showed me what that was all about.

Dr. Wilcox's diagnosis in the fall of 1979 that I was sexually frustrated hadn't been the truth at that time of my life. Later, however, Joe had shown me how sexually retarded I was. He made a woman out of me at age thirty-three. Dr. Wilcox missed diagnosing my illness, and that had cost me big time.

The clock in the den chimed nine thirty, bringing me out of my reverie once again. My tea glass sweated, leaving a ring on the walnut end table next to my chair. I took a sip, discovering it tasted watered-down and bland. It seemed as if eleven o'clock would never arrive. I went back to the kitchen and poured out the lukewarm tea. I needed some more since tea was my comfort food. I filled the kettle and used three bags to make it the right strength, the way I preferred it. While I waited on Tilly, my mama's teakettle, to sing, I sat down at the kitchen table.

My gaze traveled to the wall and settled on the framed photo of my dad in his World War II captain's uniform. That picture and the flag in the triangular glass case were my treasures. I studied my dad's features and remembered how much James had reminded me of this image of him. I'd felt a sick thrill at being sexually attracted to a man who reminded me of my dad. I hadn't experienced shame until I had sex outside of the marriage with Barry, the man I cheated with in October of 1980.

Chapter Fourteen

I had never done things for the same reasons or in the same way other people did. As I continued to ponder my past actions, I felt a ghostly realization that everything I'd accused Joe of doing to me I had done to William. Just as Joe had built all those resentments against me and never let on that he felt them—much less confronted me with his changing feelings—I had done the same thing with William.

I'd been angry with William about his dishonesty, yet, I appeared to have let it go. I don't think I realized at the time how much that smoldering anger consumed me. It had taken a strange thing to make me act on my newly emerging sexual desires. I had loved all the men's attention, yet I denied that any of them made me the least bit interested in doing something I considered morally wrong—adultery.

William and I had owned a beautiful reddish-brown Doberman pinscher named Rusty, as well as two of her daughters, Alice and Red. Since we wanted to breed Dobermans, William had given me Rusty for my thirtieth birthday. I loved that dog. When canine parvo virus first made the scene, my Rusty contracted it and became very ill. We took her to Auburn University as our only hope of saving her.

"Do whatever you need to do to save her life," I told the attending vet. "Money is not an issue. But promise me this: if you see she is going to die, call me. I want to come and get her, because I don't want her to die in a cage. I want her to die at home."

Worried sick each day, I prayed for God to save Rusty while I continued to work at the mill. As usual, all the men were more interested in trying to hit on me than realizing how worried I was about my dog. All but one man— Barry. He listened to me and seemed sympathetic and understanding that I could be upset and concerned about a dog. A quiet man, he'd never made a pass at me. We were friends and coworkers. I think he mentioned casually that he thought I was pretty, but that was the extent of his trying to flirt with me. He was one of the few men who worked beside me, told me when I did a good job, and treated me as one of the crew.

I was not sexually attracted to Barry, rather I think I was drawn to him by respect. That was exactly what set both Barry and Joe apart from all the other men at the mill. I respected them because they both treated me with respect. Being able to talk to Barry about how afraid I was that Rusty was going to die set the stage for what would happen next between us.

I was working the three-to-eleven shift on a Friday in October of 1980, and the vet had called us that morning. After the arsenal of canine drugs had failed, he'd borrowed drugs from the local human hospital and had given her intravenous drips. He'd tried everything to save her, but he realized she was dying and told us to come get her while she still had some sense of consciousness.

We drove to Auburn with heavy hearts. My beautiful dog was a skeleton with sunken eyes. I'm not sure she recognized us or was aware that she was no longer in the cage. If I had it to do over again, knowing what I know now about parvo, I would not have boarded her at the vet's. As she got sicker and sicker, I would have let her stay home rather than having to be in a cage in a strange place. As a dog, she wouldn't have understood it was necessary in order to save her, and being home would have made her last moments more meaningful to her.

When we got home, she weakly climbed onto the couch with me and put her head in my lap. I petted her and watched her ribs rise and fall with each labored breath. Her eyes dropped back in her head while I kept talking to her, telling her we were there and how much we loved her while I stroked her head. She had an odor of death that sickened me—emotionally, not physically. Finally, she kind of jerked and blew out her closed and clenched mouth, her lips sagging as she did so. Then her ribcage stopped moving.

Oh, how I cried! I wanted to call in to work for funeral leave, but of course I couldn't. And since I was still in my probationary period for permanent employment, I knew I couldn't call in sick. My supervisor knew my dog was ill and would have been on to me. Because I was a woman, they were already looking for an excuse not to let me make my ninety days. William and I needed the money way too much for me to blow that job.

I think Rusty's death may have been one of my largest resentments toward William. I think I subconsciously piled it on top of the hurt of betrayal that clawed at my love, finally shredding it into unsalvageable pieces. There I was emotionally devastated, yet I forced myself to get up, get dressed, and go to work. I couldn't even bury her. When I looked over at William, he didn't even have tears in his eyes. He never showed his emotions. I knew it was his coping mechanism for what had happened to leave him paralyzed, but that day, when I saw him looking unaffected while I was going crazy, it made me furious.

I was angry that William would get to bury her when his brother came over to dig the grave, and I had to go to work and couldn't go with them. I seethed because he'd sat there with this same expression on his face that he wore whenever we drank coffee together. Mainly, though, I was angry with God who had allowed her to die.

When Rusty got sick, I had bargained with God that, although I'd been tempted to have an affair, I would promise I'd never, ever be unfaithful and break my marriage vows to Him as well as to William if He would just let Rusty live. When I went to work that day, I was furious and wanted revenge against God. I was going to show Him. Now I realize I also wanted to punish William by keeping a secret from him as he'd kept Rachelle a secret from me. My anger at God had been only an excuse.

The teakettle's call paused my reflections long enough to make my tea. I added a pinch of baking soda to the hot tea to rid it of foam, next I measured out my sugar. I filled my grand-Maw Maw's cut-glass pitcher with the sweet elixir and sat back down at the table. Since it was dark outside, the two windows looking into the sunroom reflected my own image back to me, and I smiled as I thought that the woman I saw looking back at me didn't look like a murderer. Maybe that would work in my favor. How could a lady surrounded by crystal, china, silver, and fresh-cut flowers commit such a heinous crime as murder?

Precious, my Pomeranian, barked at a passing car. Rusty had never done that. She had been far too serious. I drifted back to the day she'd passed away.

When I arrived at the mill, I was relieved to find that my workstation for the night was working with Barry on the winder. I couldn't have tolerated any of the crude sexist remarks cracked by the other men or their callous lack of understanding for my emotional state over the loss of my dog. Barry and I talked that night, and I felt incredibly close to him as a result. In fact, to be honest, I realized that he had shown more emotion over Rusty's death than William had. He seemed genuinely sorry and identified with loving a dog the way I did.

For the first time, I noticed how sexy and blue his eyes were, and I felt myself attracted to him. He had such a gentle manner and was never crude. He voice had a nasal quality, but it was soft and kind. I looked at his face and, for the first time, observed that craggy look, high cheekbones, and his longish hair. Barry was clean. He was the only man who could work in the coating room never getting a drop of coating on him. His mouth was small and tight, and his nose was triangular with clean nostrils.

What turned me on were his high cheekbones and thin face—the opposite of William who had a round face that happened to be malnourished thin. William's head sported thinning hair with a scruffy beard, while Barry was clean-shaven. I felt my heartbeat increase each time we stood close to each other, and I sensed that he was feeling the same thing. There was no denying that we were aroused.

"Hey," I said, "do you have to go straight home tonight, or can you go out to my farm with me and talk some more? I'll buy you a beer so we can cry about the life and loss of one fantastic dog."

I could tell he noticed that my tee shirt had lost its opaqueness where sweat had formed on my braless chest. My nipples stood erect from the cooling evaporation when I stood in front of the fan by the winder. I enjoyed his staring at me.

"Yeah," he said, "I can stay over for a while. Glenda's always asleep when I get off work on the evening shift."

My stomach suddenly had a new feeling going on in there. It seemed as if my shift would never end, but we were both finally relieved by an oncoming crew. Thank God, no double for me that night. Often when I went in, I didn't know if anyone had called in and I would be expected to double onto the next shift so they could set up for the crew, and it was hard work too. I was around all the heavy equipment on the machine floor or on the wet end making oil rounds. Even in October, it was hot as hell.

William and I hadn't moved onto our farmland yet. Although close to moving, we still lived in town. I knew Barry and I would be safe there since it was isolated. I stopped at the Jiffy Mart and bought us each two Michelob Lights. I waited for him at the end of our road and, sure enough, soon spotted Barry's little white Nissan. I was feeling too strange to misunderstand that we were going to do more than talk that night.

We drove out to the farm and went up to the empty house that loomed like a wooden crypt. When I saw my land and realized Rusty would never run on it again, I felt overwhelmed with sadness. I got into Barry's car, and we drove down the road to a little church. A security light illuminated the area enough for us to see. It was one of those dilapidated clapboard churches that looked more like a house than a church. It probably could hold a maximum of maybe five or six families. The right side of it sagged and whispered half a step going up to the back door as a blessing to the deserted place.

We pulled around and parked behind it. We started drinking, and at first all we did was talk, then he leaned over and I leaned over, and the next thing I knew, we were kissing. His hand came up to my breast, and it felt divine. I craved that kind of lusty attention. Barry uncorked raw emotions as we embraced and kissed passionately. He let down the back seat of the 1980 Stanza wagon, we both climbed in and undressed.

God, his hard muscular body looked good, and I could tell he felt the same way about me. He'd admitted to me that his wife was overweight, had sagging breasts, and could walk around naked without it doing anything for him anymore. He told me I was beautiful as he lay me down and kissed me again. Unlike the weekend William had sent me to Mobile to have sex with my friend's lover while he tried to seduce Rachelle, an experience that had been the same as screwing a corpse, sex with Barry was riveting. My heart pounded, and I felt Barry's heart pounding in his chest as well.

I finally understood what the big deal was. Barry actually wasn't a great lover. Since I'd been unable to have intercourse for nearly eleven years, it felt almost sacred to me—like losing my virginity again. The newness of those sexual sensations intoxicated me. I didn't have an orgasm that night because I hadn't graduated to that stage. I'd greatly enjoyed feeling a man hard inside of me and having him kiss me and pet me. God, it felt good.

Too soon, it was over as Barry let out a small moan and lay on top of me, still for a few minutes. William couldn't have an orgasm, and I'd gone too many years without experiencing the pleasure of satisfying a man sexually. It was such a turn on. That night with Barry, I discovered my sexual power, and it awakened something inside of me that had indeed lain dormant for too many years.

Of course, I didn't want that night and that moment to end. For a brief time, all my sadness, pain and anger were gone. I looked up at the night sky, saw Heaven, and felt Rusty's presence with me. I had to believe that something I loved as much as I had loved her had to have some part of her go on forever. It couldn't simply be the end of her. It was as if that incredible love I'd felt for Rusty flowed out of me and through my body that night, not so much for Barry as it was for understanding the vastness of love itself.

Before that night, I had never drawn a parallel in my life between love and intercourse. Even as a teen, I'd not been infatuated or sexually active. I wasn't a virgin when I married William, but he and I hadn't had intercourse while we were dating. He had the values to wait until we were married, and I honored those values in him.

I never hid losing my virginity to Donny from William. We had started out with an honest relationship, and we respected our Southern upbringing enough to only kiss and pet. Then he drew a low lottery number and shipped out to 'Nam, still a virgin. I was faithful to him because I looked forward to our wedding night. The truth was my first sexual experience when I'd lost my virginity had been about as cold and calculating as anything could have been, so I had high hopes of my next one making up for it.

Chapter Fifteen

At seventeen, I had been curious and wanted to find out what "doing it" felt like. It was 1966—before William and I began dating when we went to our senior banquet in May of 1967. I wanted to save my reputation, so I carefully chose the person to whom I'd give my virginity. I wanted someone who would have a lot to lose if he talked and bragged. I grew up in an era when nice girls didn't get their names passed around town for their indiscriminating acts. In fact, a good friend of mine made the mistake of having casual sex with an older teenaged neighbor, and everyone soon branded her as the town slut. I knew better, but I also learned from her mistake.

There was a blond-haired, blue-eyed boy named Zach that I was crazy about when I was fifteen. He never noticed me, but he did date Lisa, my best friend. His older brother, Donny, was in the Army serving in Vietnam. When Donny was home on leave, he would take Lisa and me riding around with him. Sometimes Zach would go with us, sometimes he wouldn't.

I knew Donny had given his girlfriend an engagement ring on his last leave, and I also knew he'd be home and out of the service after the Christmas Holidays of 1966. I started setting up the plan to lose my virginity. I wanted to wait until I turned eighteen. My birthday was coming up that spring of 1967, my gift to myself was going to be a nice little taste of life.

I mapped out ways for me to run into Donny accidentally. In a small town, that was easy to do. Casually talking in public in an innocent and harmless way was common, since everyone knew each other. I recognized Donny had a crush on me, because he was always joking about how cute I was. I wasn't too dumb to read between the lines that he was a virile man in his mid-twenties and I was a seventeen-year-old girl.

It wouldn't take much to seduce him into seducing me. A little smile here, a flirt there, some joking and kidding around, then I'd leave him dangling. I wasn't worldly or anything, in fact, I didn't have much experience at all with boyfriends. I'd done the traditional petting in the back seat of a car, never committing to a steady enough boyfriend to move into the really hot and heavy mode until William entered my life. He had been the self-disciplined one with manners and character. Most of my sexual experiences had been simply an intense curiosity.

At seventeen, I couldn't fathom how all those body parts actually fit together in a way that was supposed to be pleasant. I figured out that mouth on mouth felt safe, hand on breasts felt respectable, and hand down below felt good, but my hand touching them? Yuck. I only did it because I knew I needed to. I'd never gone far enough to see any male ejaculating from a hand job or even from dry humping me.

I didn't know what an orgasm was—never realizing I'd been having them when I did myself. I knew that when I put my hand between my legs and pressed them together tightly and kept at it long enough, I'd feel like I was about to pee all over myself—that is what I envisioned going on inside of my head. I was so stupid that when I had one, I couldn't figure out why I didn't actually urinate. No one taught me about a clitoris, orgasms or much about sex at all. Since no male had actually ever made me feel that sensation, I didn't really relate it to sex at all.

Sex had been a taboo subject in my family, and my idea of it was that it was something nice people didn't do. I knew I was masturbating and touching myself. Everyone told us back then that our fingers would rot off, or our noses would grow, and we'd definitely burn in eternal Hell if we ever touched ourselves "down there." I had shame, because not only did I do it, I couldn't quit doing it. I'd feel so disgraceful and guilty and swear to myself that I'd never do it again. Then unexpectedly there would come this odd sensation from between my legs, and the only way I could make it stop was to touch myself until I felt that release.

God, I was naïve. I really was extremely curious about the whole genital thing. My mom made me feel as if having genitals was the worst thing on earth—dirty, humiliating, secret, and something you didn't talk about, touch, or let anyone else touch. We weren't even religious or anything. She just had this warped outlook on the female genitalia, calling them something as sick as "toodle woodles." My sister and I both inherited it too. I always hated going to doctors because they would see my bottom when giving me a shot.

I couldn't imagine how someone could have sex, because no decent girl would open her legs wide enough to allow it. I couldn't comprehend being naked and unashamed enough to let someone see you, especially "down there." Of course, since it was forbidden, I knew I had to try it, especially if my mom thought it was terrible. Although she'd already succeeded in making me uptight, I clung to my plan like a tick on an old hound dog.

As fate would have it, I was walking home from some forgotten place when Donny drove by in his car. He offered me a ride and, of course, I took him up on it.

I remember thinking Well, it can't get any better than this. It's now or never.

"Donny, what does having sex feel like?"

He looked over at me with an are-you-serious expression, and I looked back at him with an impish grin that said Yes, I'm dog-dead serious!

"Why on earth are you asking me something like that?"

"I'm curious," I said. "I see and hear all that stuff about how great it is, and I wanted to know what it would be like. I can't imagine it."

"Well, ah . . . it's like this really good, uh . . . something kinda like . . . damn, Lee. I don't know how to tell you how it feels. Why are you asking me anyway?"

"Well, you're a lot older, and I know you've done it and know what you're doing, so tell me."

"Okay, it's like when you come, it feels too good to describe. Everybody loves it when they start doing it."

Donny didn't have the best vocabulary in the world, and he used words based on a person having had some experience in order to understand what he was saying. So my next question to him was, "Will you show me?"

Think about it. Here was this thin waif of a girl with long dark brown hair actually offering her virginity to a soldier. Of course he'd show me.

Too bad Joe hadn't introduced me to sex—my whole outlook would have been so different. Joe was the type to go so slowly over a woman's body to make her relax and want him to enter her. He also never had an orgasm until he brought her to one. Donny, no way. This was my introduction to sex: we rode out to a deserted spot where he took me over behind some bushes, unzipped his pants, and pulled down my jeans and panties low enough to slip his dick up in me.

Of course, I was standing there with my legs as tightly together as I could get them. I've since learned that often makes for a fantastic orgasm for a man due to the friction. Being a grown man and having the excitement of taking a cherry, poor Donny didn't last a minute. He used a rubber, I didn't have the sensation of anything running out of me. Hell, I still didn't know what a man did during sex. I felt something that hurt more than it felt good—nothing like zero foreplay for any woman, but most especially a small virgin, to completely ruin that first sexual encounter.

I think he may have kissed me. I'm not even sure of that. It was awful. I didn't remember too much about it other than it hurt and I felt lousy afterward. There were no emotions and no rituals similar to making love. It was a quickie fuck at best, and it was Donny using me to masturbate himself at worst. I was only an orifice.

I did learn that day that you could have sex without undressing and without opening up your legs. I guess maybe that part reassured me. Mainly, though, I learned that it wasn't anything to toot either my horn or his. Speaking of which, with him engaged, he had lots more to lose than I did if he opened his mouth to blab and it got around. Of course, neither of us said anything about it ever again.

Remembering my first encounter with sex reminded me of how strong I had become as a female. I couldn't stand the damn double standard between the sexes. By the time I was in college, I came out into the open about it when I gave a speech in my communication class titled "I Wasn't a Virgin When I Married and I'm Damn Proud of It." The sorority girls in the class nearly swooned in a modest blush, but my teacher gave me an A+ for being bawdy.

I became a women's libber, which is probably the reason I was feisty enough to prevent a rape in the fall of 1980.

The den clock sounding its ten o'clock chimes returned me to the present. Thinking about my life had worn me out. I turned on the television again to check on our progress in the Iraq war. At that time, as an idealist, I had believed in freeing the Iraqi people. However, the huge mess had turned me against the war and ended my support of Bush. It seemed as if no damn man could keep a promise. They were all after something—fame, power, sugarcoated attention. Mainly they were after sex. The TV commentator faded out as my mind upped its internal volume, remembering the time I'd told one man where to stick it. I smiled as I remembered that story.

Chapter Sixteen

I'd made my oil rounds as the helper on the wet end where the pulp and slurries were going into vats. Lots of pumps needed to be checked to make sure oil lubricated them. I often had to go through tight, dark places and use my flashlight to look at the oil gauges. There was one troublesome spot where I rounded the corner of a slurry pit made of bricks. I had to squeeze between two pumps that went from a well-lit area right into a dark area.

Even with the flashlight, my eyes needed time to adjust. I guess not eating those awful carrots as a child made me pay dearly later on with a bad case of night blindness. I had traveled through there maybe thirty or forty times before, but on this particular day, as I stepped around the corner and started to squeeze through the pumps, I sensed I was not alone. I felt a tickle on the back of my neck and came to a grinding halt. I took my flashlight and pointed it up ahead and, sure enough, there stood a man I knew wasn't on our crew because he wasn't wearing the uniform of any mill employee.

"Hey, baby," he said. "What are you doing? No one's around, and I'm going to fuck you."

To be honest, he pissed me off more than he scared me. How dare that bastard talk to me that way. I beamed my flashlight straight into his eyes

"Why don't you take your dick and stick it up your ass and go fuck yourself!"

I could tell he had been flabbergasted and hadn't expected that kind of reaction from me. As I said it, I squeezed by him and quickly moved from the darkness into the lit area of the mill. I never looked back, nor did I run. I kept on making my oil rounds and ignored him. I guess he figured he wasn't going to intimidate me and left me alone. It made me realize I didn't need to fear the men at the mill. This has served me well all my life. Another time, my lack of fear prevented another rape and once even saved a woman's life when her boyfriend was beating her up. I told him I was going to kick his ass if he didn't leave her alone. Typical of cowards who beat on women, he fled when confronted with my lack of fear.

Although I didn't fear the men I worked with, I didn't understand the treatment I received because I was a woman. My foreman had been wonderful until I made it through my ninety-day probationary period. It was strange to see the change in the men on my crew—not all of them, but a good many of them. In fact, many of them who had been hounding me for some action began avoiding me as if I had bird flu.

However, most of the black men on the crew continued to treat me as they always had. Two of them were close friends of mine, and I occasionally went to their houses to have a beer with them after work on day shift. A third man named Curtis I trusted to take my Quarter Horse stallion to breed with his mares and ended up giving him the stallion. I'd had Jet Stream, son of Jet Deck, for ten years and was phasing out my Quarter Horse breeding while concentrating on my Lipizzans. Looking back, I actually got along better with the black men than the white men at the mill overall.

I eventually found out that many of the men resented me for getting one of the high-paying job slots, thus preventing a man from getting it. Maybe they didn't realize I was the breadwinner of our household, but even if I hadn't been, I—or any woman—was entitled to work there and make that money as long as we could do the work. I'd proven to all of them that I could. I couldn't understand why my boss started acting so odd.

Sometimes, on the low end of the mill, if no crew members were out and we didn't set up, the low man—in my case, the woman—on the crew did the nasty cleanup jobs. Many of the men told me to make any job last as long as I could because I was getting paid the same amount to work my fanny off or to stretch it out to all day with some breaks. For some people, that meant taking lots of breaks, but I couldn't work that way. For one thing, I had too much pride and energy, and that just wasn't my work ethic. I gave one hundred percent every single day.

Honestly, I was so thankful to that company for hiring me that I truly felt loyal to them. When given a job, I worked hard and tried to finish. After completing a task, I felt entitled to go to the cool room and take a break. However, as soon as I'd finish one job, the foreman would immediately send me on another. I couldn't sit down long enough to eat the food in my lunchbox. It was beginning to get to me since the work in that godforsaken heat was draining, but I also knew exactly what he was up to and vowed that I'd die before they ran me off the way they'd recently run off another woman who had been hired a month ahead of me.

It almost killed me, especially when the foreman would hold up two fingers, which meant I had to stay over and work eight more grueling hours. Each day or night when I got home, I'd write in my calendar journal documenting what I'd been required to do and noting if the rest of the crew had been sitting on their butts. I kept up that pace for probably another two to three months. They were about to break me when I decided to play my hunch.

It was a day shift when all the upper management happened to be at the mill. I walked up to my foreman to get my work assignment and, as usual, he was going to stick me in a nasty, hot, horrible place doing some busy work. I had my journal with me. I opened it up so he could see all my writing. Then I gave him the bad news.

"Do you see where I've documented that you treat me differently because I'm a woman? Here, let me read some of these entries to you."

His grin disappeared. I stared at him because I knew I had him by his mountain oysters.

"If you don't stop treating me differently from the other crew members," I went on, "I am going to slap a sexual harassment suit on you. I've been a sport about all the lewd remarks and have never said a word about the men bringing dirty pictures here. I figured that I'd invaded their territory, but this is where I draw the line. You will not treat me differently."

By then, he was as white as my Lipizzan stallion, Pluto Erga. I guess he realized that if I'd taken the time to write down all that stuff, I must know my salt from my pepper and had a solid, provable case against him. Affirmative action was in full play, and the mill certainly didn't want any hassles about the men mistreating the few women out there.

I knew I'd intimidated him. Satisfied that I'd made my point, I walked off to put my book in my locker so no one could bother it. Then I worked on my assignment until I finished it. When I came back up about three hours later, my foreman let me into the cool room, and I sat down with the men. I could tell many of them thought he was selling out. I could also tell some of them respected me for being feisty and having such balls. The few who held on to their resentment never did accept me, and one of them proved to be downright dangerous. I worked with Wesley from 1980 to 1982. Had it not been my last day on the machine crew before I would transfer into the lab, I would have reported him and had him fired.

I felt myself clenching my teeth as the memory of that incident assaulted me.

Ignoring the safety light I'd turned on to show I was in the chute, Wesley had purposely dropped a load of waste that probably weighed over three hundred pounds. The safety rule stated we were to never push anything into the chute when the light was on. When Wesley ignored the light and used a forklift to push all the broke or wastepaper into the chute, I knew he had been trying to harm me. It could have been a serious accident, since I was in the chute cleaning up the remains of the last load dropped in it. I'd literally just stepped out and hadn't turned off the light yet when I heard a boom and the biggest load of waste I'd ever seen came thundering down.

I went bounding up the metal-grated stairs, taking them two at a time. I knew exactly who had done it, because he had been giving me nothing but grief for months. I'd tried ignoring him, however I wasn't about to let this offense drop.

I stood up in his face. "Goddamn you, Wesley! You almost killed me, you motherfucking ignorant bastard!"

"Shut your goddamn mouth, bitch!"

"I'm going to have your ass fired! Didn't you see the light was still on? You tried to kill me!"

"Shut the fuck up or I'm gonna knock your goddamn teeth down your throat!"

He grabbed me by my collar and lifted me off the floor. Most of the time in my life, a good ol' argument pumped adrenalin into me, and I'd hold my own. This time, I instinctively knew he meant it when he threatened to hit me. I shut up and glared at him. He had his fist reared back to let me have it. The entire winder crew gathered around and watched.

I visualized watching my front teeth fall out onto the cement floor and feeling the blood trickling down my chin, anger numbing the initial pain. Thank God a black crewmember figured out that he really was planning to hit me in the face.

"Hey, man! Let her go. You don't want to be fired. She ain't worth that. Chill out, man."

The bastard finally let go of me.

All fighting resulted in automatic firing, and the union would not protect anyone involved in a fight. If he had struck me, they would have fired us both. The rule read that any parties involved in a fight would both go out the gate, whether you hit back or not. To the company, an altercation was an altercation, and they did not happen in a vacuum.

Still, I could have had him suspended for touching me and for disobeying the safety rules. Boy, was I tempted. I knew the man's wife and children, and I could not do it to them. What really saved him, though, was the fact that it happened at the end of my shift, and I knew that after making it through that day, I'd never have to see that ugly pig again. To this day, thinking about his name reminds me of our own pet pig that ran around loose in the yard. People thought the Thames family was strange.

Going from the machine crew to the lab was like dying and going to Heaven. After making my ninety days and proving to them that I knew how to pull my weight on the machine crew, a different reception greeted me once I was in the lab. The newest woman in the mill had hired into the lab from the secretary pool. Karen was soft; even I could see that. Nonetheless, I rooted for her and stood up for her. She had a lot to learn about working in a man's world.

Although much better than the machine crew, the lab still had some difficult jobs in maintaining quality control, such as having to open and close some stout valves. Testing the product was stressful because of time constraints. We had to have all the tests run and logged in before the whistle blew that meant to go get more samples.

Karen had to have help in opening and closing the big valves. I had an advantage in this by coming off the machine crew. I was half her size but strong as a Shetland pony. The only job I couldn't do all by myself was tip a three hundred pound barrel of oil. The company safety rules called it a two-man job anyway for liability reasons. I never felt bad about that.

There was one obnoxious man named Arnold in the lab who thought he was God's gift to women and thought he was going to have me. No way was that going to happen. After sweet and gentle Barry, this man was an asshole. The odd thing about it was that they lived in the same community and rode to and from work together. I always wondered how in the world Barry had been able to come alone to meet me that night. What had happened to Arnold? With whom had he ridden home?

From the fall of 1980 until the summer of 1982, I had been a good girl. Barry and I met two more times, but the guilt I felt for lying to William was too much for me to handle. I thought I was so transparent that William would look at me and know what I was doing to him. Sad to say, William was too trusting and clueless. He never showed any signs of noticing anything, too wrapped up in his own life. It was as though I didn't exist.

I'd had it bad for Barry though. When we planned one of our encounters, I convinced William to ride with me to Barry's house. Barry had bought one of my Lipizzan-Quarter Horse cross weanlings for his son who wanted a horse. They thought owning one and letting them grow up together would be the ideal way to go.

The company had moved Barry to another shift on a crew setup. We were no longer able to see each other at work. Under the pretense of going to check on the horse, I called Barry to see if we could come over to his house. He was on long weekend, and I was on my birthday leave. Barry and I hadn't seen much of each other in months as we quickly glanced at each other when we changed shifts over to the oncoming crew. Sometimes his crew would come in and follow mine, and at other times, I'd come in and follow his. All we could do was look at each other and smile.

My eyes started to droop, and I forced them to glance at the clock that read ten fifteen. Soon this would be over. The aroma of tea filled my kitchen, and I poured myself another glass, listening to the hiss and squeal as the ice cracked when the steamy liquid hit the cubes. I swirled the tea around the ice to cool it down quickly. Maybe it was my night to get everything right, because my tea tasted delicious. All it needed was a touch of mint to make it perfect.

I walked through the sunroom out the back door to my herb garden and picked a few leaves off the aromatic vine. A golden moon rose in the sky, my "Mark moon" smiling down on me—another sign that Daddy approved of my plans to kill Joe. Thinking of my dad reminded me of the photo hanging in the breakfast room. I walked back inside and pulled out one of the ladder-back chairs at the kitchen table. The table was round with a natural wood colored Formica finish atop a country blue pedestal, a leftover from the eighties.

Something caught my eye, and I stared at the chipped, gold-leaf oval frame holding my dad's photograph. Its curved glass was irreplaceable should I break it. Seeing my dad always reminded me of James. Both had dark hair, blue eyes, long eyelashes, high cheekbones, a discreet nose, and clean-shaven faces with small yet meaty lips that broke into smiles that showed their upper gum. I had the same smile.

It had felt incestuous back in the summer of 1982 when I'd had a strong attraction to a man who reminded me of my dad, yet I hadn't been able to control myself. Identical to my relationship with Barry, my affair with James had started out platonic. Sipping my tea, my mind wandered back to the night I'd met James.

Chapter Seventeen

My assignment then was to work with the electricians. Actually, it scared me to death because of a frequent dream I had.

"You won't believe this," I said, "but I have a reoccurring nightmare of being electrocuted."

"Ah, it ain't nothing to fear. You just do what we tell you and you'll be fine."

"The dream is so real that everything goes black and I realize I'm dead." My eyes were wide with genuine fear, but they laughed at me. "When I realized I was thinking, I'd know I wasn't dead and that would wake me up. It sure was real though."

"We heard you was a hard ass. You sho ain't acting like one now. I don't want you to work with me. You'd be useless," said Charles, a greasy overweight Neanderthal. There definitely was no sexual tension or overtures going on there.

We all sat in the mill truck and drove the bumpy back roads to install a generator repaired to serve as a backup when the power blipped. The stench of the mill mingled with the stench of male sweat, and it nauseated me. Most of the maintenance men had been there for a couple of hours, and their bodies, drenched by that sweltering heat, produced a horrible odor.

The truck was a yellow Ford wearing dings and dents from equipment and inconsiderate men riding around in it. Actually, I only knew it was yellow because I'd often washed its clone, the lab truck. To look at this one coated in caustic white powder and red road dust, one would think it was the color of baby poop. Most of the men carelessly sat on the edge of the bed while I wanted to sit down in the bed. Because the generator was in there, I couldn't. They all looked at each other with a smile that I assumed meant they thought I was a pussy. I climbed over the side and decided to sit on the open tailgate. I figured that if I fell off, at least the truck would be up ahead and not run over my scared ass.

Since the mill was one continuous series of potholes and strewn junk we had to swerve around, the ride almost made me carsick. The sun beat down on me, even though it was late and the heat of the day was long gone. The feeling of wanting to throw up increased with each bump, each whiff of body odor and each bead of sweat that popped out and ran down my face and over my ribs. Already, the two weeks in the lab's air-conditioned room where I ran my tests had softened me and made me unable to take working outside in the heat.

We drove up to the spot and broke into crews. They assigned me to an electrician named James. As usual, it started out innocent enough. I was fascinated with his ability to handle the electricity without any fear. I was his gofer and either held or handed him his tools, like a surgical nurse with a brain surgeon. Each time I'd hand him something, he'd look over his shoulder and smile at me.

He had the neatest smile and the bluest eyes I'd ever envisioned. I'm more attracted to eyes than anything, and his were like sapphires. I guessed he was around forty, with an ice cream gut and squirrel-ticking gray hair. He reminded me of a picture of my daddy back when he was young—much younger than James was at that time. By the time my daddy was in his forties, he'd plain out gotten fat and had a moon face.

As the evening wore on, we had more and more jobs to do. I really became attracted to James. We cut up and laughed all night, and he smiled and winked at me. He made me feel great. He did not make a pass or hint at anything untoward at all. Apparently, that was my downfall. I was so gullible that I didn't realize a man's game plan could simply be to act uninterested, and then ease his way in for the score.

Joe later told me how he played that game with all of his women, and I now realize he played me the same way back in 1982. The only one who hadn't seduced me by that method had been Dan or the men I seduced myself when I got in a promiscuous, runaway high. With James, my defenses were down, and the combination of his friendliness and acting nice without a hint of anything sexual definitely set me up.

Later that night, we went up to the top of the electric plant to service a big main power source. This really scared me. It was one of the power boxes from the huge steam-driven mill generator. It made enough electricity to run the mill and sell some back to East Alabama Power Company. After a ride up together on the elevator, we arrived in front of the bank of breaker switches and the endless line of electrical boxes dominated by entanglements of colossal wires with mega volts flowing through them. I imagined myself like Goldfinger in that James Bond movie, falling against one of them and sizzling.

We went to tag out one main breaker that governed the boxes he was going to work on. Not only was I deathly afraid for myself, but I was genuinely concerned for James's safety.

"Hey, James, I need to ask you something." I puffed out these words after climbing some stairs.

"Go ahead, shoot."

"What if I notice that you're being shocked, what should I do?"

He had a surprised look on his face. He had to stop and think for a second before answering me back.

"Let's find a board. You can knock me loose with it. Whatever you do, don't touch me."

We looked around for a board. With my heart in my throat, he started meticulously throwing switches and opening the power boxes and doing something inside one of them. I stood there with the hair standing up on my neck, as if the voltage were already in the air, the wooden board ready to go.

Finally, James manipulated things to a point where he felt safe to undo and replace one of those heavy lines and its connectors. He moved his gloved hand in ever so slowly, as if to see if there would be a way to tell if the wire were still live or not. I heard my heart pounding in my chest as raw fear churned out the adrenalin in case I needed to save his life.

He grabbed the wire and nothing happened—thank the Lord. Next, he went about his business of taking the cable off and changing out the connector.

He turned to me and said, "You know, I really like you as my helper. No other helper has thought to ask me what to do if something ever went wrong. I'm touched that you cared."

We next walked over to the elevator to ride down from the recovery area, then on to the shop to get a new assignment and take a quick break. There is nothing more sexual than a nice adrenalin rush. After James said those words to me while I was still up, alert, and anxious, it translated into a form of excitement for me.

We were the only two in that part of the mill, and we knew it. There was electricity in the air all right, and it didn't have anything to do with that big generator anymore. We stood there in the slow service elevator, and sparks started flying between us. He looked into my eyes as I looked into his. We seemed to have a magical pull between us as we stepped toward each other and kissed. It wasn't one of those passionate kisses, because that was too risky. Instead, it was more of an I-can't-stay-away-from-you-anymore kiss.

It was magical for me, and he threw a switch in me that night. In fact, I started calling him the electrician magician. That was our little inside joke as to what had taken place. I can't remember now who suggested that we meet after work that night, but it was something that both of us wanted and wanted badly.

I explained to him how to meet me at the end of the dirt road that took us to our farm, then for him to go past our farm down to the church where Barry and I had met. By then, William and I were living on the farm. I think I arrived first, my heart pounding in my chest as I waited for him. I parked behind the church and could smell the sexual aroma I exuded. I was like a wild female in estrus. This was going to be different from anything I'd ever experienced, because the electricity or chemistry between us was powerful. I heard a car coming, and my heart raced as it pulled in and parked beside mine.

We resembled people in those bad movies where the passion is so high that shedding clothes, kissing, touching, is a flurry of activity. We both got out of our cars simultaneously and met in the middle in a hot embrace, kissing deeply and wildly. We turned our heads as if shaking off the power this chemistry produced. We undressed each other and literally almost ripped the clothes off, both of us in a passionate frenzy by the time we were naked and got into his car.

We were destined to have sex, our bodies slipped into each other and our senses were suspended. I felt such a fire as I'd never felt before in my life. I didn't have a physical orgasm that night, but I had a mental one. The sex was so intense that the whole thing from beginning to end seemed to be one big orgasm. When we finished, we were both drenched in sweat. I don't have any idea how long we stayed there or how long the sex lasted. I have no sense of time to begin with, even if I had, time ceased being of any importance.

There was no tenderness afterwards—it was too raw for any tenderness. It was lust unleashed, and I couldn't contain my desire. As soon as we finished, I wanted to go again. I never wanted to stop. I wanted to feel him, kiss him, writhe with him, and never uncouple. I wanted to feel that fire and electricity jumping from my body to his and back again. A man in his forties probably couldn't have gone again under normal circumstances, but this was powerful and hot, and as soon as I showed any sign of desiring him again, he jumped back in ready for action. We came back together as if there hadn't been a first time.

The second time, the passion was even greater than the first. We both knew how wonderful it felt, which only upped the voltage. We rolled and kept changing positions—him on top, then me, then him, then me, and on and on. His previous orgasm gave him incredible stamina before the next release, and we probably had sex for well over an hour. It was wild, passionate, draining, and immensely satisfying. I had thought I knew what the big deal was about sex after Barry, but I knew this was going to change me forever, and it did.

The only difference between James and Barry was that when I came in that night, no one could have missed that I'd been having sex. I carried the musky odor inside the house with me. I was still panting when I walked in. William was waiting up for me because I was late coming in. Since I knew he had a thing for Erin, I knew it was perfectly safe for me to be honest this go round. Besides, William really wanted to test the waters for his theory in his book.

Thinking about William's book ended the intensity of remembering that night of passion. I sighed as I continued to fold the clothes and put them away. While I was hanging one of my blouses in my closet, I saw the notorious backless red dress tucked away in the right side of the closet. I'd worn it as recently as six months ago when Joe and I had gone out to eat. Today, it would look horrible on me because I was a living skeleton. I had been a knockout in it back in 1982.

All that summer, I went completely insane over sex. Every single minute of every single day, all I thought about was sex with James. I fell hard for him—in lust, not love, although I didn't know it at the time. I'd think about him and get butterflies in my stomach. I was confused about my feelings. It was beautiful and guilt free because he was divorced and I had my husband's approval.

For about a week, we met every single night since we were working the same shift because of the outage. As life in general usually has it, all good things must end, and James suddenly stopped being able to meet me. He finally fessed up that although he was divorced, he and his ex-wife were living together. She had become suspicious of his continuous late arrivals.

He also admitted that she'd caught him cheating earlier in their marriage, and that was the reason they were divorced. Their two teenage girls also lived at home, and he claimed they were the main reason he and his ex-wife still lived together, but it seemed to me that they still had deep feelings for each other.

When James started coming to his senses, a driving hunger for him still controlled my life. It was beyond love, lust, or anything I could put a name on. It was as if the cork had suddenly been removed from my bottled-up life, and every inch of my body was vibrating with sexual desire. The more I copulated, the more I wanted, and nothing could put out the fire. I still hadn't had an orgasm. It wasn't a factor in my lusty drive. Eventually, it happened one night when James was bending me over the back of his car in the middle of the road, and I thought I was going to faint. God, if I'd thought I wanted sex before, now I really wanted it. I'd finally gotten so much more of a thrill, the fire had been drenched, and it felt divine.

As James started seeing me less and less, I wanted more and more, and I went to others. I even went back to Donny who was also working at the mill. After all those years, he was still a dud, and by then I had a barometer and a means to judge who was a good lover and who was a poor one.

Then along came Joe that summer of 1982 when he transferred to my crew.

Needing a break from the deluge of thoughts and memories, I walked back into the den to check the time. The clock in there was more accurate than my watch. I kept it five minutes fast so I'd arrive only five minutes late. I glanced around the house now devoid of Joe, a house where every crevice and corner had once been filled with him—photos of Joe or us, things he'd made as a child, artwork or porcelains he'd given me. And my favorite, the Dutch iris stained glass lamp.

That lamp had been a surprise birthday present while we were up in the mountains back in 1999. Most of the presents he'd given me—jewelry, sexy lingerie, and most of our collectible irises—had been returned to Joe. I told him to give the jewelry and the lingerie to his girlfriends. Maybe he could impress and dazzle them with his romantic ways, even though I knew he'd already showered them with flowers, cards, and meals out in fancy restaurants.

However, the lamp I hadn't been able to part with. It was too beautiful, too peaceful to look at with its cobalt blue petals against emerald green blades set against cream-colored glass. They actually were upside down, the green originating at the lamp's top with long beautiful stems fanning out to the skirt in a chorus line of irises dancing in unison, trimmed in ruby-colored glass border pieces. Stunning to look at, it was brilliantly colored when I turned it on. It was almost the same as a Christmas tree's effect on a child. No, more than that, it represented the best of Joe—the man I had fallen in love with.

My mind reached back to hold onto that Joe, if only for a moment. It was the Joe I would cry for after I killed him and realized I'd killed that part of him too. I wanted to carry some part of him around in my heart, but nothing could stop my determination to end his savage treatment of me. There were two of him, and both had to go if I wanted peace.

I turned on the lamp, sending the cobalt and crimson light slicing through the dark, soothing me as I remembered the good Joe.

Chapter Eighteen

We'd started three-to-eleven when my supervisor sent me upstairs to train under Joe. I trained testing the board as it came off the reel for about an hour, then returned downstairs and ran that job because they'd let someone go home. Right off, I noticed that Joe was different. He was kind, patient and listened to me. He never poked fun at me when I stumbled in learning something. We talked in-between the testing of the board, and he told me he couldn't understand my husband not listening to my ideas, because he could tell I was bright. Of course, that was exactly what I needed to hear then, because James had begun avoiding me, and William, wrapped up in Erin and the book he was writing, ignored me too.

The fact of the matter was that I really cared for Erin and enjoyed her company when I was at home. We'd sit around the kitchen table talking. In fact, that's what we were doing when I'd had that huge Freudian slip. I guess William had changed his heart about me then. My betrayal in our open marriage devastated him as much as his betrayal with Rachelle had ravaged me. We were never the same after that night. We remained civil, but there was definitely a strain between us, which left me vulnerable to Joe's friendly attention.

Of course, when Joe talked about my mind rather than my body, it was exactly what I wanted to hear—validation that wasn't sexual. I'd always felt intimidated by William when it came to smarts. Joe's compliments hit a spot in me starved for recognition. I received no compliments of that sort from William, or at least that was how I felt. William stayed so engrossed in his writing that he didn't notice his neglect until we started having more and more arguments. We had been together for twelve years and could count our arguments on one hand. Both of us were blind to the fact that I was vulnerable to an emotional affair along with the sex.

Joe and I hit it off early on as good friends. If he hadn't trained me on the L4 job, we both worked downstairs, him the L3 and me the L5. We were constantly together and discovered how much we had in common. We shared a love for coffee with creamer and Sweet'N'Low as well as pimento cheese sandwiches followed by sugar cookies bought out of the mill's snack machines.

We also had a mutual friend we often discussed. Oddly enough, this friend of mine had been an old girlfriend of his. In fact, he had taken Sandy's virginity. At least I can say she must've had a wonderful first experience. Mainly we discussed how mistreated I was in my marriage, and he told me how miserable he was in his.

Since he had such an adorable baby-faced look, I kept asking him repeatedly if he had any kids. He didn't look old enough, even though he was in his thirties. Actually, he had two kids—a boy named Jeff and a girl named Rose. We remained in the platonic, good-friends stage for almost a month and a half. Often, after the three-to-eleven shift, a group of us would go to a local nightspot called The Studio for a drink.

My brother-in-law owned the place, and often my mother-in-law, Gretchen, would be there and would join us at our table. I always thought of Gretchen as my mentor. She kept herself young in both looks and actions. She was an adventurous whirlwind with endless energy who exuded a zest for life. Both Aries—domineering, self-confident, and not a bit afraid to say what we think, we respected each other because neither of us bullshitted the other and knew exactly where we stood on any issue. We both were attracted to people similar to ourselves, so we hit it off immediately.

I'll never forget the night at The Studio when Joe first realized I was a woman. Since the coating from work covered me, and I looked a mess, that night I decided to go home and change clothes. William was already in bed and didn't want to go out. I changed into a strapless tube top sans any bra, white short-shorts, sandals, and I braided a feather into my hair. At this stage of my life, besides the physical work at the mill, I swam and jogged daily. Muscular with a golden tan, I looked as if I were in my twenties. I also put on some makeup, something I rarely did while working.

Joe told me that night: "When you walked into the bar, all at once I realized you are a woman, and a beautiful woman at that."

"Why thank you," I said. "You look kinda different tonight too. I sure am glad today is closing. This was a hard set of three-to-elevens. Did you know that yesterday was William's birthday? Yup, on August 9, 1949, a genius was born."

"What did y'all do to celebrate?"

"Are you kidding? I had to work and pulled a double the night before. I was busy catching up on my beauty rest. We're waiting until the long weekend to celebrate. We'll probably go to Gretchen's house for a gourmet dinner, and we're going to surprise him with a new wheelchair. He's about worn the one he has now into warped wheels. I'm really excited about our surprise."

"You love him, don't you?" Joe asked with a slight sadness in his voice.

"Yes, I can't imagine my life without him. We get upset with each other, but overall we get along pretty well. We don't fight like you and Regina. If he'd just let me have some say in how our farm is going to be fixed, we'd rarely fight. He's the boss, and I'm the rebellious child."

"I don't see how you do it, Lee. If I worked as hard as you, I'd want all the say in where the money went. He's lucky to have a wife willing to work so hard and turn all the money over to him. I don't think that's fair."

"You know, he's always handled the money. I've never really thought too much about it. It bothers me only when it comes to spending on the farm. Then I get pissed."

We were sitting at the bar during this conversation, then Gretchen walked in and we joined her at a table. We sat with Gretchen, laughing, talking, and having a great time together. Joe's laidback nature made him easy to talk to when he was able to unwind with a few beers. Even though at work he was reserved, shy, and serious, I discovered that he could be witty. He tickled my sense of humor, and it felt good.

Joe and I went into the game room and played Foos-ball. I'd never been much of a game player and was pretty much a pathetic klutz. It surprised Joe that I didn't know how to play the game and had never done it before. He was an excellent teacher because he was so tolerant with me. He never laughed unless he saw me laughing at myself. I did that plenty and ended up having the time of my life that night. For once, it wasn't sexual. It was just nice. I really liked Joe a lot. I had loads of respect for him because, even that night, he hadn't made a pass at me. He treated me as lady should be treated, and that was so refreshing.

Joe and I continued to work together in the L-shaped lab. He'd be over in his section of the lab when he worked downstairs, usually reading a book. I liked that about him, that he was the gentle, scholarly type who preferred to read rather than catcalling like most of the other men. I thought he was the sweetest and dearest person on earth.

Although I really didn't know diddly about his wife at that time, I became incensed that anyone could treat him any way other than kind. He would talk about their fights—how she'd bitch at him and he'd yell back at her. I couldn't picture the man ever raising his voice. He seemed too mild-tempered. I have to admit, even with all the hell I put Joe through and the screaming I deserved, he rarely yelled at me. We fought verbally, but he displayed too much self-control to resort to screaming and rarely even cursed. When he did either, I knew I'd really pushed his buttons. Realizing that made me feel so bad that I'd turned into a bitch. At times, I'd made him feel the same kind of anger he'd felt with his first wife.

Whenever we worked off those three-to-eleven shifts, I found myself looking forward to the times that Joe would join us for drinks. One night in September, he didn't show up although he was supposed to join us. College students who were working as summer help out at the mill filled The Studio, and I saw Erin with them. They motioned me over to their table.

106

The girls were all in their early twenties, and I was thirty-three. I was most definitely on a high that night, because I left the bar with them and we cruised around acting like fools. I smoked some dope with them, and it stoned the hell out of me. We stole a watermelon from somebody's field, then we snuck into the Country Club and went skinny dipping in the pool.

One of the guys, a nineteen-year-old named Bill who looked damn good, flirted with me rather than the younger women, which flattered me. Since I was stoned, off-center, and typical of the way I'd been acting all summer, he and I screwed right there in the pool, and it didn't matter to me if anyone watched or not. It was hard to do, although not impossible. The craziness ended with daylight breaking, and I had to work a three-to-eleven shift again the next day.

By then, William was never surprised at what time I would drag myself home. Each adventure was but another entry into the journal. He kept one about me and my exploits, as well as some of his feelings. I found out about this much later when William asked Joe and me to clean out his office for him. Since William and I remained friends after our divorce, he wanted us to pack up some of his things and keep them so they wouldn't be stored at his mother's warehouse. When I finally read that journal, I was ashamed of myself. I was as inconsiderate a bitch as God ever had put on the face of the earth that summer.

That brought on a pang of guilt, almost braking my destiny as I realized everything wrong in my life hadn't been all William's or Joe's fault. Sure, I was culpable, but I still believed Joe had deliberately used my vulnerability against me to hurt me to the max. Normally, I was a go-with-the-flow kind of person and didn't let life get me down. Joe had always made innuendoes about that, laying a guilt trip on me. He was jealous of my love of life, my zest for living, and my enjoyment of teaching.

"Damn it, it's not even ten thirty yet!" I screamed in frustration. "Eleven o'clock is never going to get here!"

I decided to go sit by the pool and smoke a cigarette. After the separation, I'd taken up the habit at the expense of eating and had lost around twenty pounds. The water was tranquil, a muted aqua and orange with the moon's reflection. I lit two floating candles, hypnotized as they floated toward the skimmer—concentric fireflies lapping the pool's edge.

The acrid smell of the dying cigarette didn't mask the chlorine odor of the pool or the scent of my "Mark roses" growing along the privacy fence. The tree frogs abruptly stopped their courting, making the night deadly quiet—perhaps a premonition? I heard my thoughts as a dialogue within my head, reading my life's story. My mind played its home video.

I stripped off my clothes and dove into the pool. The water was probably around seventy-four degrees, but it felt chilly to me. I swam to the floating candles and blew them out, then I turned onto my back and felt the moonlight bathe my face as I remembered the last time Joe and I had made love while swimming at night. I started shivering and knew that time was drawing near. I exited the pool and missed the way Joe always held up a towel for me. The emptiness was overwhelming. I decided to go and smoke another cigarette while I air-dried. The cold suited me. Inside all my rage and the indifference to Joe's life, a small flame still burned for the memory of our first date on September 16, 1982.

We had laughed and talked all the way to The Studio. William's mother, Gretchen, was there with her best friend, Christine. Joe and I joined them at their table.

We really were not up to anything we shouldn't have been up to at that point, so there was no need to be afraid to go and sit with Gretchen. She often saw me with Joe as well as many others from the mill. The only thing different about that night was that, once again, I'd gone home and changed clothes because Joe had said he was going to shower and change clothes before going out that night. That was when I decided to dress up and asked him to pick me up. Most of the time when I went to The Studio, I never had over two drinks, but since Joe was about to go back to his old shift and leave our crew, we decided to make a night of it. For some reason, I wanted to look good for Joe. I chose a revealing dress. I bathed, perfumed, put on makeup, and looked different from usual when I heard Joe's car humming up the driveway.

As I walked out, I felt his eyes go over me and take in my body and my appearance. I could tell he was pleased. I'd never seen him in anything other than work clothes, and he, too, looked different. He had on an oatmeal-colored shirt and khaki pants. The colors really became his hair and eyes. I could see he was a neat person and very clean cut, mainly he had something I really loved in a man—beautiful thick, long hair—not long as in ponytail long. It was down to his collar. I wanted to run my fingers through it.

He opened the car door for me, as if letting me know he was my valet de chambre. When I stepped on one of his kid's toys in the floorboard and we laughed, it released any awkwardness between us. By the time we got to The Studio, the night was set.

We danced, talked, drank, and cut up with Gretchen and Christine. We'd just finished dancing to some hard rock-and-roll when a slow song came on. We danced to it too. While dancing, he tilted my head up and kissed me in front of everyone, including Gretchen.

My cigarette butts filled the conch shell we used as an ashtray. I smoked three of them—one right after another, with tears dripping off my chin. Was I crying for the good memories or for the greater loss I was going to create? I wasn't sure.

I grabbed my clothes and walked back inside. The house felt warm, and I felt like staying nude. Why not? I returned to the bedroom and remembered all the times Joe and I had made love there—wonderful, exquisite love. I sat on the bed, sobbing with big, gulping tears. I guess Joe had finally had enough of me, just as William had done when he threw me out. How had I failed at two marriages? I couldn't blame William for what he'd done. Why was it so easy to blame Joe? I lay across the bed remembering when William had thrown me out and Joe and I had started living together on Freya's birthday, November the thirteenth. Freya was the first foal born to me, and I thought of her as my lucky charm.

Chapter Nineteen

William had given me specific instructions on the Thursday we worked off the three-to-eleven shift. Joe and I were going on an overnight trip to Montgomery that evening after work. Both men had me caught in the middle of a power struggle to test my loyalties. Joe called me before work.

"Hey, beautiful," he drawled in his deep, mellow voice. "I want you to bring your clothes to the mill and change over at my place. I love watching you undress."

"William is insisting that I come home tonight and change clothes at our house. He also wants me to wear my sexy teddy for you."

William had told me he'd chosen the teddy because my pet name for him was Teddy Bear. William called me Wonder Woman—not as in all the spectacular things I could and did do, but because I was always wondering about things.

"A sexy teddy?" Joe said. "What color is it? I'd love to see you in sexy lingerie. Regina don't like to wear nothing like that. Damn, woman, you know what thinking about that is doing to me?"

"It's black, lacy, and see-through," I said. "But I wanted to wear a dress that shows off my bare back and not wear anything underneath it at all. Which would you prefer?"

"Nothing underneath? Do you realize the pain I'm in right now picturing you without any underwear on? I'm going to have to take me a cold shower. Wear the one without panties. I can always catch you in the lingerie later."

"Okay," I said.

"And you don't need to drive all the way back out in the country to change clothes," Joe added. "William never made an issue out of telling you what to do before. Why should tonight be any different? We'll be running behind schedule for that drive all the way to the Rodeo Club as it is."

As I thought about that night, I resumed hanging up my clothes almost mechanically until I again spied that dress, so I grabbed it out of the closet. That dress had caused William and me to divorce. I balled it up and threw it on the floor in a rage.

"Son of a bitch!" I screamed at it. "You caused my marriage to end. If I hadn't worn you, William would never have kicked me out and I'd never have married that scumbag."

I hated that I'd married Joe, but whenever I thought of Jolly, I realized that no matter what the pain, I'd do it all again to have her. I meandered back to the day William had changed what was in his heart because of that damn dress.

I had agreed with Joe about changing clothes and had taken my overnight bag, makeup and my dress with me when I left for work. The thing that had most likely caused William's anger and made him do what he'd done was that I'd forgotten to pack the teddy and left it on the kitchen table. He was busy writing when I left for work. I hoped he wouldn't notice that my dress was hanging behind the seat.

Maybe he watched me leave and spied it. Maybe when he went into the kitchen for coffee and saw the teddy still on the table in a crumpled heap instead of with my things in the bedroom for me to get ready that night, he decided to kick me out of the house. Maybe he had paid attention to many things. Something about that day was William's breaking point. He typed me a goodbye letter and threw me out.

Looking back, I know he did it in both anger and love. He must have known I'd never leave him for Joe but figured out that my heart was Joe's and not his. His theory sucked. He had allowed our affair to flame and was the one scorched in the deal. Sad to say, due to my deep love for Joe, I was oblivious to William's heartache and pain. However, I can say here and now that what goes around comes around, and both Regina and William got their day of revenge against me. Joe was the only one who came out of both marriages happier than when he went in.

On our way to Montgomery, Joe asked me to have his baby. That stirred something inside me: love I could no longer deny that I felt. My biological clock was ticking, and I finally understood the difference between sex and making love. I knew I'd never experienced the feelings I was feeling that night with Joe. I wanted to have his baby. I wanted our lovemaking to produce a child, but I would never bring shame to William or Gretchen by becoming pregnant. Little did I know that William was already setting me free so that Joe and I could marry one day and create our baby.

After spending the night with Joe, I drove up to my house the next morning on Friday the thirteenth, normally my lucky date. At the last minute, Joe and I had decided to cancel the Montgomery trip and turned around and gone back to his place. We were too eager to make love to drive hours to get to a motel.

I drove back home around ten o'clock that morning. I walked in and called for William, but he didn't answer. When I saw the note on the table, my heart froze and a cold sweat popped out on my body. I knew what it was before I read it. I couldn't imagine William ever telling me to get out—

goodbye, our marriage was over. That was stupid on my part, since he should have done it months earlier. I picked it up, read it, and started crying. I walked back to the office and discovered the locked door. I called his name, no answer. For a minute, I got scared that maybe he'd done something drastic.

"Just let me know you're okay," I called through the door. "I'm worried that you might be hurt. I deserve this treatment, and I'm going to pack my bags and leave you in peace. Please let me know that you are okay."

"Go away," he answered finally. "I'm fine. I'm the best I've been in months. Go to Joe, you made your choice last night. I asked you to come home to change clothes and wear the teddy, but you did nothing I asked. You've shown that I don't matter to you. I managed my life before you came along and, although it will be hard at first, I'll get along again. Now get out and leave me alone."

Tears were streaming down my cheeks. It wasn't supposed to turn out this way. I loved Joe, yet in a bizarre way, I also still loved William and didn't want him out of my life.

"Please give me a chance," I said. "Let's talk this over. I made a mistake. I didn't realize how much it mattered to you because you never gave me any instructions before. I didn't think it was a big deal."

By now, I was talking and gulping from crying so hard. I loved Joe, yes, but not enough to leave William. I steadied myself on the doorjamb and tapped again.

"Please unlock the door and let's talk."

No answer.

"Come on, William. Don't do this to me. You're making way too big of a deal out of my changing clothes over at Joe's place. Why should it matter?"

Still no answer. I tried maybe five more times to get him to come out and talk to me. He was done. It was finished, and I had to leave. I didn't even pack a suitcase. I grabbed a work outfit for Saturday morning when I started my day shift. With a heavy heart, I started my truck and drove what seemed like an endless ride to the river—to Joe's place. Lucky for me, as I drove up, Joe was driving out the driveway. He was shocked to see me and even more shocked to see me crying so hard.

"Can I stay with you?" I said. "William's thrown me out." Snot was running out of my nose from all of the crying. My eyes were red and swollen, and my lips were chafing from the salty tears pooling in the corners of my mouth. I was ugly—ugly to look at, ugly in my heart, plain ugly.

Joe ran to me and held me. He kissed my damp hair and told me to go inside the camp house. He'd been on his way back to Cusseta to pick up five-year-old Jeff to take him to a football game for the state playoffs in Birmingham. They had a crack at being the champions in their school division. He wanted to be with me, but he'd promised Jeff. Since this was all unexpected, I told him to go on, that I'd stay there and be okay. The reality of it wore me out, and I slept most of the day.

I was exhausted emotionally from the two emotional extremes: beautiful lovemaking the night before and the horrible crash of my marriage. As sad as I was, the years had played like a video in my mind and reminded me of why I had loved William. A poem nagged and nipped at my conscious mind. I had taken out the old blotter paper I kept in my purse to draw on and ended up writing this poem:

Lost in the Moment

By

Lee Peterson

I look down my own body
My eyes lock into yours as
Your large pupils hypnotize me
They will me
To submit my most secret of secrets
Then my gaze becomes unfocused
As I draw my conscious self
Deeper and deeper into my body
Down I drift as I literally feel myself disappear
I cease to be
I am muscle, skin, heartbeat, and nerve endings
I am fire and earth—the sun and the stars
I am gasping for breath and then I cease to breathe
I am poised for a second
In the land of immortality
I sprout wings and soar
Long gone from my own mortal body
I tremble, and then I scream
I don't even hear
Because I AM NOT THERE
I am the center of the universe
I am an atom that explodes
Fragmenting into a million particles
Magnetically swarming together
As I again perceive that—I am me.

The poem had expressed how I felt when Joe and I made love—how an orgasm felt. It was something so powerful that images and words exploded inside my head and heart. I couldn't contain my love for Joe. I'd heard the ballpoint pen roll through the soft paper and felt the drag as it tore minute fibers, etching the poem's blue lines into the paper. Then I'd drawn us kissing before making love, with a fair likeness of both of us. Contented, I'd gone back to sleep.

Thinking of the poem now reminded me that it had christened my career as an author. The Alabama Review magazine had published it that spring.

I checked the time and saw it was still only ten forty-five. I grabbed the copy of the magazine from the coffee table in the living room where I kept it to remind me that I was a writer first and a brokenhearted woman second. It served its purpose and made me happy whenever I glanced down at it. The magazine had also published my art on the cover. It had published two drawings on the opposite page of my poem. Tonight, I took the book into the den and sat by the iris lamp so that I could read it. I wanted to enjoy my tribute to our love the last night that Joe would be alive. His love was already but a memory, and I savored the thought that soon he would be only a memory as well.

I felt the corners of my mouth lift in a smile even as a tear rolled down my cheek. Funny, Joe had convinced himself that I'd left his place that night and met James one more time before I moved in with him, and he'd used that belief as one of his primary justifications not to trust me and to cheat on me. It was true that I had met James one last time to make sure he didn't control my heart anymore, and I had lied to Joe about where I was going. That had happened in August of 1982, and I didn't move in with Joe until November.

Years later, we found the record of that night in one of my calendar journals, and Joe had used that misconception to build layer upon layer of mistrust and dislike for me because he felt I'd cheated on him first. He'd started keeping score, and I didn't have a clue that he was doing it. He hadn't meant one word about us getting together and having a baby. He'd said it, and professed his love for me because he read me and knew it was what I wanted to hear. He also knew it would keep the sex hot between us.

Later, I found out he had told many women the same thing over the course of the years, verbatim except for the part about wanting them to have his baby. He'd added that part for me because he knew how much losing James's baby had meant to me. I think Joe did love me as a man loves the mother of his child, and we had eventually grown into love because we got along well, at least until 1998 when I caught him cheating on me.

Jolly admits that she never thought of us as fussing or fighting until after that. I also have to admit that when I was sick, I did things that were destructive to our marriage—complaining all the time about the money I'd spent, ruining any fun we'd had or being a super bitch. I was sick when I did them and was unaware of what I was doing. Joe's lies, manipulations and snow job were from his sexual addiction, and my mood swings and temper rages were from my bipolar illness. I guess we were both too sick to grow up and have a truly mature relationship based on love.

I had thought we had something special, but life had ripped us apart. For most of the marriage, we'd had a wonderful sex life with passion right up until the end, nearly twenty years later. What was that? I realized now it was shallow and obviously not real love, at least not the till-death-us-do-part type of love anyway. On my part it could have been, but never on Joe's. I'd wanted a trial separation to save the marriage. He'd wanted to end it.

By January 2003, he couldn't stand me anymore. He had ruined our fifteenth and now our twentieth anniversary by cheating on me. In 1998, I had given him a second chance, but today there would be no third. What I had wanted to believe was our beautiful love affair had come crashing down. Today would begin a new way of thinking and living: LWJ—life without Joe.

Such bravado, but whom did I think I was fooling? Even as I planned to kill him and tried to prepare myself for life without him, I wasn't sure it was possible. I loved him too much and doubted I'd ever get over the end of our marriage. All my actions were proving that was the truth.

I glanced at the clock on the mantel. Joe would be getting off work soon. Adrenalin kicked in at the thought, then I began to feel too scattered, the voices getting louder and confusing me. I'd cried myself dry. My eyes itched from the dried tears crusted around them and on the corners of my nostrils, I grabbed a Kleenex out of my iris tissue box. Blowing my nose cleared my head for a moment, but all too soon the voices started in again.

I headed back to the kitchen and took my two Ambiens, a light sleeping medication that calmed me down enough to stay focused. It was easy to fight the urge to go to sleep and have a twilight zone of up to an hour of actions with no memory. The perfect drug for a murderer. I fired up my anger again when I saw the clean spot left on the wall where a plaque had once hung: Let's go over the hill together. Yeah, Joe had put a stop to that.

With too much time on my hands, I waited for my destiny by immersing myself again in the past. I remembered when I had caught Joe cheating on me in 1998 and again in 2003.

Chapter Twenty

My first suspicion that Joe was cheating on me came in April 1998. We were going to the Pony Club Rally down in Gulfport, Mississippi. Joe stood up, and I noticed when he tightened his belt that he had lost a lot of weight and inches off his waist. Seeing that snake as he tightened his belt sent up a warning, but I convinced myself I was being silly. Pony Club Rally was something we took Jolly and her white Lipizzan cross horse, Krisco, to each spring for competition and usually looked forward to, except Joe wrecked that particular weekend.

I'd taken that Friday off from my job as a schoolteacher. After leaving the mill, I had gone back to college and began working on my master's degree in elementary education. I taught school in the daytime and commuted to classes at night, about thirty-five miles from my house for about five years of that grueling pace. We loaded up and pulled out at around noon.

On the way to Gulfport, Joe refused to look at me or talk to me. Whenever I tried to make conversation with him, he'd grunt out a one-syllable answer, never elaborating on anything. When he did talk to me, he tried to pick a fight. I rode the majority of the trip crying silently as I looked out the window with tears streaming down my face and dripping off my chin.

Things worsened after we arrived. He wouldn't sit next to me to watch the event. After a long period of his being nowhere in sight, I set about looking for him. Finally, I went to the horse trailer and found him inside all by himself, sitting on an upside down water bucket, his head bent as if studying something on the floor.

"What is wrong with you?" I asked. "You wouldn't talk to me or look at me all the way down, and now you won't come out and sit by me to watch Jolly. What have I done to make you this mad at me?"

"I'm not mad at you," he said without looking at me, his voice dragging with obvious depression. "I need some time to myself to think. I have a lot on my mind right now. It's nothing you've done."

I felt sorry for him and started into the horse trailer to hug him. He waved me away. I respected his need for privacy.

"I love you," he said. "I'm upset with myself right now. You've done nothing wrong."

That gave me a little relief, but not much. What really upset me was at dinner that evening when he took out a Visa card I knew nothing about. After we'd finished our meal, he left his American Express card on the tray for the server. She smiled apologetically as she picked it up and said they didn't accept American Express. We certainly didn't have enough cash on us to pay the bill, and it looked embarrassing until Joe said not to worry and brought out a Visa card. That bothered the hell out of me. On the way back to our motel, I let him have it.

"What are you doing with a Visa card you haven't mentioned to me?"

"Oh, I meant to tell you about it but forgot," he said. "I figured sooner or later we'd run into this situation and would need something to use as a backup card."

"That sounds like a wonderful idea," I said, "but it seems strange to me that you wouldn't think to tell me about it either when you applied for it or the day the card arrived." I trembled with anger as I said it. "Getting a credit card behind your mate's back is a pretty big deal, and it's not so insignificant that you'd forget to mention it. You've been acting so strange lately that I'm beginning to get this really funny feeling that something terrible is going on behind my back."

"Honey, you're being ridiculous. Your imagination is going wild. You always blow things up and think the worst. Why don't you give me a break?" He looked me boldly in the eye as he spoke, giving credence to his explanation. "Look, I just bailed us out of an embarrassing situation, didn't I? Why not see what I've done right instead of always seeing what you think I've done wrong?"

Yeah, he did a good job of laying a guilt trip on me that night to cover his own guilt. Later that same month, I found his stash of money. I discovered seven hundred dollars in his wallet while I was getting Jolly some money for her class trip. I nearly fainted to see that much cash on him. It further led to my suspicions that he was up to something, and I had to confront him about it.

"My God, Joe! What are you doing with seven hundred dollars in your wallet?"

"Well, you've done gone and ruined my surprise. I've been saving up some money for the past few months to go out and buy you a special Mother's Day present. Now you've messed it all up by snooping in my wallet." He looked at me with a hurt expression, as if I'd taken a swing at him.

Of course, I immediately thought maybe I was wrong for feeling all that mistrust. Maybe it was my problem, not his.

"I wasn't snooping," I said. "I never look in your wallet and you know that. I've never felt a reason to look in it and check up on you. I trust you, Joe. Jolly needed fifteen dollars for the Shakespeare Festival this morning. I only had a ten and your wallet was on the kitchen counter, so I was seeing if you had a five on you. Can you imagine my shock?"

"Well, I always seem to fuck up no matter what, and you always seem to think the worst of me. I guess I'll never learn."

No, I seemed to have been the one who never learned.

By that May, I discovered that our phone bills had mysteriously disappeared, and that was only the beginning of my discoveries. Early one morning, I awakened with some intuition telling me that Joe was hiding something huge from me. Although I'd cracked his one-night stand with a woman named Teri and gotten a confession from him in the marriage counselor's office, he kept having an upset stomach afterward. He was still acting guilty, thus I decided to search for what he was hiding from me.

While Joe slept, I went outside and searched his locked truck from top to bottom. When I dug that bag out from underneath the back seat, I went back in the house and started slapping Joe in his face. I turned my diamond and sapphire ring around so it would make contact with his face when I slapped him. Without turning on the light, I screamed at the top of my voice.

"Motherfucker, what are these! Why is there a motel receipt from Andalusia when you were supposed to be in Birmingham camping and learning saddle repair? You took everything with you to make me think you were going to be camping. Why in the hell would you need three thousand dollars, and what did you do with that money?"

"I don't remember what I did with the money," he said, blood dripping from where his cheekbone jutted out. "I swear to you I don't. Be quiet, you're going to wake Jolly up and upset her."

"Shut up! Me upset Jolly? What about you? What about when you lied to me and hid things from me? I know for a fact you screwed around once outside this marriage with Teri. Did it not dawn on you that doing all this stuff might upset Jolly? Or did you not give a shit?"

Remembering my anger made me restless again. I headed to my bedroom and checked to make sure the gun really was in the drawer. Sometimes I get delusional and can't tell my thoughts from reality. I knew I was close to that state tonight. I opened the drawer, and there it was. I hadn't imagined stopping at Jessica's house to get it. I really was going to kill Joe. Tonight it would all be over, and he would pay for his part in how we had fucked up Jolly.

I checked the time again. It was eleven o'clock by my watch, minus the five minutes I kept it set fast to prevent my being late. It wouldn't be long now.

Jolly had told me later that her life had changed forever that morning when she'd realized her daddy had cheated on her mom and our marriage could end in divorce. She admitted she never felt the same security or sense of love in our home. She'd been only thirteen. Mature for her age, she'd seen her daddy's leaving me long before I did.

The saddest part was when she'd realized he'd used her to help cover his cheating once when he'd disguised his voice and called from our computer phone line so Jolly would tell me she'd talked to the saddle-making instructor before she'd called her daddy to the phone. Of course, Joe had walked out of the office, picked up the phone, and feigned a conversation with Mr. Murdock in front of Jolly.

All of this elaborate acting from my shy and reserved husband—out of character for him. No wonder we'd never suspected anything. Jolly felt bad when she saw how much it had all hurt me. She told me she felt partially responsible for my pain and even my attempted suicides.

I tried to tell her not to blame herself, because Joe had deceived both of us. Even after I learned how he had used several loans to pay off the other and kept out a thousand for himself, he had smooth talked me into thinking I was making much ado about nothing. Yeah, I learned the hard way that denial ain't the name of a damn river!

The day after I found Joe's bag of goodies in his truck, we had a civil discussion about it while we sat outside in the swing. I knew something awful had gone down. Joe had supposedly quit smoking and I hadn't smoked in years, but he boldly took out a cigarette and lit it, then took out another and handed it to me after lighting it. For once, he was ready for my questioning.

"Why do you have a motel receipt for that Sunday you left me crying in the driveway, begging you not to go because I felt like you had another woman in your life? This receipt proves I was right. You did go to meet a woman that day, didn't you?"

"I'm so embarrassed, but it's not at all what you think. In fact, I was trying to protect you and keep you from ever thinking I was up to something. I was being blackmailed."

"Blackmailed?" I said in disbelief. "By whom? And how did they find you to blackmail you, and what on earth were they threatening to tell?"

He looked believably embarrassed. We sat in silence for a few minutes, smoking our cigarettes. Gullible isn't the word for me. I lapped up a plausible—though farfetched—excuse that he'd left me that Sunday in May of '98 for a valid reason other than cheating on me again. Two weeks earlier, when I'd discovered the hidden phone bill, I found out he'd had sex with Teri. How stupid could I have been? I knew he was a cheater, yet I'd bought his lie for a penny.

"You know I've been on the Internet in some of those chat rooms," he said. "Well, it was innocent and I was just curious, but this lady named Kat started chatting with me. Somehow, like an idiot, I gave her my name and told her where I lived. I never thought anything about her again."

He calmly lit another cigarette and lit a second one for me. This courtship ritual worked, lifting my spirits as he continued speaking.

"About a week later, a car pulls up into the driveway. This tall and beautiful blonde gets out of the car. She comes to the front door and rings the doorbell. I answer it and she reaches up, grabs me, throws her arms around me, kisses me, and then pushes me inside the house. She smiles at me and unbuttons her blouse, but then she just turns around, opens the door, and leaves the house buttoning up her blouse. I thought it peculiar and wondered what she was doing."

Joe stared at me with a pained look in his eyes. He seemed genuinely hurt by the memory of the experience. By then my eyes were misting, partially from the smoke and partially from the flood of emotions I was feeling. My throat was starting to hurt, and I tried soothing it by tickling my neck with my index finger. The lump in my throat was physical.

"The next week," Joe went on, "the same car pulls up in the drive and the doorbell rings again. This time when I opened it, she handed me a videotape. She told me to go inside and look at it, saying they had another with your school's address on it and your name on it. She said she'd let me know later what to do."

He paused for a moment, as if deep in thought.

"She called me later and told me to meet her at the Red Roof Inn in Andalusia and to bring her seven hundred dollars or she'd send the tape to you. That's why I had the money and why I had to leave you that day and not say anything to you. You were already thinking I was doing something I shouldn't. That was all I needed, and I was so afraid of losing you that I was willing to do anything."

"Oh, my poor baby," I said. "I'm sorry you had to go through all of that alone. You could have told me. I would have understood."

Disgusted at the memory of my incredible gullibility, I went back to the kitchen where I sat at the table, staring back at a fool's face reflected in the sunroom's windows.

I had actually believed Joe until my sister Margaret had pointed out to me that innocent people go to the police. She said he was either guilty of doing something with the woman, or he was making the whole story up to cover why he had so much cash and why he had been in a motel in Andalusia. By now, as adults, Margaret and I were very close. We had united in not allowing the dysfunction of parenting to go on for another generation. We'd vowed to be good parents to our children. I now looked up to Margaret for advice. She was right about the blackmail.

No matter what, he had lied about where he was that night, and it got worse than that. I found out later that he'd gone to meet yet another woman, Jane Kelly, the weekend before the Pony Club Rally while Jolly and I had gone to the state science fair on April tenth. No wonder he'd been such an asshole at the rally. He had told us he couldn't go to the science fair because he would be working, although he'd missed the regional fair in March by meeting Teri, using the saddle-making workshop as his excuse then. Prior to this year, he'd never missed a science fair.

As soon as Jolly and I left, he had met Jane in Andalusia, and they'd had a love affair. To cover his ass, he had programmed our answering machine so he could retrieve any message I left on it and could call me back, acting as if he was home and had just stepped outside for a minute. Oh, he was a sly fox, that's for sure.

And not only had he cheated on me, he had been doing the mattress mambo with Teri while seeing Jane, so he'd even cheated on his mistress! Oddly, that gave me some kind of weird satisfaction and a sense of closure. Still, at the time I'd discovered these women, I had wanted to die rather than face the truth. Joe had been the love of my life and my soul mate. To discover that he'd fallen out of love with me and in love with another woman had broken my heart to the nth degree.

The outcome was a total breakdown and a suicide attempt. For the first time in my life, I entered a mental hospital. One of the oddest outcomes from Joe's cheating was that I associated horses with the cheating, since he'd treated me so badly at the Pony Club Rally in between his two visits to Jane. Horses had been my lifelong passion. I drew a horse at the age of three and would spend hours drawing them as a child, even in school. I had perfected my drawing while listening to the teacher and keeping up so that when I was called on, I could answer the question without picking up my pencil. From age seven onward, I'd had a dream to see, then own, then breed Lipizzaners, which I had done. My next goal had been to watch them perform at the Spanish Riding School in Vienna, Austria, so I had taken us to Austria in 1997.

However, after Joe cheated on me in 1998, I stopped loving horses. The memory of my passion for them in happier times was too painful for me. We had often ridden as a family on wonderful trail rides. We took our horses to shows where Jolly had shown her pony or horse, and we'd ride in the cakewalk or around the show area.

Joe and I had even trained young horses together. He'd had a buckskin Saddle Horse gelding named Chief, and I had a paint-colored Paso Fino-Saddle Horse bred named Magic. That majestic animal had chosen me at a sale one Saturday in Opelika, Alabama. He wouldn't let anyone ride him but me. He'd run away or rear up with everyone else. I figured he loved my light hands on the bit.

In 1998, I quit riding Magic. He loved it when I rode him and would run up to me when I showed him the bridle. The last time I'd worked him, right before I discovered Joe's cheating, I rode him bareback and took him for a swim across our five-acre lake. And the horses and I weren't the only ones who suffered from this oddity. Jolly paid the highest price because she had to give up our trail rides as well as showing her horse. Fortunately, that hit about the time she got interested in boys. I had always felt guilty that I'd let Joe's cheating have that effect on me.

We tried hard for a while to put our marriage back together, but he laced even that with lies, and I complicated things with my suicide attempts that began with ambulance runs to ICU and ended with another hospitalization in a mental ward. I constantly fought the conflicting impulses to leave him or to love him passionately. Finally, I had the courage to depart temporarily in December 2002.

The Ambien was taking me to a place of calm, a place of clarity in my thoughts. I went to the refrigerator for another glass of tea. On my way through the large opening to the den, I passed the bookshelf that held the iris journal I'd kept during our separation that December of 2002. Titled "My Journey to Discover Myself—Learning to be Independent," the journal now appeared prophetic.

My mind went back to the time I had stayed in Mobile, trying to come to resolution with my life. I'd had such great hope that I would return home to a happy marriage and a renewed love and commitment. While I was gone, I realized that I'd handed Joe too much of my power and placed a burden upon him. I knew I'd changed from the independent woman he'd fallen in love with to a clinging, pathetic mess. I decided that things such as learning to fix the computer myself were going to free me from those tentacles that ensnared me to Joe. I planned on returning home a changed, better woman and wife.

Chapter Twenty-One

_____

January in Mobile that year wasn't very cold. I was out in only a long-sleeved shirt with no jacket as I took a swallow of my daily indulgence down at Kentucky Fried Chicken, tasting its sugary sample. Mobile tea is renowned for its heavy-handed sweetness.

While separated, words spoken by Joe had satisfied me on the one hand and scared me on the other. I guess my radar was up, but my voice of reason had calmed me down. I somehow accepted the words Joe said. I convinced myself to trust him to be faithful while separated. I fully believed he had been faithful to me since 1998.

We struggled with our marriage, love, and my trust. What complicated things was the fact that I couldn't stop thinking about the past. I'd try—God knows I'd try to live in the present and appreciate that Joe had come back home and was willing to love me again. What made all of it difficult was the painful realization that he'd stopped loving me. I had caught Joe lying many times concerning his affairs.

In both 1997 and 1998, he had cheated on me with three women. The first was in July of 1997 with Lynn, which had been only an emotional online affair without any sex. I called her in 1998 when I found her e-mail address in a book where she had left her work and her home phone numbers.

"May I speak to Lynn, please?"

"Lynn, someone wants to talk to you," I heard someone say. "I don't know. It's a woman."

"Hello, who this?"

"I'm Lee Thames, Joe's wife. I want you to tell me all about your little affair with my husband."

"I swear we didn't have no sex," she said. "He wanted to meet me, but I'm overweight, and I told him I'd meet him when I got skinny."

"I don't believe you. I think I'll call your house and tell your husband."

"He already know about it. He caught us last summer. That why we stopped e-mailing and calling after August. He threw my computer away. I called and warned Joe that he might tell on us."

"What about the phone call in September? I noticed a call to this number one time then."

"He telling me about you trying to kill yourself over him smoking. Boy was he pissed off with you. He need a friend, that all."

That made sense to me. I hung up and left her alone. I laughed to myself when I remembered reading that she'd written him an e-mail message saying she thought he was sophisticated. Damn, after talking to her, I was surprised she could even spell the word.

In March of 1998, I caught Joe with Teri. I'd finally found the damn phone bill, and it had her number on it a couple of times. He'd called her from our computer phone line. I called information to find out whose number it was by lying and saying this person had been harassing me, and I wanted to know who it was. I got her husband's name.

When I confronted Joe with it at our marriage counselor's office three days later, I had to keep a straight face and act as if I knew nothing. I told him I knew he was cheating with a Mrs. Brown. He confessed to calling her and e-mailing her but swore they'd never had sex. Well, I decided to call her and find out the truth. He'd slipped and given her first name as Teri in the counselor's office.

A sexy voice answered the phone when I called her number.

"Teri, this is Lee Thames. I know you've been having an affair with my husband. I want to know if you two have had sex or not."

"Why don't you ask him?"

"Why don't I call and tell your husband?"

"He's sitting right here. Do you want to tell him? He already knows. We have an open marriage."

Well, that blew my advantage, so I had to try a new tactic. She obviously wasn't a semi-literate bimbo like Lynn.

"Unlike your husband," I said, "mine has been hiding this from me and lying about it. He swears you were too overweight to have sex and that he turned around and drove back home."

"We did have sex. He is a liar."

"How many times?"

"Why don't you get him to tell you all of this? It's not my place."

"Because he's a lying motherfucker, that's why."

"We only met that one time in March," she said. "We had sex only once."

"Thank you." Now I had some shot to shoot him with when I asked him about it when he arrived home that day. "He's taken our daughter to a movie."

When Joe got home, I was loaded and ready. I even warned him.

"Joe, I'm going to ask you a question that I know the answer to it. Don't lie to me. You'll only make things worse if you do. Did you and Teri have sex?"

"No, I swear to you," he said. "She was a blimp, and I couldn't get it up. I left, and she was screaming and dog cussing me for not fucking her."

"Asshole, I've talked to her," I said. "She admitted that y'all had sex but said it was only once. Now let's try this again. Did you have sex with Teri?"

"Okay, we did it once. I had to force myself because she was fat. It was a quickie because I didn't care about her one bit. I did leave her cussing me out. I'm sorry, Lee. Please forgive me."

"By missing Jolly's winning first place at the Regional Science Fair, you punished yourself. How many years have we been waiting for that moment? You were too busy fucking a whale to see our daughter finally win first place. I hope that makes you as sick as it makes me."

"It does make me sick. I'm ashamed of myself."

I was glad that something back then had made him feel truly ashamed of himself.

Finally, the clock chimed eleven times. It registered in my brain, but it didn't bring me out of my tortuous memories.

Why hadn't Joe stopped with Teri? We could have smoothed things out. She had been a fuck and nothing else. It had bothered me, but not as much as the third one that I'd discovered in May. Their affair had lasted three months—April, May, and June. Jane Kelly had begun as another online affair. It had progressed to a full-fledged sexual love affair. I remember now how it had all started. I was so stupid that I didn't notice it going on right in my face. If I'd been astute, I could have stopped the train wreck. Well, maybe.

Lynn and Joe had been e-mailing during the summer of 1997. I walked into the office one night, and Joe didn't realize I was there. Since I didn't have my glasses on, I couldn't really see what he was involved with, frantically typing away. He finally stopped when he realized I was there, and the computer screen flipped to a game of solitaire. I was so computer illiterate back then that I didn't even realize that wasn't normal.

"When are you coming to bed?" I asked. "I miss you. Besides, I'm feeling a little frisky tonight."

"Not tonight," he said. "I'm about to win this game. You go on to bed. I'll be back there in a little while." Normally, Joe would have fallen all over himself to get on back to the bedroom for some sex.

I laughed because I actually thought he was playing a joke on me. "Are you sure about that? Since when did you prefer a card game to having sex? Are you sick or something?"

When he never got up, I realized he had been serious. What I didn't know was that when the screen had flipped, he had been hiding a hot e-mail message he was writing to Lynn.

I found her e-mails to him when I discovered the bag under his truck seat with the bank loan notes and motel receipts, which had led me to Jane. The only reason Lynn and Joe had never screwed was because her husband had caught them. Joe had sweated that her husband was going to call me and tell me. After all, Lynn had called Joe often, therefore he had our number. She thought Joe was the hottest, sexiest, most sophisticated man she'd ever known. Well, that told me that she was one first class redneck. On a scale of one to ten for sophistication, he was a three at best.

When I first met him, he had been a point five. His idea of a date was to take me back home to his high school football games on a Friday night. Believe it or not, he took me to their Homecoming Dance when we were both in our thirties. I thought it sick that people still participated in their high school doings decades after they graduated. I'd never returned to my high school and attended a football game. In fact, I didn't know one person I hung around with who did or would have even wanted to.

Joe learned about fine wines and dining, first class hotels, art, theater, symphonies, and ballets from me. I taught him about wearing a tuxedo and going to a dance as well as eating in places where there were more than three utensils at the table. Joe had learned to be romantic because I had given him a rose "from Jolly" on the night she was born. I sent him cards or made him small gifts. I wrote him poems and talked to him in romantic terms.

By doing these things, I had indeed turned Joe into a lady's man. I found out he'd sent virtual flowers and virtual love cards to his women, and he'd bought Jane a dozen red roses and had them delivered to her at work on the day they were to meet for the first time. Was that romantic or what? I wonder what she would have thought about him if he'd suggested that they go out and watch a high school baseball game in the sweltering heat.

Yeah, I had groomed the man well. I think that probably bothered me as much as his cheating did. He'd sent me red roses only once, and I later chanced upon the fact that he marred that occasion by posting an ad for a dating service on the Internet the same week he'd sent me those roses for my birthday. To say the least, that had canceled out the effort of his being romantic with me, although he'd had no problem at all being romantic with Lynn, Teri, and especially with Jane.

While in the den, I sat in the old brown wooden office chair that had belonged to my dad—worn from fifty years of use. The chair, an old type seat with an added backrest that screwed in with a large knob and a pedestal resting on four curved legs radiating out from the swivel seat, rolled along on castors that squeaked while the uneven legs rattled the chair as it rolled across the floor. Dark brown in color with two butt-induced racing stripes caused by sliding into and out of it for nearly a half century, I found it surprisingly comfortable.

I sat at the computer to check my e-mail, wondering if this evening would ever end. My sister and Jolly had written to check up on me, concerned because I hadn't answered their messages earlier in the day. Margaret would be asleep by now, but Jolly would still be up. I didn't want her calling the local cop to come check on me again, so I typed a reply and told her how good I was feeling and for her not to worry about me. Sitting at Joe's Systemax computer that was now mine reminded me of the day in December '98 when I'd found a deleted e-mail message from Jane on our IBM computer.

I had accidentally deleted something I needed while cleaning out my e-mail Inbox. I opened my Recycle Bin and, to my shock, found a message to me from Jane, my husband's mistress. The subject line was "I hope that will do." Maybe she was finally admitting to the affair and apologizing to me.

Lee,

I hope the letter last night was what you needed. I got emotional writing that. I don't bare my soul easily. I found all the e-mails from Joe and still have them. If you still want me to send them, I will. I don't recommend you read them. I think you should close this chapter and go on.

Jane

My breath caught in my chest as the memory of reading that message came back to me. Imagine how upset I was to see something from her in my trash bin. I had worked hard the five months prior to that at just getting her to admit that she'd had an affair with Joe, because I wanted her to apologize to me. I knew Joe was behind its being deleted. I couldn't understand why he would deny me the chance of freedom from some of my anger. After all, he had admitted to it. What was his problem? I remember how he had lied to me while I was in the hospital.

In June of 1998, I had tried killing myself after I'd discovered that Joe had been unfaithful. While in the hospital, I confronted him and asked him to tell me all about it. I'm the type that needs the details in order to put it behind me. I was journaling when the hospital staff paged me for a phone call.

"Is there anything you want me to bring you when I drive over tomorrow?" Joe asked.

"I need some long-sleeved shirts and a sweater. It's so cold in here."

I was wearing jeans and a short-sleeved shirt since it was June, but my terry cloth bathrobe failed to keep me warm. Rules prohibited our having belts or sashes, because we could potentially commit suicide by hanging ourselves. There was a shake in my voice because of the way my body trembled from being cold.

"Honey, I'm so sorry," Joe said. "You know I love you, don't you?"

"I've been thinking," I replied. "I need to know all about your affair. While I'm in here and being treated is the time to come totally clean with me. I'm surrounded by doctors, nurses, therapists, you name it."

"Okay. I don't feel comfortable, but I'll tell you the truth if you insist."

"What is her name? I know she has a salon and lives in Andalusia. Tell me who she is. You owe me that much, Joe."

"Her name is Kat. I don't know her last name."

"Joe, you're lying to me. I've already called the salon to make an appointment. I left the name Mrs. Joe Thames in the appointment book. I asked who all worked there. No one named Kat works there."

I heard the phone drop.

He picked it up and said, "Sorry, I was folding clothes while listening to you and dropped the phone off my shoulder. I meant that her screen name was Kat. I think her name is Jane. I don't know her last name. It wasn't serious. She was dumpy and not attractive."

I remembered his description of Kat the blackmailer as a tall, gorgeous blonde. Had he subconsciously been describing Jane?

"Then why did you send her the dozen roses?" I asked. "Why did you go back and see her the second time? I don't believe you when you say you don't know her last name or that she's fat. Man, you fucked her for nearly three months." My voice got louder and louder as the anger rose in me.

"Please hold it down, Lee. Everyone's going to hear you."

"Well, big boy," I said, "if you're man enough to fuck another woman, then you should be man enough to let the whole goddamn world know it."

This I practically screamed. The staff started eyeing me, and that quieted me down some before I continued.

"You were e-mailing her and talking on the phone. I'm sure you know her name. And you left me screaming that Sunday. Are you telling me you left me for a fat, dumpy woman? That's worse than leaving me for a beautiful woman!"

"I promise you, I don't know her last name. I wanted sex with her. She didn't mean nothing to me. We were on a first name basis. In fact, the first time we met, she admitted to me that she was married. I didn't even know that until then, and I don't think she knew I was married. We never discussed it one way or another."

Maybe it was due to the mega doses of medicine they had pumped in me, but I accepted what he said. I dropped it, too depressed to fight and too defeated to stand up to him. I had wanted to believe that it hadn't been a love affair, that she hadn't meant anything to him and wasn't pretty. I had believed most any stupid thing Joe had told me.

From his cell phone records that I'd wrestled from the wireless company by worrying the hell out of them until they gave them to me even though the phone wasn't in my name, I knew the phone number and name of the place where she worked. After he told me her name, I decided I'd go straight to "Kat's" mouth to find out the truth.

I had to talk to Jane and get her to tell me her side of the story. I called the salon and asked to speak to her. Someone called her to the phone. My heart raced in anticipation of hearing the voice of Joe's mistress. When she answered, she sounded sexy, sweet, and young.

"Hello, can I help you?"

"Jane, you don't know me, but you know about me. I'm Lee Thames, Joe's wife."

"Pardon? I don't understand who you are."

"Yes you do. My husband Joe was in Andalusia on April tenth and again on May third. I have the motel receipts to prove it. I also have your number here in his cell phone log. Don't act dumb. You know my husband. In fact, you know him well. Let's say intimately."

"Yes, I remember now—Joe Thames. He was here on business. He said he was checking out old cemeteries to do rubbings for a genealogy project. He came by my shop for a haircut."

"Listen, honey, cut out the bullshit. I have digital photos of Joe that show his hair growing longer during those weeks. Right now, I'm not trying to fight with you or accuse you of anything. My beef isn't with you. You never made any promises to me—Joe did. You're simply a victim. I'm calling because, as his hairdresser, he may have confided something in you that I need to know."

"Go on."

"I've discovered bank loans for nearly $3,000 that he hid from me. Right now, my mind is convinced that he was having an affair with you and spent the wad on wining, dining, and gifting you. If that's the case, let me know. He's acting as if he can't remember what he did with the money. I'm tired of his lies. Help me, Jane. According to him, your husband cheated on you. Joe confessed to me and told me everything about your tryst. I just want to know what he did with that much money."

"I promise you we didn't have an affair."

"I can't prove you had a sexual affair, although if I described you naked to your husband, he'd probably think I could prove it. Joe has described your naked body in vivid details. I know what your snatch looks like and that you are a natural blonde. However, that's not important. You and Joe have been e-mailing, talking on the phone, had some kind of face-to-face meetings and, according to my American Express statement, flowers sent to you compliments of Joe using my card. Thus, by those actions alone, you two have been having an affair. Let's quit being in denial, okay? I'm not here to harass you about sleeping with my husband. You made no vows to me. I have no anger toward you at all as long as you'll quit lying to me."

She finally told me he'd said he used the money to help his grown kids and paid off a loan for his ex-wife, Regina. I found it funny that Jane would know more about something like that than me, yet she kept insisting that they weren't anything but friends. I knew she was lying, and I knew I had to find out more to let her know she wasn't fooling me one bit. I concocted a plan to trick her into giving me her full name as well as her address.

Thinking about how I had outfoxed Jane brought a genuine smile to my lips. I felt my face crinkle and the slight breeze from the ceiling fan on my gums as my lips rolled under, lifting them like a window shade or a curtain after the finale. I realized Jolly would call and spoil things because I'd stupidly e-mailed late and shown her I wasn't asleep. Thank God I hadn't sent it yet. Best to leave her message unanswered as if I were asleep.

Whew, that was a close call. I deleted the message to Jolly, which took me right back to what I'd been thinking.

Chapter Twenty-Two

After I got my own cell phone, I called Jane again. At least she wouldn't recognize the phone number if she had caller ID.

"Hair and More, how can I help you?"

"May I speak to Jane please?"

"I'm her. What can I help you with?"

"Jane, my name is Addie. I'm going to be back in Andalusia in about a month and I want you to cut my hair again. You did the best job of anyone who has ever cut my hair. Put me down for September 10. In fact, I was so impressed and had so many comments about my hair that I'd like to send you a little 'happy' to show my appreciation."

Of course, I'd never been in Andalusia in my life.

"Okay," she said. "September 10th at two o'clock. Will that be okay for you?"

"Yes, that's perfect. Now, I need to get your name and address to send my little gift to you."

"Now, who did you say you were, and when did you come in?" she asked with some caution in her voice.

I gulped.

"Oh, you remember. I'm that little blonde that was a walk-in this past spring. Addie Jeffery. Remember, I was visiting my sister down there. I'm hurt you don't remember me." I laughed.

"Oh, yeah. I remember now," she said to cover up a cardinal rule of business etiquette: you never forget a client. I heard the puzzlement and the blush in her voice when she realized she hadn't remembered me and felt foolish for having questioned me.

"Okay," I said, "now, spell out your name for me. I don't want to make any mistakes. I can't hear too well, and this way I'll know I have it right."

"J-a-n-e-K-e-l-l-y at 1602 River Drive, Andalusia, Alabama, 36780."

My heart pounded as she spelled out everything I needed to know. I could look her up on the Internet and get all kinds of information about her.

"Oh, honey," I said. "Thank you. I'll put your little gift in the mail today.

It's not much, but I wanted you to know how much I appreciated all you've done for me."

Yeah, I appreciated all she'd done. She was a bigger dummy than I was.

I started laughing aloud at the memory. Boy, what an idiot she had been. After I'd hung up with Jane, I immediately got on the computer. In a matter of seconds, I had her e-mail address. That led to my catharsis of e-mailing her daily. I used it as a journal entry.

Before I started e-mailing her, I opened an e-mail account using a name similar to the one Joe had used when they were lovers. I figured enough time had passed by then that she wouldn't pick up on the subtle difference. I used the numeral one for the lowercase "L" that had been part of his handle. He'd use random letters and numbers so I'd never figure out his secret e-mail name and address. Wrong. Once I suspected he was cheating on me, Miss couldn't-turn-on-the-computer found a cache stocked with information such as every e-mail address used on it. It wasn't the history file, as he'd slyly deleted it each time he signed off the computer. Desperate, I played around on that computer until I went into its operating system to trace or backtrack any little tip I could glean.

Once I had created an e-mail address for "Joe," I was ready for my ruse. I e-mailed Jane as him. I wanted to get her to confess her sins.

Mon, Sept 7

Jane, Listen, you'd better watch out. Lee knows all about what we did and she has threatened to call Warren and tell him everything. I know that I shouldn't be writing you again and maby I'm taking a chance for Lee to catch me. I feel like I owe you this. After all, you and I had something special, didn't we?

Joe

Then I waited for her to respond. Nevertheless, to make it more believable, I e-mailed her as myself.

Saturday, Sept. 12

Jane, this is Lee Thames. I'm Joe's wife. You have denied that you had an affair with Joe. Well, let me tell you the definition of an affair. Anytime one spouse does anything with anyone other than their spouse and doesn't tell the spouse, then it is an affair because it is done in secret. Besides, Joe told me everything and I can describe your genitalia to your husband should I decide to call him and have a little chat with him. How would I know something that intimate unless Joe had seen you up close and personal? You can save yourself a lot of grief by telling me the truth and that you are sorry for hurting my daughter, Jolly, and me. Joe's been honest and he's come clean. He's told me that he is so sorry. To heal completely, I need your apology.

Lee

Then I sat back and waited. Of course, I was impatient. I figured in time she would fill in some gaps. I knew Joe was hiding something from me, but I didn't know what. Besides, I had some kind of sick longing to know how she felt about Joe as a lover. It was strange, because whenever Joe and I made love at that time, I always felt as though she appeared in our bedroom as a third party haunting me. She was faceless, an apparition of humiliation calling out taunts to me, ruining everything. The fact that our sex life had stalled, yet he had slowly kissed her, undressed her and caressed her in ways he hadn't done with me in years made me jealous as hell. For the same reason, whenever he tried doing all of that with me then, I'd freak out because it only reminded me of the things he had done to her. For the first six months after I caught him cheating, our sex life was in the crapper.

A full week went by, and I started thinking Jane would never reply. I gave her credit for having enough shrewdness to know maybe it had been me and not Joe who'd e-mailed her. Just when I'd given up all hope that "Joe" would ever hear from her, who should pop up in "Joe's mail box" but JKGlamor@hotmail.com? My pulse raced and I broke out in a sweat as I moved the mouse over the subject line to open it. I could tell by what it said that she was going to do the motor mouth. Sure enough, she had taken my bait.

Sept 14

Joe, listen I really want to thank you for warning me about Lee. You sure were right about her being a bitch. Why is she making threats this late day? I sat Warren down last night and told him everything. I won't be threatened by her. I don't know what you two want from me. We had fun talking with each other. We shared our Mon dreams and goals. Nothing was meant to be anything but fun. I never meant to hurt anyone. Besides the way you talked about her, it seemed like she never would have cared, one way or another, what you did. I didn't make your problems or Lee's, and I can't fix them either.

Jane

Okay, she hadn't actually admitted to having sex with him, but she sure as hell had something to hide from me. She'd admitted that she'd done something she figured I wouldn't care about, yet it had ended up being fun and had hurt me. Reading between the lines, she'd made a weak confession. The thought occurred to me that maybe she wouldn't come right out and say she'd slept with Joe because she did have a feeling it was a bogus e-mail message.

I probably could have kept on e-mailing her as Joe, because I knew his speech patterns and the words he consistently misspelled. I could have pulled it off and probably gotten the fool to meet "Joe" again at the same Red Roof Inn. I could have continued the ruse by telling her "I" couldn't talk on the phone because Lee had it tapped. I could even have convinced her that Lee had alerted the nurses at the mill not to allow any calls to "me." I could have moaned and complained that things had gotten unbearable again since Lee had discovered what "we'd" done.

That would have been a fun tactic to screw her over for screwing my husband. What stopped the plan was my own honest self. No, I had to go and blab it all to Joe. It really pissed him off that I'd set her up. He made me promise that I would never write to her as him again. The thing about me is that when I make a promise, hell, I keep it. That's one reason I never did follow through on my plan of setting up another tryst with Jane finding me rather than Joe waiting for her in the motel room.

I decided the next best thing was to write her as me. I'd cultivate her conscience and try to make her feel guilty—which I did. However, as I wrote her these long, cathartic e-mail messages, I ended up changing my feelings toward her. My messages became more and more compassionate, friendly, sincere, and less contrived. By November, I'd had a complete change of heart.

Nov. 3, 1998

Jane, I finished reading the most wonderful book. This one book has done more to help me, thus helping my marriage, than the six months of marital therapy that Joe and I have been through. Somehow, I accidentally ordered the book, Passionate Marriage, by David Schnarch, Ph.D. Joe underwent what this book is all about, both in the spring when we were having all of our problems, right down to my discovery of what he had been up to and the subsequent marital discord and crises that followed.

As you know, the discovery led to my suicide attempts and hospitalization for acute depression. Even after my release from the hospital, Joe continued to manipulate me and lie to me. My therapy at the hospital gave me the courage to draw a line in the sand. I told him that I would tolerate no more lies or manipulations. He had to go get help or I would leave him. I told him I would take Jolly and move to another area of the country or even the world, because I could get a job anywhere due to teacher shortages. That shocked him to reality so he did get counseling, and his therapist put him on Prozac.

In the meantime, I left for three weeks to attend teacher workshops, and he tasted what life would be like without me. To make a long story short, he underwent a complete metamorphosis. No joke, now, I can tell when he is bullshitting me because my bullshitometer is fine-tuned. As time rocked on, we went into marital therapy, and I went into individual therapy.

I have become obsessed with reading books on marital therapy and surviving infidelity. All helped to a small degree, but the above book really made me look at myself as well as our marriage. To wit: all marriages must undergo gridlock in order for couples to differentiate and grow. This personal growth unlocks true intimacy and sexual potential that becomes spiritual in nature.

I've finally truly forgiven you, and I offer you this chance for you to get your life and marriage on track. According to Joe, your husband tried to control you. He, too, cheated on you. I understand now the desperation in seeking the Internet for companionship and happiness, as well as validation.

Please get this book and read it. It will show you how to find self-validation and personal growth. The change in the dynamics of the marriage will cause Warren to wonder what it is that you have gotten, as I did with Joe. Anyway, you could find real happiness rather than a shallow attempt at "other validation" via the Internet.

I am not sending this to hassle you but in a real spirit of love and concern. You are no longer my enemy. In fact, we share my husband as a common denominator, and he joins us in some cosmic way. May you find true joy and happiness one day.

Lee

I'd labored for months to get her to be honest and apologize to me. She'd finally e-mailed me that December of 1998.

Lee, I poured out my heart to you in that last long e-mail.

What last e-mail? I wanted to know exactly what all she'd said in it. I knew that Joe had been uneasy about her ever responding to me, so I decided to call her and talk to her about the message she said she'd sent. After I called and talked to her, I knew why Joe hadn't wanted her talking to me.

Chapter Twenty-Three

The clock read five minutes after eleven—surely Joe would be home by now. Soon, this would be over. Joe should be pulling up in the parking lot at his apartment. I'd allow him time to take off his helmet then roll his cycle back behind the apartment building to his back door. He'd wheel his Harley inside the kitchen because he didn't want all the college kids around him to mess with it.

While I waited, I reread Jolly's e-mail message to make sure she was okay. I worried about her worrying about me. Jolly's message begged me to go back to Dr. Hopkins within the week. She expressed an uneasy feeling that something bad was going to happen. Jolly was a empath and was rarely wrong. She could read tarot cards and do divination. She could also read Nordic runes. Jolly practiced Stregarrian witchcraft—the real deal. She used herbs to make healing potions that worked. She wrote in her Book of Shadows any knowledge she gleaned from her teacher, a woman who had been a fourth generation witch and knew the trade.

I'd grown up thinking witchcraft was evil and satanic, but I'd discovered it was a matriarchal nature religion. True witches didn't believe in Satan. How could they worship something they didn't believe existed? There was no "black magic or devil worship." Jolly believed in the Rule of Three: "Whatever thou doeth shall return to thee thrice." Kind of an ancient Golden Rule, which predated Jesus: "do unto others" combined with "reap what you sow." I'd learned from Jolly that witchcraft was a peaceful and pastoral religion.

Of course, having been raised a Christian with all the lies propagandized about witchcraft, I was very concerned about Jolly's involvement at first. She'd come home once and logged on to her e-mail and my password keeper had kept her logon name and password. I knew it was wrong; however as a parent, I felt I had to check things out. I didn't want Jolly's getting mixed up in something that could hurt her in any way.

I went into her e-mail and read what the teacher had to say. After I verified that Jolly had told me the truth and was satisfied that nothing evil was going on, I erased her logon. I'd always felt bad about that breach of privacy. I eventually told her what I'd done and why I'd felt compelled to do it. She was mad at first, but then she told me she understood. I started researching the religion so I could talk to her knowledgably about her life. I have to admit, Jolly's thinking as a pagan resulted in my first seeds of doubt about my own religious beliefs.

As I sat there, I felt something hit the front wall of the house, waking the dogs. Since I was jittery, I jumped until I heard the familiar grunt of Pigger. He was clueless that he was a pig, thanks to Jolly. I remembered when she'd tamed him down. Jolly possessed a way with animals as well as having a sixth sense. As a child, she caught wasps that never stung her, snakes that never bit her, and she trained a baby pig into acting like a dog, including a barking noise he emitted when strange dogs entered our yard.

The squealing had sounded as if we were slaughtering Pigger when Jenny Mackie first gave him to us. In reality, Jolly had picked him up to hold and pet him—an adorable black piglet with a white star on his forehead between his dark chocolate eyes. It wasn't long before Jolly had him coming when called, and he spoke on command, "barking" rather than squealing.

Joe hadn't been much of an animal lover until I came into his life. We had four dogs, four cats, and we'd always had horses and ponies. This menagerie later expanded to chickens and one pet rooster named Sweetie Pie who watched TV with Jolly as a child. We had a cockatiel named Freddie and even pet goldfish out in our front fishpond that were trained to come eat when we tapped on the edge of the cement pond.

I really believed Jolly had some mystical power to catch critters without hurting them or their hurting her, including a pet Black Widow spider. She did a study on them that evolved into a science project when she was in second grade. She kept the spider through the winter in a jar. She even found a male to mate with her pet, but Jolly plucked the lucky male from the jar and saved his life. The female spun an egg sack, and thousands of tiny spiders hatched. We kept a photo log, and Jolly scrawled her daily observations in her scientific log for six weeks in her second grade inventive spelling. She won first place in her school and fifth place in the regional fair.

She'd never entered a science fair in which she didn't win first place at her local school level, but the only regional fair she'd won had been when Joe had gone to screw Teri, too tied up to attend it with us. I took her to the next competition at the state level, and while Jolly was winning third place for the state of Alabama with her project on how to make kudzu into paper, Joe had been busy screwing Jane.

Jolly had brains and beauty, but mainly she had a compassionate and a forgiving heart. She always took care of so many creatures great and small— even wild ones such as squirrels, raccoons, and even a pet coyote. While she studied at the Alabama School for Gifted Children from tenth grade through her senior year, Joe and I took care of all of the animals.

When Joe left me for good, I was stuck with running the farm alone—or rather, I tried to run it. I began to appreciate Joe for all the things he'd always done outside that I'd taken for granted. In fact, I realized I had taken many things for granted. In a lot of ways, Joe was a good man. How many men would come to their wife's classroom and read to her children or help them make booklets? All my students had loved "Mr. Joe." How many men surprised their wives with a dozen yellow roses brought to the classroom "because he loved me"—no holiday, no anniversary, nothing special, just his thinking of me? Of course, he did this after he had cheated on me in 1998. At many of Jolly's functions, Joe would be the only dad there most of the time, especially at the Pony Club meetings. I guess it was his sweetness that made the hurt feel bitter to me.

I'd vacillated between feeling appreciative of all the years that he'd done so much and feeling exasperated as well as overwhelmed by the many things I needed to do after he was gone. Since I was single, the farm—once our dream—was no longer fun. It became a huge burden, and I felt it was unfair that I had to deal with it alone.

Remembering that anger led to the memory of the biggest lie Joe had told me about Jane and him. The old wounds of 1998 ripped at my mutilated heart, much like our mangled family photos I'd destroyed after reading Jane's deleted e-mail message.

When Joe got home that day, I met him in a total rage. I hadn't thought it was possible for me to get any angrier than I had gotten when I found out he had been involved in an affair, but this had crossed a line. He should have told me all about what he'd done when I was in the hospital. While I was there, while the doctors were pumping me full of drugs and I had around-the-clock staff to make sure I would come around emotionally, I could have better digested what he'd done and been on my way to healing by the time I found out about the deleted message. What made it even worse was that Joe had looked me in my eyes while he swore he'd never lie to me again and that I could trust him. The whole time, he had been lying to me!

After I discovered Joe had deleted the long message Jane sent me, I picked up the phone and dialed her number. The dial tones seemed to echo in the room. My adrenaline-fueled anticipation enhanced everything I expected her to tell me—my heartbeat a tympani drum rolling in the climax of a fugue. The phone rang three times, and I suddenly feared she'd recognize our number and not answer. Let's face it—she'd heard from Joe often during those three months they had been lovers. He even called her from work using our AT&T calling card, although he told me the company had cracked down on their calling and he'd ceased calling me during that time. I prayed she didn't have caller ID. Finally, before the fourth ring, I heard someone pick up. I waited for the hello and hoped it wasn't Warren. Right then, I didn't want to get her in any trouble. When a soft voice answered the phone, I knew it was Jane.

"Hello, Jane. This is Lee. Listen, somehow your e-mail message went to my trash, and I never got to read the long letter where you poured out your heart to me. Can you tell me what you told me in that message?"

"Well, Lee, mainly I said I was sorry for the pain I caused you and Jolly. I never meant to hurt anyone. It was supposed to be for fun, and no one was supposed to find out. We were good friends and we could talk about anything. He was so easy to talk to."

Was she talking about the same man? Joe rarely talked to me. I tried to start many conversations about all kinds of topics and, at best, I'd get a one-syllable answer from him. That made me jealous too.

Jane went on. "It got out of hand when he told me that he loved me and would marry me in a minute, especially when we had oral sex."

I nearly dropped the phone because, for a split second, I blacked out from the intense emotional pain. I felt myself being numbed and losing any conscious thought.

"I'd never done that with anyone in my life," she said, "and it made me feel close to Joe. I was beginning to fall in love with him, and I knew that he had fallen in love with me. I knew it would never work out because he lived so far away. He would never give up his job, and I would never give up my salon. It was getting too intense, and I was afraid one of us was going to do something really stupid, so I broke it off."

We ended up talking for over an hour, but that little bit is all I remembered. My heart was devastated to realize Joe had fallen in love with her. He'd presented it to me as being only a sexual thing, with no emotions. He'd also told me she was slightly overweight and not nearly as attractive as I was, and he'd convinced me she was a dud in bed.

I realized his claim that she had been too inhibited to have oral sex was a joke—though it wasn't funny. Of course, when he'd first admitted to having the affair, I had asked him if they'd ever done that, hoping that at least some part of our sex life remained sacred between us. Now I knew that he'd lied and misled me all along. I also knew that Joe was responsible for her mail going to my trashcan.

When he got home, I started screaming at him. I grabbed all fourteen framed family photos off the wall—one for each year we'd been married—and started slinging them as hard as I could at his lying head. I truly wanted to kill him that day.

"You sorry son of a bitch! You didn't have any oral sex, did you?"

"Honey, have you flipped out? Of course, I didn't do that. I wouldn't. That's something I only did with you. I never wanted to do that with anyone else."

God, had he walked into it!

"Quit lying to me! I talked to Jane today, and she told me all about it! She said you told her you loved her and would marry her in a minute. Damn, this is so much worse than I ever imagined. No wonder you didn't want me getting any e-mails from her. How did her message end up in my trashcan?"

"I blocked her from coming into your Inbox."

"Why, when you knew I e-mailed her for nearly three months trying to get her to apologize to me?"

"Honey, I did it to protect you. I didn't want her to upset you." His eyes widened with fear—something I rarely saw in Joe.

"Don't honey me, you shithead. You did it to protect yourself! You did it to keep me from finding out the truth. Damn it, Joe, why didn't you fess up when I was in the hospital? Why hold back and keep on lying to me?"

Sweat trickled down my chest from the exertion of throwing all of the frames. My hair was wet, and the perspiration and tears had my eyes burning. My heart felt as if it were melting away from the fire of my anger.

"Remember when you got down on your knees last month and apologized for lying to me after the discovery?" I said. "After reading our saved e-mail messages and my journal entries, you said you realized the lying was as bad if not worse than the cheating itself. You can't claim ignorance now. You knew how much lying undid all the progress we had made. I'd find out about some new lie and had to deal with the whole affair as if it were D-day all over again."

The hallway glistened with the broken glass and the mauled wooden frames I'd thrown at him. It was a miracle I hadn't cut him to shreds as I had truly wanted to hurt him. The only thing that saved him was my sorry aim because of my cursing, crying, and screaming at him. It had been hard to see where he was through my blurred vision. In fact, I'd actually seen four of him as my tears acted like a prism.

We made our way to the bedroom, and Joe lay down on our bed, looking pale. I'd never seen him look so defeated. I think he thought he'd had this thing licked, and we were in the home stretch. We'd recently picked out new wedding bands and planned to renew our wedding vows and truly commit to a lifetime of love for each other.

"Joe, you have a truth that you must face," I said. "It's something I've felt in my soul, but you have denied repeatedly. You did love another woman, and to have done that, you had to have fallen out of love with me. Did you?"

He looked tired and haggard as he replied.

"Yes, I did fall out of love with you. In fact, I fell out of love with you the year before. I grew to resent you for buying me all that stuff. I started keeping score and holding things against you. By the time we were in Europe, and you wouldn't have sex with me while we were over there, I was done with you."

I looked at him incredulously. "I can't believe what you're saying. I was good to you, and you quit loving me then? You stopped loving me one year because I showered you with my love, and then the next because you said I didn't pay attention to you while I was suffering from depression. I was damned if I did and damned if I didn't! How unfair is that? Besides, Jolly was in the same room with us the whole time we were in Europe. How in the world could you have expected me to have sex with you then?"

By then, I was truly incensed. I began to sense that something wasn't right with Joe. The idea that he'd wanted to have sex in the room with a twelve year old who had gone through puberty turned my stomach. Doing that would have traumatized Jolly.

Once I knew Joe had lied about what he and Jane had done and what she had meant to him, I began to suspect that he'd lied about her appearance as well. My next project was to meet her in person and see what my competition actually looked like. I knew I'd have to convince Joe to let me meet her. I'd really have to work on him.

As I said, our sex life had its good moments occasionally, and at other times it sucked, because I couldn't help imagining Joe making love to Jane. During that first year after the discovery when I imagined Joe doing those things to Jane as the other woman, I was incapable of enjoying sex. In my mind's eye, no matter what Joe had told me about her, Jane was gorgeous with a perfect body—long-legged, big breasted, round hipped, with an hourglass waist. In comparison, I felt ugly and unable to compete with her. It always left me crying or angry with him, and of course I was unable to have an orgasm. Talk about frustration: he cheated, had all the fun, and I couldn't enjoy sex at all anymore. Was that fair?

I convinced Joe that if he let me meet Jane, I'd be able to put a face with the name and close that book once and for all, which would vastly improve our sex life. Bingo—the magic words. He agreed but said he wanted to go with me to make sure I didn't cause a scene. Obviously, he was still protective of her.

There came a point in time after I met her that I fantasized I was Jane, feeling the excitement she had felt to have Joe as her new lover. I had some great orgasms then. I literally played out the first time we laid eyes on each other, the first time he touched "me" as Jane, and when he entered "me" the first time, I nearly had an orgasm right then. Afterward, I'd always feel dirty—sick that it took thinking of Joe's cheating on me to get off. Pain seemed my only comfort.

Tonight, I'd end that pain forever.

Chapter Twenty-Four

I tried calling Joe, but the line was busy. We were both on dial-up Internet access since we lived in rural areas, so I knew that might be the reason. Anger sharpened my memories and my determination. I hated the possibility that he was either talking with Yvonne, his latest girlfriend, or online schmoozing her with romantic e-mail messages like he used to send me daily. I thought about how I had worked at staying thin and sexy for Joe. I'd tried to look attractive to him through all the years, except the one time I did something just for me and hadn't cared if he liked it or not.

For some reason, maybe to prove what a wild hare I was, I decided to have my hair dyed. Instead of doing what normal people do, I dyed it "manic mauve." Punk hair color at the age of forty-nine decked my thin body. I don't know, I guess that hair color gave me the courage to face Jane.

In December 1998, right around New Year's Eve, Joe and I planned a trip to Biloxi, Mississippi to sell our cabin on the beach. That was going to be my opportunity to swing through Jane's town. We stopped in Andalusia so I could meet the vision of my mental nightmares. At last, I would put a face on that ghost who laughed at me and taunted me that she possessed Joe when I didn't. I had to know if I was worrying over nothing or if her beauty was a real rather than imagined threat.

We drove down and checked in at the local Hampton Inn, then we rode by her salon, expecting her to be open, but she wasn't there. Well, ol' Joe thought he had won that round and that I'd give up. No, not me. I was even more determined to meet her since I was that close. I went back to the motel and called her up.

"Hello."

"Are you going to be open today? I need my hair fixed for a New Year's Eve party."

"No, I'm only open by appointment today. But I do have a ten o'clock and could work you in around ten forty-five."

"Great. I'll see you then. Put down Mary Anna for ten forty-five. I want you to put my hair up."

I was grinning like a child let loose in a Nintendo store when I hung up. Joe could tell his day was fixing to take a downhill turn. My stomach was churning as I waited for ten o'clock to arrive. Of course, I was going to do my thing as soon as she opened her doors.

We got there around nine forty-five. We wouldn't miss her when she drove up and unlocked the shop. We had to wait until five after ten when she finally arrived. Her customer beat her there. Then I remembered Joe's telling me that was one of the things that turned him off about her—she was always late.

He told me that on their last rendezvous, she had pulled into the motel parking lot a full hour late. The day he left me screaming, crying, and begging him not to go because I knew he was up to something. When she was so late, he said he decided he wasn't interested in her anymore. He figured I was hot on his trail and determined she wasn't worth the risk.

He'd stopped at the Sleeping Pines Mall and bought her a diamond necklace, by the end of that meeting with her, he said he was so mad at both of us that he threw it out the window on the way home rather than give it to either her or me for Mother's Day the following weekend. He'd bought Jane the necklace with the seven hundred dollars I'd found in his wallet. This he told me later. Who the hell can believe Joe? I sure can't.

He said they called it quits that day. Nevertheless, after the discovery when I was so angry with him about Teri—or rather his lying about things—he said he'd called Jane up and set up another tryst while he was going to be on vacation. The brazen liar actually planned to pull the going camping trick on me again! With tears in his eyes, he stood there and told me a black minister had told him to go find himself and God before making things right with me.

I didn't bite that time, though. I told him to go camping and find God in our pasture. Right under my nose, he was going to risk everything to see Jane again for one more fuck. Even when I knew he was out on the prowl, he couldn't give her up. This time, it was Jane that called it quits—after he manipulated her into an angry fit. He never had the balls to break up with any woman. He's a passive-aggressive who does underhanded things to make their partner walk away.

He'd purposely lied to me about being with his grown son Jeff in May because he wanted me to catch him and then leave him. He'd set me up. I went to my sister's house, and he called Jane. With me gone, he was as free as a mockingbird. Later, he told me that after he got what he wanted from Jane, the thrill was gone for him. Because of her hang-up about oral sex, when she finally gave in, it was as if the hunter had slain his prey and the inert form was no longer fair game.

The first time I actually laid eyes on Jane at the salon that day in December of '98, I got the shock of my life.

A Yukon pulled up and Joe said, "That's her. Try not to cause a scene."

We had parked two buildings down and across the road because Joe didn't want her to see him and recognize him. She exited her car, and I took stock. She was a tall woman, and I could tell she dressed nicely in expensive brand-name clothes, but I wasn't close enough to see her.

My moment was near as I opened the truck door and stepped out.

Joe pleaded with me. "Please promise me you won't do anything stupid. You said you'd only introduce yourself and leave. Please, for me, if you love me at all, please do that."

"Oh, Joe, take a chill pill," I said. "I'm only going to do exactly that. I want to see what she looks like, that's all."

I glanced at myself quickly in the reflection of the truck's window. I had purposely put on something that showed my thin body and firm breasts, which still did not sag in spite of my age. Anyone could tell I was braless and see everything was pert and alert. I walked up the steps and rang the doorbell. I was anxious, but at the same time, I was miraculously calm. I heard her footsteps, imagining a person who sounded as though they took confident yet dainty steps. A lady for sure.

The door opened and there stood the most beautiful woman I'd seen in a long, long while. Damn. Joe had described her as fat, dumpy, and plain. Shit, she could make a rose bloom in cement. She had her hair fixed so becomingly, she had the prettiest green eyes, nice clothes, and expensive jewelry—all of which were my antithesis for sure. I noticed her gorgeously manicured long nails on a hand with gracefully long fingers, and I thought of my recently bit off ones on my stubby fingers.

I scanned her up and down, mentally undressing her since I knew what she was supposed to look like naked. But who could trust Joe with any descriptions now? He had one thing right though. She did have big breasts, although Joe had claimed they sagged and weren't as nice as mine. My astute eyes took in the ever so slightly off-centered tilt of her points, which suggested that, without her bra, they hung down rather than stood out. At least that part was true. She was six years younger than I was and didn't have one damn wrinkle on her face. In a millisecond, I tallied the score and came up with her winning for beauty but me winning for body.

As my mind worked all this through my head, I was actually reaching for her hand and saying, "Hello, Jane. My name is Lee Thames—Joe's wife. I've heard so many nice things about you that I wanted to meet you."

Although she lost her poise for only a second as it registered who I actually was, she regained it rather quickly and extended her hand out to mine. "Hello, Lee. It's so nice to meet you."

To her surprise and to Joe's relief, I simply turned around and walked down her steps, I'm sure leaving her wondering what the hell was going on. She was a classic lady, and I was a classic manic-mauve-haired-seductive-tight-clothes-wearing tomboy—computing in my mind whether I had anything to worry about in the future.

145

Well, in spite of her beauty, grace, poise and style, I knew that Joe did prefer his kinky, uninhibited wife to that lady. Sure, the difference had been a huge turn-on for him at first. In the end his preference for someone who was more spontaneous, erotic, and daring made him decide that what he had at home was more to his liking. I was always coming up with unique ways for us to have sex, or places to have sex, or times of the day to have sex. Bottom line, in the sack I was hard to beat.

Thinking about our sex life made me think of the time I'd sold out everything to Joe, trying to hang on to him by swinging.

My own jealousy had opened the door. I wanted the courtship, attention and anticipation of a new lover. A friend of ours who was a recovering sex addict and knew about Joe's addiction had proposed swinging as the perfect solution, since Joe was not going to stop having sex outside the marriage and didn't want to change or even admit to his problem. This friend caught on to both of our problems: that Joe was a sex addict and that I suffered from multiple personality disorder. Knowing that, in and of itself, made me desperate to try anything to keep Joe married to me.

The prospect of an endless supply of new pussy with my blessings made Joe the nicest to me that he had been for our entire marriage, although he was already a kind, caring and considerate person. I never imagined he might be upping the attention in order to get what he wanted rather than its being genuine. For two months right before we split up for good, we were in a brand new courtship better than our original one.

We had the love, the history, the magic to take our lovemaking to another plane—a spiritual one as far as I was concerned. I felt secure during that time, until we met Daryl and Ginger when we joined Adult Friend Finder, an online swinging group.

I'm sure my suffering from different personalities—especially promiscuous Dee Dee—set me up for swinging. I'll never forget the time she seduced Joe while I was in a blackout. When strange things began happening, such as forgetting how to paint, I went to a new doctor who introduced me to Dee Dee and Nancy.

Chapter Twenty-Five

I realized something was wrong with me that summer of 2002. First, there was the incident when Joe claimed we'd had sex that I didn't remember. That really bothered me. Also, I once ended up in a strange city with no recall of having driven to it, and I lost my ability to paint. I wondered if I had lost my mind. I made an appointment with Dr. Diamond, a psychoanalyst, knowing I needed to understand what was happening to me. I didn't know how, but I felt in my gut that my flashback had something to do with all these things.

I walked into Dr. Diamond's formal office bedecked in ecru walls trimmed with mahogany paneled wainscoting.

"Hello, I'm Lee Thames," I said as I extended my hand to him.

"Please, have a seat," he said rather formally.

He obviously loved sailing, as an exquisite model of a schooner in a bottle rested on his glass-topped desk. Dr. Diamond, neat with no clutter on his desk, presented a minimalist look in his office. Behind him, an oil painting replica of the same schooner in stormy seas caught my attention. I sat in the deep Van Dyke brown leather captain's chair on the left, nearest to him. His huge desk emphasized his importance.

"Dr. Diamond, too many strange things are happening to me. I can't draw or paint. I'm having blackout spells with no memory for large spans of time. What really told me that something besides my bipolar is going on was when my husband claimed that he'd screwed me while I thought I was in bed asleep. I think Joe screwed another woman right under my nose while I slept."

Suddenly, I couldn't move my eyes from the Prussian blue skies in the painting.

Although I didn't know it until later, I had another blackout spell then. Still clueless as to Dee Dee and Nancy's existence, I quit looking at the painting and turned my attention back to the doctor.

"Dr. Diamond, can you help me? Can you find out what is wrong with me?"

"Lee, I will have to run some more tests before I can definitively diagnose you. I'm going to set you up for bi-weekly appointments. Do Tuesdays and Thursdays at three o'clock in the afternoon sound good to you?"

"That often? Can't you give me an idea of what's wrong? I can't stand not being able to paint."

"Lee, I suspect there are three of you living in one body. The personalities are variations of you, not some totally different personality. Hopefully, one day I will merge your different personalities into one. This will take extensive therapy to accomplish, but it will make you one whole, healthy individual. Hypnosis may be used if necessary."

I couldn't believe what I'd heard. It put my problems with Joe into perspective. Finally, some of the flaky things that had happened the past two years began to make sense. I was starting to blackout again when I heard Dr. Diamond's voice reel me back into the room.

"Lee, do you remember what just happened?"

"What do you mean? Of course I do. I was telling you about how Joe claimed we'd screwed but I thought he had screwed someone else."

"No, Lee, that's not what happened. You talked to me about 'banging' Joe. Does that ring a bell?"

"You're starting to scare me. What's really going on?"

"I'll mail you a copy of the transcriptions. Your time is up, and I have another patient to see. The notes will help you understand things better."

It was bizarre. He had recorded our session as he does all of his sessions, to be transcribed verbatim. A week later the transcripts arrived, and I couldn't believe what I was reading.

> *"I can't stand men. I don't trust them. I use them the way they use women. I hate that wimp, Lee, even more. Yeah, I got back at Lee by banging Joe."*
> *"Who is speaking right now?" asked Dr. Diamond.*
> *"Dee Dee. What's it to you?"*
> *"Where is Lee?"*
> *"Who cares? I hope she never comes back. She's stupid but not as bad as Nancy, who dresses up in Lee's mother's tattered pajamas and shuffles along. She's as old as Nordic runes. I can't stand that bitch."*
> *"How old are you?"*
> *"Twelve. I broke off when a doctor gave Lee a pelvic and traumatized her."*
> *"Do you want to tell me about that?"*
> *"Nope."*
> *"Who is Nancy?"*
> *"She's mean. She came out when Lee was seven years old. We detest each other. She reminds me of my vile mother."*

"Does Lee know about you two?"

"No, only through her thoughts. We do things to her all the time, and she takes the rap for them."

"Do you want to harm Lee?"

"Yes! The two of us are the voices inside Lee's head. That's why Lee takes overdoses. I want her dead. Depressed Nancy stays out the most. She's the one interested in suicide. She can't forgive Joe. Me, I despise him. I love teasing him with hot sex, then I let Nancy turn a cold shoulder to him. That drives the asshole crazy. Wimpy Lee loves Joe and wants to save the marriage. Boy, do we ever fuck her up. Getting Lee to kill herself is easy to manipulate. Joe loathes Nancy, loves me, and is indifferent to Lee—although he doesn't realize this. Crazy Lee wonders why Joe is so moody. What Joe did to Lee was almost as bad as what happened to her when she was a child. We also have the Secret Keeper, but she never comes out. Just us."

I found myself feeling weak. How could this be true? I knew I was crazy, but this was more than insane. This was sick and perverted. In time, through therapy, I learned to accept the truth.

While under hypnosis a couple of months later, I told Dr. Diamond the following story. He gave me the choice as to whether to remember it or not. I chose to wake up knowing what Dee Dee had done. I wrote this as the beginning of a short story in my journal. When I read my journal entries, sure enough, I could distinguish a distinct difference in many of the entries. Sometimes the writing was good, while many entries were completely immature. I wondered which of us loved to write. I hoped it was Lee. By this time, I was aware of Dee Dee and Nancy, although I couldn't control them. I think I was the one who wrote this in my journal:

Joe broke young twelve-year-old Dee Dee's heart. She couldn't forgive him for his infidelity. Dee Dee often disappeared, upsetting Joe because he couldn't find her. Whenever she threw one of her fits, she climbed a tree. No one thought to look up. Dee Dee listened from her treetop perch as Joe frantically called Lee. Nancy, always in a bad mood, refused to have sex with Joe while Dee Dee taunted him. Nancy told Joe that she forgave him, but she never treated him with any kindness, making his life hell.

Joe's affair woke Lee up out of her matrimonial slumber when she realized that other women desired him. Once Lee forgave Joe and their marriage went through another courtship, things improved.

One day in June of 2002, Lee decided to lie down for a nap. Although it was a beautiful spring day, she couldn't shake the distrust she felt toward Joe. Realizing that fighting harmed them,

N.L. Snowden

she decided to retreat into her bedroom. They fought often—mainly when she'd bring up those damn affairs. He always denied any wrongdoing. Drained emotionally from her constant nagging, Lee thought the bed looked inviting. Soon she fell into a deep sleep.

"Joe, you want to go to the pool for a quick dip?"

Dee Dee had a wicked glint in her eye, a sexual come-hither look. Joe loved her passionately when she was uninhibited and childish. He stopped working on the stirrup he was repairing. With an impish grin, he followed her to the pool, loving the youthful look on Lee's face.

"Let's go over to the gazebo," she said as she stuck her foot into the water that wasn't warm enough to be comfortable.

"What do you have planned?"

Joe played it dumb. He wanted Lee's full seduction. They walked into the gray gazebo made of latticework holding up red climbing roses, with a weathered wooden bench along the back wall. Joe pulled the chain on the ceiling fan. A whoosh-whoosh sound emanated from it as it turned slowly, stirring up a soft breeze. The day burned warm enough that the gazebo's shade was a necessity. The pasture's scents from right behind the gazebo carried the sweet aroma of horses that sweated as they grazed on the blooming clover.

"Oh, I want to show you how much I appreciate you. You know, she always was such a drag to be around with her constant moping and whining," Dee Dee said with a seductive wink. "You deserve better than that."

Dee Dee started removing his belt and unzipping his pants.

He untied the halter-top from around her small breasts. "God, I love these."

She wore white short shorts sans any panties—her body golden, tan and firm. Dee Dee knew she looked good, and the woodpecker tapping of Joe's heart agreed.

"No woman's ever made me feel the way you do."

Joe panted out these words as she started on him—stirring him into a sexual frenzy.

"You need this, don't you, baby?"

Joe looked at her with a curious look as if he didn't understand what she was saying. Caught up in what was happening, he ignored his confusion.

"Woman, if you only knew what you do to me." His huge and dreamy bedroom eyes locked into hers as if a tether tied them together. "I feel so lucky to have a woman like you. Why can't you always be like this?"

"Shhh, don't talk. Enjoy this."

Dee Dee left him drenched with sweat, sitting on the bench with his eyes closed in total contentment. She tiptoed away and went

150

back inside the house, stopping by the laundry room, pulling off her clothes and dropping them into the washer. Then she eased on back toward the bedroom and climbed into bed.

A few minutes later on that June day, Joe shook Lee awake. This is what she remembered.

"God, that was wonderful."

"What on earth are you talking about? What was wonderful?" Lee felt groggy and resented his waking her up.

"The sex was the best we've had in months." He had an incredulous look on his face.

"What sex? I've been asleep. What's going on?" Lee yawned and stretched.

Joe's upbeat mood faded. "You're putting me on. I fucked you hard, and you gave me the best blowjob ever in my life out under the gazebo. You don't remember? Come on, quit joking. It ain't funny."

"You're right. This isn't funny. Why are you doing this to me? Are you trying to hurt me again? Why would you say that?" Tears started forming in Lee's eyes because he seemed to be making fun of her. "Why pretend like we had great sex while I took a nap?"

Then it hit her—maybe he had sex with someone else and wanted to throw her off. Lee casually leaned over and sniffed him. There was the definite scent of musk. For sure, he'd screwed someone. She knew he hadn't screwed her.

Lee's tears turned to anger as she shouted at him. "You've been messing around right under my nose! I won't tolerate this. Who was it?"

"I swear to God it was you and not another woman!"

Joe looked Lee straight in her eyes, leading her to believe that somehow he was telling the truth. However, it didn't add up. Remembering her recent pledge to quit fighting with him, Lee refused to pursue it.

Agitated yet getting somewhat sleepy, I walked downstairs to my studio. It reminded me of the time Nancy had taken over and kept me from painting or drawing that summer of 2002.

The popular Rooster Day Festival had been coming up in about a month, and the committee from Cusseta, Alabama had approached me to donate a painting for their silent auction. I walked into my studio and sat down at my drawing table, staring at the palette with confusion, because I couldn't remember if I'd laid my paints out on the palette from warm to cool or from bright to neutral colors.

I tried to figure out whether to use Titanium White or the Zinc White, since one was more opaque and the other had a bluish gleam to it. Normally, my eyes would have easily seen the difference, but these eyes couldn't discern anything. Next, I tried drawing an outline of a rooster but couldn't remember whether to use an aught or number one brush. Should I dilute the paint with turpentine or oil medium? It clumped on the canvas rather than brushed on in a fluid line. My rooster ended up looking like a second grader's work rather than the typical photo-realism I was capable of painting. I pondered how to blend colors. If I thought the drawing was bad, the muddied colors were even worse.

I reposed my head on my drawing table and cried. To my horror, over the next twenty-four hour period, my talent disintegrated. Nancy controlled my mind and body, but I didn't know it.

However, nothing was as bad as the car incident. Joe and I had wondered what in the hell was wrong with me, especially when I blacked out and lost my way while Nancy drove the car. That was scary. When these episodes endangered my life, I knew it was time to get some help.

The truth was too strange. I often lost time because of Dee Dee and Nancy. The worst part was hearing their different sounding voices arguing in my head. I once called Dr. Hopkins, my psychiatrist, frantically explaining that I'd gone totally insane because the voices wouldn't shut up. He told me to take an extra sleeping pill and knock myself out. He suggested that I see Dr. Diamond, as he suspected more was going on than my bipolar illness. Both doctors had their offices in Birmingham, Alabama, about three hours from my hometown.

Dr. Diamond confirmed that I had dissociative identity disorder. It took going to him twice a week for nearly five months to attain cooperation between Dee Dee and Nancy. Our insurance capped out, and we ended up having to pay a good bit of it out of pocket. I will forever be grateful to Joe for helping me pay that huge bill.

It took Joe years of dealing with my mental illnesses before he hardened his heart. I sincerely believed he went a little insane himself during this time. He couldn't escape the fear of my wigging out—of his having pushed me into killing myself. Conversely, over time he couldn't escape not caring. Normally, he loved our daughter enough not to hurt her by giving up on our family, but my illness became too much for him. We all paid the price dearly, but I did most of all. Swinging turned out to be the end for us as a couple.

Chapter Twenty-Six

The irony was that by 2002, I finally trusted Joe again when we decided to swing, or maybe I'd taken another one of my stupid pills. A couple needed to be extremely open, close, deeply in love and trusting to allow the other the gift of being pleasured sexually by someone else. I thought Joe and I were at that point.

All was going well until we decided to meet our first couple, and Joe was going to have sex with another woman. Up until that time, we had been involved in threesomes with another man named Sam who lived in Birmingham. I sold out my soul as the good co-addict who would do anything to keep her drug of choice—her sex-addicted husband. The encounter with that couple turned into my worst nightmare.

Daryl and Ginger answered our ad on a couple's swing-board. We contacted them via the Internet and phone calls. I told them the first time we had sex, I wanted it to be a threesome with me just watching. I explained the deal about Joe having been unfaithful, and all three of them promised me they would stop if I felt uncomfortable—that Ginger's husband would start things out and Joe would join in. And, of course, Joe would use a condom. Ginger hinted that she didn't require one, but Joe and I promised to keep semen sacred between us.

They invited us up to a University of Alabama football game. We'd planned to have dinner with them first, go to the game, then go home to have drinks and spend the night. None of us mentioned sex, but we all knew it was going to happen.

The first sign of trouble was when, after a couple of drinks, Ginger seductively invited Joe over to sit by her. They started making out as Joe undressed her while doing her orally. That kind of got off on me although it actually turned me on to watch "the master" do his magic from a totally different perspective.

We all moved into the bedroom, and her husband joined in. I was sitting there observing in a sick, voyeur-like way when he came over and grabbed me, pulled my little dress off, pushed me down on the bed, opened my legs and screwed me against my will. Thank God, he was all bravado and no machismo. He didn't last a minute.

Joe watched this, yet he wouldn't stop him. By then Joe was screwing Ginger, and I watched his pelvis move in that wonderful figure eight, slow and sexy. I changed positions so I could see his eyes, and I noticed as he pulled out for one of the thrusts that he wasn't wearing a condom. He'd broken another vow and betrayed me again. His first time out with a woman, a time when he should have been overly sensitive not to upset me, he messed up big time by doing everything he'd promised he wouldn't do.

I grabbed a condom and tapped him on his shoulder in the heat of the moment, right before he climaxed, causing him to lose his erection. He never got it up again, even when she worked on him orally. He tried reaching over to have sex with me so he could have his orgasm, but I pulled away and turned my back to him. That killed things for everybody. We got up, dressed, and drove home.

Thinking back on that night now, I realized I am healing to a degree, because I heard myself chuckle aloud as the picture of them all entered my head. I wish I'd picked up his clothes and our suitcase and just left his naked ass there while I drove back to Senora. Let 'em fuck like rabbits, I didn't give a shit.

Once we were in the car and on the way home, I started in on him.

"How could you do that to me? How could you allow Daryl to push me down, have sex with me against my will, and then totally ignore our rule about safe sex and sacred semen? You don't care about me! When you say I love you, they're just empty words to manipulate me into getting your way. How could you betray me this time?"

"Stop it," he said. "You're overreacting. I didn't like what Daryl did, but, to be honest, I was enjoying myself too much to stop, and that's what happened with the condom. I couldn't stop. It had nothing to do with my feelings for you."

"No, you're wrong there. You would never have gotten to a point where you couldn't stop if you had been at all conscientious of my need to be secure during—"

"Shut up! Don't start fussing at me!"

"—during all of this!" I said, refusing to let him cut me off. "You've ruined swinging. I never want to do it again! You can't control yourself because you're a sex addict, and this proves it. You've got to get some help, because this marriage will never withstand sexual addiction."

"For God's sake, woman. I'm just a man and not a sex addict! I'm tired of you accusing me of being one. Ninety-nine percent of the men in the world would have done what I did under the same circumstances."

"No, you're wrong. Most men would have cherished the gift of sex with another woman and would never have done anything to blow such a good deal. They'd think with their head and not their dick when it came to a supply of new pussy."

"Damn, I wish you'd shut the fuck up!"

Joe was screaming at me by this time, which got my attention. We drove home the rest of the way in total silence.

Things only got worse after that because of his sexual frustration at not getting to show Ginger what a stud he was. He started a new tactic on me. He tried to get me to start having sex with other men one-on-one so that he could have sex outside the marriage again. He suggested our friend up in Birmingham that we'd visited for a threesome, figuring I'd go for seeing Sam alone.

"You know how I feel about that," I told him. "I'd never have one-on-one sex. That has too much potential to lead to something it shouldn't. I learned from William and my open marriage when you and I became lovers that it can stop being purely sexual and become emotional, and that leads to the end of a marriage. I'm not willing to risk that. Besides, I have no desire to have sex outside this marriage. I love you, Joe, and I'm not interested in that kind of sexual activity. Please don't ask me to do that again."

The sound of the refrigerator cutting on brought me out of my reverie. As I sat there waiting to kill Joe, I kept thinking about the swinging incident and got madder and madder at the way Joe had manipulated me all the time. Although mad, I was beginning to feel the Ambien.

He'd repeatedly insisted he wanted me to go out and have sex with someone without him present. I finally figured out that it was because if I did that, he could go out with Ginger. He openly lusted for a return visit where he could have sex with her and not have me around. It was a manipulation guaranteeing he could have new women with my blessings—sexual addiction heaven. I knew then that he had a serious problem and needed help. In my soul, I also knew he was going to cheat on me again, but I couldn't quite grasp this with my conscious mind. Dee Dee knew. Lee was in denial as usual.

Finally, I realized that Joe had stopped making love to me and had only been screwing me. No man who made love to his wife could have done the things Joe did. At least I wasn't in denial of that fact. I understood that Joe used me for his pleasure, but I meant nothing to him.

I remembered the night I confronted him about it.

"There will be no more sex until you can make love to me," I said. "I don't care to be used as your sex object. You have a problem, and I'm sick of our marriage."

I emptied my coffee cup and went into the kitchen to get another cup for both of us. Joe sat in the recliner by the window, and when I took his coffee to him, he looked me square in my eyes with an expression that could have killed me.

"You know what?" he said with a sarcastic grin. "I've been screwing you for the past fifteen years. Sex is fun and has nothing to do with love. I know how to make it feel like making love, but I have always viewed sex as separate from my emotions. That's why I can have sex with other women, and it shouldn't threaten your emotions, because mine aren't involved."

Remembering those words silenced my breath and stilled my heart for at least a beat. I wanted to stop the memory of it. Since I knew it was the very thing I needed in order to go through with my plan, it forced my mind back to that conversation.

"Let me remind you," I said, "that you had sex with me and fell in love with me, then you did the same thing with Jane. Sex can become an emotional thing for you, can't it? Besides, we did make love and you know it. Fifteen years ago, yup, that's when I caught you almost cheating on me and your feelings for me changed. I simply became your dumpy wife."

I was trying not to cry as I realized what I was saying to him. I flashed on what he'd told me, and anger cleared up the mist.

"Yes, Joe, I agree that you haven't made love to me in a long time. I realize that men who are good in bed can certainly fool a woman. You're the best and have it down to an art, but I can't live this way. You have to get some help."

I glared at him with a growing hatred. My throat tickled to the point of feeling as if I were choking. I grabbed it, trying to stop that irritating sensation. I was so upset that the usual tactic didn't work. I started coughing almost in a spasm.

Joe's eyes softened as he put down his coffee cup and got out of the recliner. He walked over to me, gently taking my hand into his and moving his eyes back and forth across my face, as if drinking in the fullness of me— something he hadn't done in a long time.

"You know you are the sexiest, most beautiful woman I have ever known, and no woman will ever take your place. And I lied. I do love you, and I do make love to you. And I want to take you back there right now and make passionate love to you."

"Which is it, Joe? Which one is the lie and which is the truth?"

"I lied when I said I didn't make love to you. I was angry and wanted to hurt you. You know I love you more than life itself. I don't know why I can't be honest with you." His voice was a soft whisper filled with shame.

Of course, this is what I craved hearing, and I let him schmooze me right back to our bedroom for some fantastic sex. I thought we'd solved our problems, because Joe had finally set up his first appointment. Maybe things were going to work out after all. I warned Joe that if he mentioned us having an open marriage again there would be a consequence. Like a fool, I walked right into the trap he had set because he knew me so well.

"I know you had a spark for Sam," he told me one day. "He really turned you on. And I know you and Bruce have the hots for each other. He wants to have sex with you and not have me around. Honey, let's go and do what you know you want to do."

Suddenly, the AC and the refrigerator both cut off, and the silence in the house wrapped me in its arms. The house was my casket rather than Joe's, at least for a second or two.

The Ambien was making me a little too sleepy. I had to keep thinking about the things that would stimulate my adrenalin and stoke me up so I could stay awake.

Oh, Joe appeared to be such a selfless giving man, didn't he? He knew that was going to wig me out, cause me to leave, and he was right. That was the day I started looking for a room to lease. I wanted to write my book. Mainly, I needed to get away from Joe. I ended up taking a room in Mobile and moved out in December of 2002.

We celebrated Christmas at Jolly's apartment that year. Joe and I were civil but not a loving couple. For New Year's Eve, Jolly and I drove home to celebrate it with Joe. There was a chill in the air over the holidays, and it had nothing to do with either the weather or our ghost.

Once we got to Senora, Jolly caught up with her best friend, and I went alone to Jessica and Edward's annual New Year's Eve party. Joe had to work three to eleven. Jolly and I needed to leave right after New Year's Day because we both started classes on the third, and I would start my new writer's group on the fourth.

We left on the second and returned to Mobile on an overcast, cold day. Joe loaded up the Jeep Wrangler with his photography gear and told me he was driving over to Georgia to one of the national forests to take photos. I denied the uneasy feeling trying to take hold of me. After the betrayal with Ginger in front of me then manipulating me so I'd leave, I couldn't forgive him. I knew I still harbored a good bit of anger toward him at that time, but mostly I couldn't trust him. However, I didn't think he would try cheating on me again that soon. Our recent courtship filled with tenderness was still too fresh in my mind.

By the time Jolly and I had driven home, we'd run into some bad weather. As a courtesy to Joe, I called him on his cell phone to see how he was doing and to let him know we'd made it back to Mobile safely. His phone rang and rang and rang. He didn't answer. This was around four in the evening, so I wasn't all that occupied with any foreboding yet. I figured he was out capturing the beauty of winter's gloom with his camera. When I tried an hour later after it was dark and he still didn't answer, I became concerned.

I called the house to see if maybe he was home and the cell phone's battery had run down or something, because now the voice mail was picking up on the first ring. Either the battery was dead or he had turned off his phone. I tried until eight o'clock but generated no answers on either the house phone or his cell—only the answering machine and voice mail. I thought maybe Joe was looking at the caller ID and screening my calls. I decided to enlist Jolly's help.

"Jolly, I'm worried sick. I've been calling your dad now for four hours and he's not responding. He should be home from Georgia by now. Can you try calling him in case he's choosing to ignore my calls?"

"Sure. Now, don't start worrying and make yourself sick. Please, Mom."

"I can't help it. That's part of my illness. I envision the worst case scenario and go from there."

"There's nothing we can do even if something has happened, so there's no use in worrying about things." It was eerie, almost as if she were Joe's shadow—how many times had I heard him say those words to me?

We both tried for another two and a half hours. By then I was calling the Georgia and Alabama Highway Patrol to see if there had been any wrecks involving a Jeep Wrangler.

Jolly called me back and said, "Now I'm worried. I've left messages on his voice mail. This late, he should be home. Did you call the Highway Patrol?"

"Yes, no accident occurred in the area he was headed to today."

"If we don't hear from him within the next hour, come pick me up and let's go look for him."

"I'm ready to go now," I said. "I'll trust your judgment and give him one more hour."

I sat in my room watching the hands on the clock. I tried reading, writing, even cleaning up, but I had an intuition that something terrible had happened that January day in 2003. I'd already picked up my keys, ready to head out the door to pick up Jolly, when the phone rang.

"Lee, I'm okay," Joe said. "I was driving back from Georgia and got sick to my stomach and pulled off the road. I threw up over and over again."

"Why didn't you call us and let us know? Joe, I'd have come to get you and you know it."

"I figured with the three hour drive to Mobile plus the two hours to reach me here in Georgia, I'd probably be either better or dead by the time you got here. I'm sorry. I didn't mean to worry you. Besides, I didn't think you'd care one way or another if something did happen to me."

"Don't be silly, Joe. I do love you. I'm confused right now and need some time like you did back in 1998. I moved to Mobile because I do care and want our marriage to survive. Being around each other and fighting all the time was not helping either of us."

My heart raced as I thought about how angry he'd made me and how scared I'd been.

"Thank God you're okay now," I told him. "I can finally go to bed and get some sleep. I'm so up that I know it will take two sleeping pills to get me to sleep. I'm sick with nerves and fear."

"Diddleleedee," he said, using his old pet name for me, "I didn't mean to scare you or worry you. I'm really sorry. It won't happen again."

The endearment warmed my heart and calmed me down.

"Do you forgive me?" he said. "You know I love you and would never do anything to worry you or hurt you in any way."

"Yes, Diddledumps," I replied. "I realize that. I love you too. Do you need me to come home and take care of you? I'm wired and can easily drive home tonight."

"Naw, I'm fine now. I threw everything up and I'm okay now except for being a little weak. Get a good night's rest. I'm heading toward the bed to get prone right now myself."

God, worry had sure turned off my bullshitometer that night. I was so much more than merely a fool. I'm sure some of my suicide attempts were from me turning the anger inward at my own stupidity.

I needed my comfort food—another glass of tea—so I got up and walked into the kitchen. I could barely read the dial on my watch. I guessed that it said eleven fifteen. I noticed my American Express bill on the top of the day's mail sitting on the kitchen counter and opened it.

"Shit on him!" I yelled in frustration, my anger renewed at the memory of what he'd done to drive me to my current insanity.

Chapter Twenty-Seven

What finally triggered my homicidal bent were two key things that Joe had done. The first one was finding out that all the time I was in Mobile, he'd quit paying any bills that were in my name and ruined my credit—again. I had platinum credit before that. He had also gotten a secret American Express card and run up huge bills in wining and dining his women in the fanciest places. He even put an ad on Match.com and Yahoo personals, presenting himself as divorced although he was still married to me. He thought he was Mr. Big Shot, worldly and sophisticated thanks to my inheritance money. He cut corners at my expense since he had to pay off his American Express bill each month. That set into motion the final, deadly chain of events.

In mid-January of 2003, I took Joe's computer back to Mobile with me because I knew he was e-mailing at least one woman named Carolyn. When I got the computer home, I discovered he had locked me out because of his Windows password. I knew Jolly could hack into the system. I invited her over to help set me up and clean up anything that might upset me.

The gods must have been smiling down on me then, because Jolly called her dad in total innocence to get the password from him, and he freely gave us four choices that I wrote down. Actually, she was on the computer typing them in, so he gave them to me. What a lucky break. Later, this would save my neck from a lawsuit, because Jolly and her boyfriend Johnny were both witnesses that Joe had given me his passwords.

At some point, Joe had cleaned our mutual Netscape box—or so he thought. He'd given me the password to it in order for me to check up on him. I guess he thought it would prove he was being a good boy. By the end of January, there was an e-mail message hiding among all the hundreds in his old Netscape Inbox, and I opened it up. It was a welcome message for his new e-mail account, so I knew he did have a secret box after all. It was a new Yahoo account.

I tried the passwords he had given us for the computer and bingo, I was in. He actually had three other e-mail accounts he'd registered through this new one. I also saw a message to him from Daryl, thanking Joe for the great sex between the three of them that January 2. My blood pressure shot up when I read that date. That was the night he said he'd been sick.

I monitored that box and soon discovered that three other women thought Joe was in love with them. He'd promised some poor Native American woman that they would build a shack together, and he would watch her make dream catchers while he "set on the front porch." Joe never did use the correct word. Poor Yvonne was one of the women he schmoozed the most, stringing her along as Mr. Faithful. My luck held out, and I was able to access the other three e-mail accounts with those passwords. To my surprise, he was courting and schmoozing about twenty women. He'd literally gone fucking crazy. I kept a watch on his e-mail for around two months, until he caught me. Boy was he pissed.

However, little did he know that the most damning of the e-mail messages already sat in my lawyer's folder for our legal separation. I laid low for a couple of months, then I went back in to his e-mail Inbox. It was damn easy, even though he was afraid I'd get in again and was constantly changing his password. I knew that, and I used it to my advantage.

I'd go into his mailbox, change his password, and read his mail. That's how I found him telling one of his women the exact same love expressions he'd said to me back in 1982. They had been a damn line and nothing more. He had at least two women on the string to whom he professed his undying, faithful love. Ha! What a damn load of crap.

I finally got tired of hearing his bullshit and quit reading his e-mail. I figured I'd lucked out that he hadn't caught me again. Unfortunately, I confessed to him that I'd been reading his e-mail during one of my Ambien fogs. He threatened to divorce me and cut off my medical insurance if I ever did it again. That scared me and I learned my lesson—don't piss him off enough to prompt a divorce.

The second thing he did I found out one night when I received a phone call from our mutual friend Sandy, who'd been his first girlfriend and whose cherry he had taken. After she heard we had split up, she called and told me something that made me first decide I was going to kill his sorry, cheating ass one day. He had tried to get her to go out with him in 1999, right after we had renewed our wedding vows.

Two days ago, on May 3 of 2003, I had decided to confront the bastard.

By then, Joe was living in an apartment over in Opelika. I drove over to his place, found the door unlocked and went storming in. He was sitting in his recliner talking on the phone to one of his girlfriends. I screamed at the top of my voice so she'd know what he was really like. I'm sure he'd convinced her I was a wicked witch, and he was some poor, misunderstood, unloved, unappreciated victim.

"You cheating son of a bitch! I know you called Sandy six times from work and asked her to come to the house when I was out of town back in

1999, right after we renewed our wedding vows!"

He tried to cover the phone so his woman, Yvonne, wouldn't hear what I'd said, but I grabbed the phone out of his hand. I'm damn strong when I'm mad.

He jerked it back and slammed it down. "Get out of my house, you crazy bitch! I'm going to call the police."

"No you aren't. You're going to talk to me. You owe me an explanation."

"I don't owe you anything," he said with a sneer in his voice.

"Yes, you do. While we were married and really getting along, and I thought the marriage was rebuilding, I found out you were trying to get one of my friends to go out with you! You sure as hell do owe me an explanation."

Joe looked as if he were going to get up and start wringing my neck. I knew I was pushing things, because he truly had no feelings left for me by then. When he gets angry, he hits, chokes, and smashes things. I'd be easy to hurt in an instant. I was at my breaking point too and fed up with his crap. I was mad enough to chew crowbars and spit out bobby pins.

Of course, Joe denied that he had called Sandy. He kept telling me to leave, and I kept refusing to leave. The phone rang again and he went to answer it. Before he could say anything to his honey, I went and unplugged the phone. That made him so mad that he grabbed me.

I felt him pushing me backward, even though I was trying to dig in my heels and not lose my balance. His hands held my arms, and my own hands went numb where he had the circulation cut off, but I glared at him rather than surrendering. He pushed me all the way through the living room to his front door, hurting my back and hip as they crashed against the doorknob. I broke free and grabbed him, and with adrenalin pumping madly in my incomprehensible brain, I pushed him backward all the way into the hall.

He went and picked up his cordless phone to dial a number. "Yes, this is Joe Thames. I want to report a disturbance in my—"

Before he could finish the sentence, I walked up right next to him and purred, "Oh, baby, that was good. You're the best."

He held his hand over the phone and glared at me. "This is the police I'm talking to."

"Oh, honey," I said, "are you playing a joke on me? Are you inviting the police to join us? What fun!"

Naturally, that didn't sound like a couple involved in domestic violence, and Joe knew they wouldn't pay any attention to his call.

"If you don't leave in one minute," he said, "I'm getting a lawyer tomorrow, and I'm going to divorce you."

That threat jarred me. Along with all his other promises, he'd sworn that he'd never divorce me and make me lose my insurance. If that happened, he knew I'd end up homeless and in the streets with all the other mentally ill people who couldn't afford their medication or treatment by doctors.

When I looked into Joe's cold, heartless eyes, I knew he meant it and wouldn't flinch at leaving me destitute by his actions. Suddenly, I turned and went to the refrigerator to pour myself a glass of milk. Now, that's a sane thing to do at a time like that, isn't it? He told me the seconds were counting down. I asked him if I could finish my milk. I took my time and studied his face. Who was that man? He couldn't be the man who'd promised to love, honor, and cherish me for the rest of my life.

I finished my milk and left, sure that Joe hated me because he couldn't escape my torments—my constant reminders of things he had done to me even though we were legally separated and living two cities away from each other.

Just before I left, I glared into his eyes and said, "I hope you can live with yourself when you have my death on your hands!"

I meant it too. I wanted to die. I didn't want my life to go on—horrible, lonely, and now even my good name and credit were ruined. I was hurt enough to want to die, because living was too hard. I convinced myself it was the best thing for everybody. Jolly could collect my life insurance and never have to fool with me again. That was my depression lying to me. Anger convinced me to kill myself to hurt Joe, depression lied to me that he cared and that it wouldn't hurt Jolly. Both ways, I was doomed, but I decided that night would be the night.

When I got home from Joe's, I took a handful of three different kinds of pills, then I locked and dead-bolted all the doors. I didn't want anyone to save me this go round. God, I hated doing this to my baby, Jolly. She'd never understand. Life was too damn painful to keep on trying. Each time I thought I was getting better or over Joe's messes, he always sent me more to deal with. He thought he was leaving me alone. No, his legacy of lies and things he tormented me with popped up day by day, grabbing me and slinging me down over and over again until, finally, I was too beat down to fight it anymore.

As I thought about Jolly, I decided I had to hear her sweet voice one more time. I wanted to tell her that I loved her. As if there were some gods watching over me or Jolly and we had mental telepathy, the phone rang. Apparently, the medicine had already started working on me, because I had trouble answering the phone. Jolly realized I had taken something, so while she had me on the phone, she used her cell phone to call Tom Vault, our local cop. She kept his number on speed-dial. I must have been out of it, because I never realized she had called him.

"Mommy, are you all right?"

I never realized that she was on to me. Jolly was wise and mature for her tender age of eighteen. The honest-to-God truth was she'd adjusted to and understood my mental condition much better than Joe ever had. Maybe it was because she had grown up with it and experienced it as part of my personality, or maybe it was her talent in the field of psychology. She had graduated from a difficult high school with a cum laude in psychology and won a gold medal for excellence. No matter what the reason, she instinctively knew I needed help and was in grave danger that night. I couldn't fool her one bit.

According to Tom, he knocked on the front door and windows while calling my name, but I'd passed out in my chair. Jolly gave him permission to kick down my outside door and break the glass on my pantry door to get to me.

The next morning was when I woke up in ICU with a tube in my nose— a painful first for me. They'd wanted to send me to the mental hospital then, but I convinced them to let me go see my regular shrink, Dr. Hopkins. I had an appointment with him set up the next day on May fifth.

The ICU team stabilized me enough to go home. Tom picked me up. Washed out and numb from the overdose the night before, I slept most of the next day. I remembered little about that day, other than Jolly calling and checking on me a couple of times.

As that day dragged on, I became more and more depressed again. I felt cheated out of life, love, happiness, and now my credit standing. I worked myself up all over again. When Jolly called for the third time, I cried for an hour and a half. She tried being strong and compassionate, and she even used the tough love approach.

"Mommy, Daddy doesn't care about you anymore, so get over it. You don't want him anyway. He's an asshole."

"But, Jolly, you don't understand. It doesn't matter that he's an asshole— I still love him. I don't want to take him back, at least I understand that much. I grieve over him and miss him and his love. I want and need someone to hold me and tell me he loves me and cares for me right now. I want to mean something to someone."

"You mean something to me."

"Oh, Angel, I know that, and I'm so grateful for your love. I feel so blessed to have you as my child. You know that a mother-daughter love isn't a man-woman love. You know that. You have Johnny, and it's not the same thing as the emotions you have for me. All I've ever wanted out of life was to be a mother and a wife—to love and be loved. Both of my parents emotionally abandoned me as a child, and Joe's love meant everything to me because it healed me. I'm so damn lonely."

Jolly kept on with examples, reasons, pep talks and even exasperated threats as she tried to get me to stop crying. By the time I hung up the phone, the corners of my eyes burned from the salty tears.

Fortunately, I had the appointment the next day with my psychiatrist, because not only was I suicidal, I was starting to get homicidal as well.

Chapter Twenty-Eight

That appointment with Dr. Hopkins had been the one earlier that same day when I'd told him about how I wanted to kill Joe. After I told him that, he'd been required by law to send me to the mental hospital again, however I had escaped before they could commit me.

I felt good that I had circumvented the nurses from locking me up, but I knew I needed to let Jolly know what I'd done. That's why I'd called her cell phone and told her I was supposed to have been hospitalized but had fled. I told her that being up there all alone and locked up would have done my mental health more harm than good. I said I wanted to be back with my dogs, cats, china, crystal, books, computer to write, as well as my studio to draw and paint.

So that's how I'd gotten to where I was now, waiting for the time to arrive when I would kill Joe. I had thought eleven o'clock would never get there, but it was finally time to take action if I could just get Joe to answer the damn phone!

I tried calling him again using the portable phone in the living room. This time, there was no answer instead of a busy signal. Maybe he hadn't been on the 'Net earlier after all. Maybe he wasn't even home yet and one of his "honeys" had been calling him at the same time I'd been calling.

Damn, it was nearly eleven thirty. Where the hell was he? He must have stopped at the post office to check his mail, or maybe he'd stopped to get gas. I was woozy by this time, so I turned on the TV and happened onto a channel with a hot love scene going on. Of course, that reminded me of the passion Joe and I'd had when we made love, and I knew I needed to do something to get my mind off those kinds of memories.

I waited a few minutes, and memories flooded in when I thought of Joe doing those ordinary things I'd taken for granted. I thought of our kissing and sleeping together, and that led me back to thinking about making love. I'd never dreamed we'd end that part of our relationship—sex between us had always been so good.

Thinking about our sex life jumpstarted my memories of Joe in a pleasant way—why I loved him. He was there for me during some of my roughest moments. For instance, when we had made "Mark Moons" a symbol of our faithfulness and the strength Joe provided for me during difficult times. I'll never forget that day—May 12, 1995—as long as I live. Everything about it is imprinted on my soul.

I still remember the cloudless May sky with a hint of summer in the air. How could such a beautiful day end up such a tragedy? After all, it had been a Friday, so the weekend was finally there. I pulled into the driveway after dropping off ten-year-old Jolly at Jessica's house. What struck me as odd and out of sync with the rest of the day was the rooster perched on the back of the swing, crowing at four o'clock in the afternoon. Since darkness didn't descend until nearly seven thirty, the rooster's crowing produced an eerie feeling in me. Also, I'd never seen him do either of the things he was doing— roosting on the swing in our cats' range, or crowing so early in the day.

A chill shook me as I thought about him trumpeting his song like "Taps" on a bugle. I entered the house with Mother Nature's call tugging on me, then the phone rang. I almost ignored it, but something about seeing that rooster made me pick it up. It was Margaret.

"Lee, I have something to tell you."

"Can I call you back? I'm about to wet my britches. I've had to pee ever since I left LaGrange."

"Go ahead, I'll wait on you."

I knew something sinister had happened. My sister had never not let me call her right back. When I returned filled with dread, I wasn't prepared for what she said.

"Are you sitting down?"

"No, why?" I asked. "What's wrong?"

"Sit down, Lee. I've got some really bad news."

"Did Mama die during her surgery?"

My daddy had called the previous Thursday afternoon to tell me about Mama's surgery. I thought he'd sounded unconcerned about it. Adhesions had plugged her up for a second time. Dr. Henry planned to heal her by cutting out the section that had closed up in her intestines. The adhesions were from old scar tissue left over from an earlier surgery.

"Don't worry about missing work tomorrow," Daddy had said. "Laura's as swollen as a basketball, but the doctor said she'd be fine and there's no need for either of you girls to be there for the surgery. He considers the surgery routine. Just come on over this weekend to see her. She'll be in room 236. I just got back from the hospital, and she's looking good. They plan on doing the surgery first thing in the morning."

"Daddy, are you sure?" I said. "Don't you want one of us to be there with you while you wait?" As I talked to him, I ran my hand up and down the phone cord, sometimes twisting it in my fingers. The dark paneling in the room had seemed to swallow me like a cave that evening.

"No, this isn't emergency surgery," he said. "Back in 1965, we rushed her to the hospital while on vacation at the beach, but this time they found it early. I'll be fine. For once in her life, I guess she wishes she could shoot a firecracker. She'd feel a whole lot better. She's in pain. They've given her something to knock her out. She's sleeping right now."

"Well, okay," I said. "I'll see you on Friday afternoon after I drop Jolly off with a neighbor and feed all the animals. Joe will be working the evening shift, so I'll drive over and check on both of you. Daddy, thanks for calling."

Little did I know how important that conversation had been. After Margaret told me what she'd called to tell me, I wished I had gone over that Thursday evening when he'd called me. At least I would have gotten to tell him goodbye.

"Lee, Daddy's dead."

"Oh, my God! No, not my Daddy! I can't believe it!" I started squealing.

"Daddy never showed up at the hospital for Mama's surgery," Margaret interjected. "Daddy's never missed Mama's surgeries, so they knew something was up. They called me to ask where he was, and since Harry was visiting his other grandmother KayKay, I told him to go check on things at the house. I told him where they hid the house key. He walked in and found that Daddy had died peacefully in his sleep last night."

"What an awful thing for Harry to discover," I said.

"Joe's on his way home from work early. I called the mill first and told him so he'd be there with you as soon as possible. Lee, that isn't all of the bad news."

"Don't tell me Mama died too."

"No, but when they opened her up, they found that ovarian cancer traversed her abdomen and was everywhere. Dr. Henry told me that Mama's writ for survival is about up. He feels that she can't know about Daddy, because the shock of it might kill her. Adam and I are leaving in a few minutes from Meridian, and we'll meet you at the house. You go on over there, because Mama is asking about Daddy. You have to tell her that he's sick and the hospital won't let him come see her right after surgery. If she asks about calling him, tell her he's sleeping because he's been throwing up and he's taken one of those anti-nausea drugs that knocked him out. Stall her for tonight anyway. Poor Harry had to call the funeral home to come and get Daddy."

No sooner had she said that than I heard the studio door open, and in walked Joe.

"I have to go," I said. "Joe's home now. God, what are we going to do?"

I hung up the phone and heard Joe's footsteps approaching. The next thing I knew, I felt him holding me and running his big, rough mill hands tenderly over my hair.

"Baby, I'm so sorry about your Dad," he said. "I really did love Mark. I'm going to miss him."

I turned around and kissed my husband. "Joe, I love you so much. Please don't ever do anything that will take you away from me."

"You have my promise, Lee. Nothing will ever take me away from you. I love you more than life itself. Now let's head on over to see about your mama."

My sister had to drive all the way across the state of Alabama, but I lived only about thirty minutes away from Mama. Joe and I packed a suitcase, asked our neighbor to keep Jolly for us, then we fed all our critters—dogs, cats, horses, chickens and a pig. I believed in God, but I wasn't necessarily religious. In fact, we didn't go to church on a regular basis. To be honest, my faith was lukewarm at best.

On the way to Opelika, the strangest thing happened. By the time we got everything taken care of, the evening had turned to dusk, and a huge, full, peach-colored moon had appeared on the horizon. I cried as I looked at it and exclaimed to Joe, "That's my daddy looking down on me."

Instead of the seventy-six-year-old gaunt man who'd recently passed away, I was remembering the moonfaced dad of my youth. At that moment, a peace that passes understanding descended upon me. The oddest part of it was that my sister—coming from the opposite direction—also looked up at the rising full moon and had said the exact same thing to her husband. She, too, had felt calm and at peace. I knew that God was letting us know that Daddy was safe in Heaven with Him. To this day, whenever I see a full moon, I call it a Mark Moon after my dad.

Joe and I made a pact that night that whenever we saw a Mark Moon, we'd always stare up into the sky and remember my dad, each other, and our love. That was what love and marriage were all about—the difficult times when your mate carries you and when you know they are there for you.

I had felt extra close to Joe that night, and thinking about it brought tears to my eyes instead of anger to my heart.

Seven weeks later, my mom died from chemotherapy complications. No one had even had the heart to tell her how useless undergoing chemo would be. None of us told her anything more than that she had ovarian cancer, not the degree to which the small tumors had already invaded her body. Having been an alcoholic and a pill abuser, her liver couldn't detox her body during the chemo.

In the meantime, since my mother's diagnosis with ovarian cancer, the doctor had also checked me. They found a couple of small tumors on the one ovary I had left after the hysterectomy I'd had in 1986. Since I taught school, we scheduled my surgery for July so I'd have time to recuperate before starting my second grade classes for the next school term.

No one expected Mama to die that soon after Daddy. It turned out that I had my surgery on the evening of the same day we put my Mama in the ground. No dinner after the funeral. No visitors or relatives. Joe whisked me off to LaGrange, Georgia for my surgery. My hospital pre-admit bracelet adorned the arm I used when I reached out and took a yellow rose from Mama's casket.

The mill sent me a yellow rose bush to plant in memory of both my parents. Mark Moons and yellow roses would always symbolize the sadness I felt in never saying goodbye to Daddy and not having time to make my peace with Mama. I dug up that old rose bush and lugged it around whenever I moved. It was as if I thought that letting the rosebush die would kill the memory of my parents and the remaining love I felt for Joe.

I'll say this much for Mark and Laura Snowden—they had brought me up to be tolerant and non-judgmental. Daddy had hired a black man to be a DJ at our radio station when it was unheard of in the South, and we'd received bomb threats to both our house and the station. I was also one of the few whites who'd welcomed the black students to our newly integrated school. When I was in college, I spent the night with two black girls to help them with biology, and we'd had to dodge rocks going into the cafeteria. My parents had stood up against the Jim Crowe South and taught me to do so as well. They'd had their flaws, but they had taught me integrity. That part of me would miss my parents and mourn their deaths.

After Mama's death that August, my sister and I cleaned out my parents' house right before school started. While cleaning out the attic, I found an old diary. I wasn't supposed to do any lifting and needed to sit down after working myself like a pack mule. I really couldn't keep up with my sister that soon after my surgery, but I tried because I didn't want the bulk of the job falling on her shoulders.

I took a break, poured myself some tea and opened up the book. The death of my parents had activated my bipolar gene. A doctor from Georgia had diagnosed me in 1996 when I'd stayed depressed. That doctor had prescribed Paxil, and it had thrown me into a hypo-manic state in 1997. Stressful situations made me crazy, literally.

Most of my life, I'd fancied myself a writer. I thought about when I'd moved to Mobile to write the next best blockbuster novel—in only six months. Mainly, I used the time for Joe and me to have a respite from all of our fussing and fighting. I'll never forget my surprise the time in 2003 when I came home unannounced.

Chapter Twenty-Nine

I tried calling Joe again, and the line was busy for the second time. This time, I knew he had to be home. I figured I'd e-mail him and get him to call me, so I walked back into the den where I kept my computer. On the bookshelf above the monitor was the cheap carnival horse I'd bought as a child. It was raw-boned with a jug head and as ugly as pigeon poo. Always the one to feel sorry for any underdog, I'd felt no one else would buy it, so I did.

I'd kept it through college, two marriages, and eight moves. I pondered why I'd let so many of my beautiful childhood horses go but had kept this one. I'd owned Lady Snowfire, a plastic gray Arabian mare, and DC-un, brought back to me when I was four when my parents went to Washington DC. He had been buckskin covered in beige hair with a black leather saddle and bridle. I'd kept him for years, even when all his hair had worn off and I'd galloped three of his hooves off him, leaving his legs as nubs. Finally, while in college, I'd given my best ones away and had finally trashed poor one-footed DC-un. Yet the ugly one I'd carefully packed and carried with me for over forty years.

I sat down at the computer and typed: Joe, call me. EMERGENCY!

I put nothing in the body of the e-mail. He'd call if for no other reason than curiosity and worry about Jolly. Typing on the keyboard reminded me how this computer that had been Joe's and had come into my possession when I came home on January 14, 2003 to surprise him.

How could something that was supposed to have been wonderful have turned into something so horrible? When I'd sat down at his computer that day, my hands had been shaking because I knew I needed to go into his e-mail to find the truth, but I also knew it would probably end us as a married couple.

Until then, Joe had been my life. We'd survived a hard five years and were struggling to put a broken marriage back together again. We'd promised our daughter we would never divorce. She saw us working hard to right a tilting ship, a matrimonial Titanic.

Two days before, I'd sat alone in the austere room I had rented in Mobile during our separation. A photo of an iris that Joe had taken hung above my bed, and my Tiffany lamp of cobalt blue Dutch Irises with scarlet stripes illuminated the room. Irises—the symbol of our committed, never-ending love for each other—were everywhere. On my bedside table sat a clay iris that Jolly had made for me when she was fifteen.

The room also smelled of stale coffee and cigarette smoke—a habit I'd recently acquired to minimize the stress of my marital strife. My landlord didn't allow smoking indoors, but that morning had been unusually tense, so I'd turned on the bathroom fan, hoping to hide the odor. Lucky for me, the landlord rarely came up the stairs.

I got up and lit my one pumpkin spice candle to mask the taboo scents— another no-no per my landlord because it was a fire hazard. My bed was unmade and filled with manuscript pages, because I routinely typed out one draft then another before I hand-edited them. I'd thought I was going to be the next author on the New York Times bestseller list when in fact I was ridiculous.

I sat at my computer to play a CD of "Eye in the Sky." My own saline burned my eyes as the music transformed me back to September of 1982, until the ringing of the phone interrupted my thoughts. Straddling the fence between the present and the past, I studied a drawing stashed in my notebook as the song played and I picked up the phone.

"Hey, beautiful," Joe said that January fourteenth, "what are you doing?"

As he talked to me on the phone, I decided to send him the drawing. I scanned and resized it before e-mailing it to him, the drawing beckoning me like the Muslim call to prayer, filling me with intense emotions. Joe's low and steady voice centered me, stopping my chaotic thoughts as I sent him the picture.

There was so much tenderness, love, and passion in the kiss depicted between Joe and me in that drawing, rendered in pen and ink. But as I continued to look at it, a chill ran down my spine as I suddenly realized the last time Joe had kissed anyone with newly awakened desire, it had been Jane and not me.

God, that tore me up. I hated the idea that he'd felt the same steady pull to her mouth as he'd once felt toward mine. Images of their heads slowly moving together in synchronization, their lips ravenous to feel each other's passion, put my heart in an aching vise that squeezed out my sense of security.

There was no way it wouldn't have happened, since they'd both pined for it. She, an answered prayer, had owned his heart. When he'd met her after his online affair, she had been as beautiful to him on the inside as she had been on the outside, and he was totally smitten. The kiss had been a gift of years of loneliness and frustration healed in one sacred moment shared by them.

The same had once been true of us. He'd also experienced the same emotions with Regina when he'd left her for me, when I had been his answered prayer. Strange how history had repeated itself, even though we had vowed never to take each other for granted.

"Why are you crying?" Joe asked, interrupting my thoughts again. "Aren't you happy that I called? What's wrong now?"

I could hear a tiny bit of irritation in his voice, but I was too self-absorbed in my own emotions to focus on it. All I cared about was that Joe had heard my tears before I told him I was crying. He'd heard them with his heart, because I wasn't making a sound. I sat there looking at the drawing with tears dripping off my chin. I don't even sniffle when I cry like that.

"It breaks my heart to look at this drawing and realize that the last time you felt that kind of tenderness, it wasn't with me. God, that still hurts even after four years. How could you forget our passionate kiss that night at the Studio and give it to another woman?"

Joe was silent.

"I really want to know the answer to that question," I said. "Look at the drawing I sent you and think about us that night. Can you do that now? On the other hand, do you only think about kissing Jane when you see that kind of kiss? You know, it's unfair that you've gotten to feel that kind of passion again. You had a nice little break from the ho-hums of long-term marital kisses. You have to think of Jane when you think of passion now. I couldn't compete with that in a million years. How unfair."

Finally, Joe broke his silence. "Why do you always associate memories with the negative instead of the positive?"

"Joe, there would be no negative to associate with the kiss or the drawing if you hadn't cheated on me." There I went throwing it up to him again. I couldn't stop doing that.

While I talked to him on the phone, I continued to pull papers from an old notebook of love poems I'd written to him. There were two more drawings showing us kissing. The original drawings were on pieces of twelve-by-twelve-inch blotter paper. They had yellowed from the twenty-one years since I'd drawn them, and the blue ballpoint pen lines had a greenish cast to them now. Still, they showed a good likeness of both of us when we had been in our thirties. We were nude and embracing, and I held his chin in my hands.

Joe never initiated anything with me anymore. He expected me to be in charge of our sex life, then held it against me when it wasn't what he wanted. He expected me to read his mind. It was never often enough, yet he never made an effort to show me he was interested. The passion between us had dried up years ago, although the cheating had brought us another honeymoon period of a sort. Lately, he'd been paying more attention to me. I thought he was such a good husband for trying hard to make things right between us.

"I'm looking at more drawings I did of us in 1982," I told him. "The depiction of our passionate kisses makes me so sad to realize my wonderful, naïve belief in love is now gone. God, how I believed you when you promised to love only me and to love me forever. I believed you to the point that I overcame my own fear of abandonment, and I entrusted my wounded and scared heart to you—asking you to keep it safe and to cherish the gift of my love. I'm such an idealist, aren't I?"

"Lee, please don't start going back," he said. "You're only going to upset yourself and end up in the hospital again."

Again. Yeah, the first time had been in June of 1998 when I'd tried to drown myself in our pool after I discovered that Joe had sent Jane a dozen red roses and had the nerve to charge them to my American Express card. Then he'd thrown the bill away and hadn't paid it, messing up my credit. When I called American Express because I couldn't find the May bill, they'd mailed me a duplicate.

The bill had shown a charge for flowers from April, the same day Jolly and I had been at the Alabama State Science Fair that Joe couldn't attend with us because he'd claimed he had to work and couldn't get off. They'd been purchased from a flower shop named—get this—Jolly Time Flowers and Gifts in Andalusia. How could he?

I remember the rain had been pouring down hard that day in June. I locked the gate and jumped in the pool with my clothes on and sat on the bottom. Joe climbed the fence around the gazebo. Going into survival mode, I guess, I came up for a breath against my will. Joe could see I was serious and was intent on killing myself.

Right before I jumped in the pool, I'd tried to take a handful of Depakote, an anti-seizure medication that had a warning about over-medicating. Joe had slapped them out of my hand as I was directing them toward my mouth. I screamed—an animal, guttural, from-my-soul piercing scream—then I ran to the pool. I didn't remember coming to the surface. The next conscious thought I had was realizing I was in a hospital. Joe was talking to nurses and a doctor, and I was freezing.

Placed at first in a room with a video camera pointed toward my bed for the suicide watch, I had felt nothing. The staff monitored me the entire time I was in my room. Since I wouldn't get out of my bed for nearly two days, the camera stayed focused on me. At the time, I couldn't have cared less about my lack of privacy. Eventually, the medicine kicked in, and I improved. I got out of bed, warmed up and finally started eating and socializing. The nurses brought our food to us rather than letting us go to the cafeteria in another building, because all of us were on suicide watch.

The first day I came out of my room to eat, the strangest thing happened. Sitting to my left was a woman, probably in her fifties, who always carried a baby doll around with her. Trying to be friendly, I reached over to touch her as I tend to do when I talk. As soon as my hand made contact with her, she made some kind of excited, throaty sounds that weren't anywhere close to words and started this repetitious rocking. With terror in her eyes, she pulled back from me.

She scared me to death. Now, that was an indisputable crazy person. Of course, the personnel came running out to see what had happened, because it sounded as if I had attacked her. They finally got her calmed down, and she went back to her room.

I surveyed the people around me, feeling rather smug that I wasn't as crazy as they were. To my right was a disheveled man who looked as though he hadn't had a bath or combed his hair in about a week. To his right was a young girl who looked to be in her early twenties. There was also one middle-aged, nicely kept lady.

One thing about depression—we avoided mirrors, so it never dawned on me that I looked just as ratty and dirty as the man did. With unwashed and uncombed hair and the same clothes I had worn into the hospital, who was I to judge him? I had become energized enough to get out of bed and eat but not enough to think of the daunting task of putting on a new outfit or cleaning up some. This was totally out of character for me, since I normally took two baths a day at times and washed my hair daily. When I don't wash my hair, you can bet it's because I'm depressed to some degree.

"Hello, my name is Lee," I said to the man. "What's yours?"

"Randal."

Mighty talkative, wasn't he?

"My name is Fran," said the girl to Randal's right, her voice sounding a tad too excited for her to be on suicide watch. "What ya in for?"

"Well, I tried killing myself with both pills and drowning. What did you do?"

I noticed the other woman and Randal sat there without speaking. The woman appeared to be listening to the conversation, but Randal seemed zoned out.

"I'm a cutter," Fran said. "I like cutting my arms and legs with razor blades. I enjoy watching myself bleed."

Oh, dear, I thought to myself. This can't be real. What am I doing here with these nuts? As if reading my mind, the other woman spoke up.

"My name is Betty, and I work for BellSouth in the complaints department. I worked there twenty years being nice to people who were being butt holes. One day, I lost it and told everyone off—customers, my boss and people working around me. Then I left and haven't been back. I didn't try to kill myself, but everyone thought I would. I guess you could say I cracked up."

"I can identify with that," I said. "I cracked up too. My husband broke my heart, and I didn't want to live any longer. God, it's cold in this place. I noticed that y'all are wearing sweaters. I'll have to get Joe to bring me one. My daughter Jolly packed my suitcase, and I only have shorts and tee shirts."

My teeth chattered as I talked—clicking like a Spanish dancer's castanets keeping time to a lunatic's beat.

"She's only thirteen," I went on, "I think she did a good job. The only thing I remember before coming here was hearing her tell her daddy that she had forgiven him while he was drying me off. I'm glad she can, because right now, I can't."

"Yeah, the cold is nothing but your depression," Betty said. "We're all cold when we come in. Actually, they watch us, and when we start showing them we're no longer cold, they let us have more privileges."

Betty didn't sound crazy to me, and I thought to myself that there must be more to her story. Randal still sat at the table without saying a word, but he did stare at us. I wondered if he followed us mentally or not. He gave me the spooks. I looked where the lady with the doll had been sitting and felt even more crept out. I didn't know her name at that time, so I asked.

"Who's the lady with the doll, and what's her problem?"

"That's Mabel," Betty said. "No one knows exactly why she's in here. She won't talk to any of us, and she won't let anyone close to her—even the nurses when they try to give her the medicine or take her vital signs. She shrinks away, acting as if someone is beating her or something. We're all curious . . . everyone excluding Randal."

With that wisecrack, we laughed. Randal still didn't show any emotion. We weren't being mean, just honest. That's one thing you get in a nuthouse—complete honesty. You've never heard it all until a mentally ill person gives you an assessment of yourself.

I looked at my plate. I'd barely eaten anything, but I was full. Food tasted flavorless. Life was so damn bland. In fact, it wasn't only bland right now, it pure-dee-ole sucked. After I noticed my food, I wrapped my arms around my body, trying desperately to capture some heat. Thank goodness Joe was coming the next day for a family session. Maybe he could bring me some long-sleeved shirts and a sweater. There it was June, and I was dressing as if it were March.

It sure wasn't cold this night. In fact, it was unusually warm for this early in May. Still no call from Joe, and I was really starting to get sleepy. I probably needed to move around so I could stay awake. I went to the kitchen and found I still had some coffee left in the pot. It would taste like shit reheated in the microwave, but at least it would help me to wake up.

While waiting for it to heat up, I went back to remembering what it had been like in the hospital the first time. Even after that awful beginning with Mabel, we'd ended up being friends. She had loved butterflies, and I ended up drawing her some after seeing her reaction when she saw a girl coloring a butterfly in a color book. That had been really funny to see a bunch of adults coloring in color books. Not me! I would draw instead. To be honest, though, I didn't even color in color books when I was a child.

When I saw Mabel making her little sign of happiness by hugging herself as she watched the girl coloring the butterfly, I knew what I could do to make up for the scare I'd given her when we first met. She never talked at all, but she did say thank you when I gave her the butterfly drawing. Everyone noticed too, because those were the first words she'd uttered in nearly two months of care.

Joe called me at the hospital later that day. "God, honey, I would give anything if I hadn't hurt you, but I can't take it back. Please live in the present and accept my love for you now. Don't cry, baby."

I heard genuine concern for me in his voice. "Promise me you'll never ever cheat on me again," I said. "I don't know if I could live through it again. You are my world, Joe. All I've ever wanted in my life is someone to love me. I have never wanted 'stuff.' That time we lost the blue two-story house and had to move to a mobile home, I was fine. And you know why?" I choked up as I asked him.

"I know," he said. "You don't have to remind me. You were so happy having your family and my love that nothing else mattered."

"Right. Even in 1988, the writing was on the wall. You became involved with your old girlfriend, and I felt uneasy about the direction the friendship was taking. I noticed you stopped talking to me but spent lots of time on the phone talking to her. I stopped you before you two actually met each other. I gave you an ultimatum, and you chose me over having an affair. In my heart, I knew from then on that you saw me as 'the wife' and never again as the mistress I had once had been in your life." I was sobbing because my heart was broken.

"Stop it," Joe said. "You're going to make yourself sick. Try to focus on what we have now."

I didn't believe him. Something inside me knew he was bullshitting me.

"God, love is so blind," I said. "Despite the fact that you cheated on Regina the whole time you were married to her, I wanted to believe that you would miraculously love me so much that you wouldn't do that to me. That's the part that really hurts."

Chapter Thirty

I took my reheated coffee from the microwave and sat down to drink it. My mind returned to the phone conversation Joe and I'd had while I was in Mobile before I decided to surprise him.

While Joe and I had talked on the phone, I kept staring at the drawings both in my lap and on the computer screen. My bipolar mind was able to talk to Joe, look at the drawings, observe the techniques I'd used, notice how detailed they were, and think about how I could develop a character in the book I was writing.

Amidst all those thoughts was a haunting one about Joe being at home alone while I was down in Mobile. Of course, I tried to push aside the thought of Joe being by himself and able to do anything he wanted, since I'd never know. That thought kept coming back to worry me and make me feel insecure—part of my addiction for the past four years since his affairs.

I'd missed him that night in January, but I knew that living in Mobile would save me. It might cost me the marriage. In the end, it was going to make me a whole person again. I had been Joe's blob for the past four years. He'd emotionally trampled me, and I needed something to make me feel good about myself.

I had always wanted to write, so when a room came available in Mobile and I heard about a creative writing class starting up at the University of South Alabama, I decided to reach for Antares—the brightest star in our galaxy. I moved out long enough to attend class and write my book. I knew I needed to come to terms with the affairs and move on or end the marriage, but mostly I needed some space.

I stayed perpetually angry with Joe and couldn't understand why. While I was away, I planned to rewrite the script of our marriage. Either I was going to come to grips with what had happened, or I was going to use the time to realize that I didn't need that kind of abuse in my life. Joe was a good man, but he was a chronic liar, manipulator, and he knew exactly how to make me dance on the end of his strings as he pulled on my heart.

I pondered all those thoughts in between words as I continued talking to him without so much as a stumble.

"Joe, your love for me was never as strong as my love for you. All these years, I actually believed you might have loved me more than I loved you, because you were always writing me letters or telling me how much you loved me. Even when you were seeing Jane back in 1998, you still wrote me love letters."

"I'm going to hang up if you don't stop," he said.

I felt angry with myself for missing the obvious. I went on undaunted.

"I was so clueless that your heart had changed," I said. "And you were so good at hiding how you felt. God, if you'd been a little bit more open and honest with your emotions, I could have picked up on your being unhappy." I rifled through some papers looking for a poem I'd written recently. "Maybe I could have done something to keep you from straying or at least falling out of love with me enough to fall in love with another woman. That was what made me sick enough that I wanted to take my life."

I realized that I blamed myself for his cheating and totally obsessed over this thing. That was from being bipolar. We had this focus similar to a stuck record and couldn't move forward or back, only around and around and around. I'd also noticed it in my writing and found it often redundant or jumping around in my thoughts.

I thought of poor Joe, sick of hearing the same thing repeated often. I'd vowed to stop, but like a drunk who was unable to resist that bottle, I couldn't resist thinking about what Joe had done to me. Worst of all, I constantly threw it all up in his face. God, I wanted to stop, but I couldn't.

I cradled the phone as I talked to Joe, looking down at my bare feet and feeling awed once again at how ugly they were. Joe must have loved me to have ever wanted any physical contact with me after seeing those ugly feet. They were these little short nubs, I was flatfooted, and my toenails were thick and brittle with that fungus they're always touting the latest miracle cure for all over the TV. I also had a hammertoe on my left foot, which only made it a guaranteed win hands down in an ugliest foot contest.

After studying my feet, I moved on up my body, taking mental inventory as my conversation with Joe never missed a beat. As I did this, I also envisioned the heroine of my book and mentally thought of the physical descriptions I was going to give her. My mind did all three things simultaneously, the hallmark of a true bipolar. We were an amazing multi-tasker and achiever, until we did so many different things inside our heads that we couldn't cut through the mental clutter and retrieve a single thought.

Once, I had been extremely crazy, and I'd bought us a mountain chalet on a schoolteacher's salary, because I'd recently inherited some money and my credit was excellent at the time. However, spending over one hundred thousand dollars wasn't what had sent me to a shrink. No, it was when the thoughts argued for the front position, and I was unable to read.

That had sent me to Dr. Stone over in LaGrange, Georgia. My illness had been causing Joe and Jolly all the difficulties then, since I was either an arrogant know-it-all bitch who had a quick and explosive temper or a sluggish blob with no emotions at all. Not being able to read had been the only thing I found unusual enough to think I needed help.

Dr. Stone had actually contributed to my problem with Joe by not informing him that I was sick. His attitude was that he, as my doctor, had everything under control. Joe figured I'd quit loving him when I withdrew during the depression in 1998 that followed my mania in 1997.

"I feel as if I could have done something to prevent the worst thing that ever happened to me in my life," I told Joe in that January phone conversation while I looked at the drawings and thought about my life. "Being cheated on was worse than losing both my parents within seven weeks of each other. What I lost from you took away my entire being. It's hard to pick up and go on when my soul is broken and scattered. I struggle now to simply put the pieces of the puzzle called my life back together again."

"Honey, you know I wouldn't do anything to hurt you now. Trust me."

I heard Joe's voice pleading with me, and I shuddered as he said those words. That Southern ring-tailed tooter was stalking me for some reason. My radar was up. My trust in him was at an all-time low, which only made me feel guilty—I felt as if I were being unfair to him.

"I realize I hurt you so much," he said, "and I'm so sorry. Please, honey, quit worrying. I will never ever cheat on you again. I'll never hurt you like that again. I love you. You know you can count on me and believe me. I promise you I'll always love you, and you'll never have to worry about losing my love again."

Joe's voice broke with emotion. This softened my feelings towards him, and I read his sob as his being genuine.

"You'll never have to fear my leaving you or not being there for you," he said. "I feel ashamed that when you were depressed in the spring of 1998, I not only used that against you to cheat on you, but I also wasn't there when you needed me the most."

As he talked, I picked up my coffee cup and sipped. I almost had to spit it out when I realized I'd left it since that morning, and it tasted vile. I forced myself to swallow but gagged in the process.

While Joe went on talking, I surveyed my hands—short stubs with no fingernails, because I was always chewing off that fine little sliver of nail that I should have filed off instead. I peeled my nails with my teeth, one millimeter at a time. There was no sense polishing something I was just going to chew down to the quick.

Besides, my left hand couldn't hold the nail polish brush steady enough to keep it only on my nails. What looks worse than a woman without nail polish? A woman with nail polish all over the ends of her fingers. I couldn't use polish remover to get it off my skin, because I was such a klutz that I'd also shake off a swipe of my new nail polish as I smeared the edges even worse.

I'd long ago given up on having feminine hands—one reason I'd been so intimidated by Jane's gorgeously manicured hands. Just before my mind traveled back to remembering that day, I heard Joe still talking to me.

"God, I can't forgive myself for the way I treated you, especially when you were sick. Honey, I promise you this tonight, I'll never be unfaithful to you again, and that's the truth. Now you promise me that you won't never try killing yourself again. I don't want to worry about you or feel guilty about what I've done. I worry so much that I'm going to lose you, and I don't know what I'd do if something ever happened to you. I couldn't go on with my own life. You mean the world to me."

"Joe, I swear to you that if I feel down or suicidal, I'll call you and let you talk me out of it. I'll never ever hurt you or Jolly like that again."

Jolly was the reason I'd finally realized how important it was for me to get a handle on my suicidal tendencies. Since 1998, even with medication, I'd tried everything from electrocution to pills, even trying to jump out of the car in front of a transfer truck. Each of those attempts had sent me back to the mental hospital. I'd definitely had a guardian angel who kept me alive.

That was the down side of bipolar. We have the highest probability of suicide due to our impulsive nature, because we're compelled to do something whenever we think life is hopeless. A truly depressed person often doesn't have the energy to commit suicide. That's why many people end up killing themselves after they had begun to appear better. They feel good enough to summon the energy to complete the task. Bipolar people are that way all the time.

When I hear a voice telling me how to kill myself, before I can separate the reality of what I'm doing from the delusions of what I think, I've already gone and done something stupid. Things such as spending a fortune, trying to commit suicide, or running down our road naked one night were typical bipolar things I did. In one of my black manias, I flew into a violent rage at Joe because I directed all my anger at him. I bottled it up when I was sane, and it spewed forth like rotten vomit when I had an episode. I made everyone sick, including myself.

As I thought of all that, my mind focused on what life would be like if Joe ever left me, especially for another woman. My ear began to hurt. I transferred the phone to the other one.

"I can't cope with the thought of losing you," I said. "That's why I've tried so many times to end my life. Sometimes, the pain of that reality is so much stronger than the reality of your love. But I promise you here tonight that I'll do everything in my power to make you feel as if you can trust me on this issue. Promise me that you'll call me if you start getting that itch for another woman again. I know it's going to be tempting since I'm down in Mobile while you're up in Senora. Promise me, Joe!" I could hear the desperation in my voice.

"Honey, I swear you'll never have to worry about me again."

I know he heard me breathe a sigh of relief, even through the phone. My tears also dried up. I still had the drawing up on the screen, and once again I meandered back to that night on the dance floor in 1982 when we'd shared our first kiss in front of William's mom.

After Joe and I finally hung up, I wandered to the bathroom sink to wash out that nasty coffee cup. A coffee pot was the only thing I had in my room besides my computer, bed and stereo—no stove, refrigerator, or even a sink. I had to do all my dishwashing in my bathroom lavatory.

I filled up the coffee pot by holding it under the tub faucet, because it wouldn't fit under the one in the sink. I sat down at my computer again, and the drawing took me right back to where I had left off in my thoughts.

From the start, there had been something different about that night in 1982. None of our other crewmembers had shown up at The Studio with Joe and me, so we'd sat at the table with Gretchen. She seemed not to mind that I was out with someone other than William. Since William was a writer, he chose to stay home locked up in his office most of the time. When I went out, it took pressure off him to be with me. I think she understood that I was moving into a different stage of my life and that William wouldn't be able to provide me with what I needed. She'd always told me I was special to her for marrying him when he was already in a wheelchair.

There we were in front of William's mom and his brother, relaxing at The Studio after work. It had started out innocent enough, but there had been complete abandon as to how our next action would affect everyone that night. As the long introduction to "Eye in the Sky" played, almost as soon as the guitars started their rhythmic call with an erotic beat, something happened to both Joe and me simultaneously. As the music led us deeper and deeper into the song, it also led us deeper and deeper into each other's personas.

Joe looked down on me as we danced slowly and sensuously. He lowered his head as I tilted mine upward. Like magnets and iron filings, we were pulled together, as if some force of nature controlled the joining of his mouth to mine and made that kiss inevitable. The music stopped, and everyone and everything faded as the full bouquet of him filled all my senses. His big hand inhaled my small one as he held it. He pulled my head down and rubbed the back of it in an exotic message. I felt his heart beating as I put my head against his chest. My right ear conducted both the tactile sensation of his beating heart and the faint but rapid sound of it. I was shocked to realize how aroused he had become.

Suddenly, I was aware of the increasing tempo of my own heart. I smelled his recently showered male body after a hard night at work, blended with the scent of his shampoo on his clean, silky long hair. As we kissed, I tasted his sweetness, his passion and his love that night. My eyes looked deeply into his, and I was able to see into his psyche. I saw something I had never seen before: a man who connected his entirety to me, opening up his all as a wonderful gift for me to receive.

I was fighting the love I was feeling, afraid that accepting it would set me up for heartache. However, his love was strong and powerful enough that he literally forced it down my throat with his tongue, sweeping my mouth and pointing itself straight toward my heart. It sent out tentacles that wrapped themselves so tightly around my beating heart that it captured and caged it. It belonged to him, and even though I didn't know it at the time, it would be his and his alone for the rest of my life.

I surrendered my heart completely to Joe—but not that night. I was too cautious then because of the way James had burned me with a sizzling infatuation. Something inside me always stopped me from totally giving my heart away. It was as if I knew that one day someone would knock a huge hole into my heart and life, and since I was a person with a low pain threshold, I guarded my heart viciously to prevent that from happening.

I guess I figured that William would be a safe bet—someone who would be forever grateful for my love. That's what I'd counted on, but I'd been surprised to find that I couldn't count on a man in a wheelchair to love me always. On one plane, William never did stop loving me, but on the one that really mattered, he had.

There I was, bruised and torn by William, burned and bleeding by James, terribly afraid of rejection and abandonment because of my childhood. That fear had been a major driving force throughout my life. It had made and molded me into a sick person. However, that night I was unaware of those feelings. I knew I needed to hold back and needed to protect my heart, but Joe overpowered my resolve. His love sealed my destiny that night with a passionate kiss.

Joe's sexy eyes had drawn me deeper into the matrix of his lies. They pulled me closer and closer to what would eventually hurt me and kill me mentally one day. I struggled against it, mentally kicking and screaming like someone was trying to drag me up a mountain and throw me off. The valley below was going to devour me when I fell. Yes, that's what Joe did—he devoured me.

It had to be those damn eyes of his. They had ended up being the biggest turn-on for me, because he would always watch me as he made love to me and brought me to total ecstasy and satisfaction. We loved looking into each other's eyes while having sex and found it erotic. We were both uninhibited, and it turned us on to watch each other's expressions.

I had never cared for hairy men, and Joe was almost slick due to the Native American blood in his pedigree. Because of his Native blood, he literally turned a reddish bronze in the summer when he worked outside or drove his Jeep around with the top down. Of course, his arms were darker than his torso, but he did have a tan because we would swim nude together in our pool.

Remembering the good things about Joe should have deterred me from wanting to kill him, but hell no! The fact that he'd robbed me of making more special memories in the future made me more determined than ever to get even with him. Good memories tended to relax me, and the Ambien was already doing too much of that. I stayed on my feet because I was beginning to feel funny. Fighting it caused my peripheral vision to see people-like shapes, moving as if on hot air waves arising from the highway on a hot July day. I walked to the pantry to see what I could pull out to eat. This shit gave me the munchies worse than any pot ever had.

"Pop Tarts!" I squealed. Not only that, my favorite ones—cinnamon and brown sugar, unfrosted. I went back to the living room to munch on my treat, and the people still danced all around me. The room had also started slanting. I focused on something to make me mad enough to remain homicidal.

Chapter Thirty-One

That night in January had awakened some painful memories. It had all started with listening to a country and western song that sounded as though someone had been with Joe and me the night we first kissed. It went something like this: Everyone thought we were lovers when we were only friends. There was this funny feeling, and I felt different that night. When I kissed your lips, electricity shot right though me. When you kiss me like this, do you mean it like that?

I couldn't remember the words exactly, but that was the gist of the song. Then, to make things worse, I listened to our song, "Eye in the Sky." Hearing that long intro once again tormented me because of our recent problems, and I yearned for Joe. It made me want to pack up everything, drive back to Senora and call off the separation. I wanted to feel Joe's love, his warmth, and his arms around me once again.

My room in Mobile was bare and lonely. I knew in my soul that I couldn't do that. Our lives were at stake in overcoming our sicknesses so we could approach our marriage in a healthy way. The easy thing to do would have been to run away from the long, lonely pain we both were going to feel from the separation, but I knew I had to tough it out.

The next day, I tried to settle myself down and do some serious writing. I did get involved in the book, and that helped. While I was writing, my mind could shut out that nagging loneliness and emptiness I was stuffing inside me. Fingers flew over my keyboard, and the steady clicking sound kept me company for the better part of the day.

When evening came, as the darkness swallowed up the day, the loneliness swallowed up my pretense that all was well. When I'm hurting, memories draw me in like a thirsty animal toward a waterhole. It's almost as if there's a crazy comfort in dealing with those awful memories. My heart had to face them. I dealt with pain in that fashion. I stuffed it and stuffed it, fussed, fought and got angry, but it was all a façade to ignore the real culprit eating away at my sanity. I realized again that I longed for Joe's kisses. All I wanted at that moment was to feel his lips on mine and taste him once again.

Thank God my class was that night. It always helped to get my mind off things. My thoughts were especially bouncy that night, jumping around all over the place. I listened to my instructor, but my mind was on what had happened the day before when I'd talked to Joe on the phone. I kept thinking about what I'd told him about our kiss, and I thought of something else. I was curious to pick his brains about how he'd let another woman have my kisses, and I decided to ask him when I got home that night.

It was almost nine when I got home. I punched in Joe's number, afraid he'd be online and the line would be busy. It started ringing, and Joe picked up on the first ring, almost as if he'd been expecting me to call him.

"Hi, honey," he said very sweetly.

I was in a mad determination to get to the truth, so I started right in without any hello or asking how he was doing.

"Joe, I need to ask you a question."

"Well, hello to you too," he barked in obvious irritation. "What do you want now?"

"What always kept me connected to you, no matter how angry, upset, or hurt I got, was the ability I always had to flash on and remember that night at The Studio when we danced and kissed and life literally stood still for us. Do you ever do that anymore, or did you stop back in 1998? Is that how you could give Jane my kiss?"

"I'm afraid so." Joe's tone had changed to tired. "I did stop seeing our kiss. All I could see was that I felt like you neglected me and no longer loved me. At first, I was going to show you, and I cheated in anger to get back at you. Then I found love with Jane and couldn't stop. She made me feel special and appreciated, feelings you had long ago stopped showing me. I needed her. Listen, I was talking to Jolly before you called, so let me go."

Although I didn't trust him, it never dawned on me that history might be repeating itself that soon.

Anyway, I had his answer. That's how our love dried up and went away. There was no image of life to infuse it repeatedly and feed it when it needed food. Just as my secret weapon with William had always been to remind myself that, no matter how much he upset me, I was thankful he was still there with me to cause my upset. His doctors had predicted he'd never live into his thirties, but he had proved them all wrong. Still, I'd always lived in fear that he would get sick and die as many people in wheelchairs often did. Therefore, just as I had used images of horses to get me through the pain in my life as a child, I had used that same imagination to create a powerful image that gave me the strength not to cave in to that love killer called life.

To be honest, when I'd left William, I had hardened my heart to him because of the way he had been treating me and because of the unfair double standard he'd kept. Mainly, I'd resented the fact that I had a man who was willing to share me. As much as I enjoyed the sex and the attention, my heart had wanted it to be from a monogamous love that never threatened my

185

security. Once that was gone, there was no foundation to preserve my sacred images.

I realized Joe must have felt the same way when he thought he had lost my love. Just as I had hardened my heart to William, Joe had hardened his heart and been unable to love me. Moreover, as my heart had starved for love, affection, and a connection with William, I had been open and vulnerable to Joe, and he'd been just as vulnerable to Jane. When she'd entered his life in the spring of 1998, he could no more have stopped himself than I was able to stop myself back in 1982.

Understanding my role in all of it suddenly opened my eyes. How could I be such a hypocrite as to judge Joe as an aberration because of his reaction to the times I had mistreated him when I'd been through the same thing myself? I had been mistreated, ignored, and put down by William whenever I suggested anything, which had caused me to lose my feelings for him. How could I have expected Joe to do anything differently from the way I had handled similar feelings?

Brokenhearted I might be, but a hypocrite—never. I decided I would look at the drawing of Joe and me and see it for what it really was: a representation of what I had done to William rather than a representation of what Joe had done to me. That gave me a sense of peace at long last, and I knew what I had to do.

I was going home to surprise Joe. Finally, I could forgive him. This trip to Mobile had really paid off. Not only had it given me the distance I needed to come to this revelation about Joe, I had been getting a lot of writing done as well as receiving some wonderful instruction from my teacher, Faith Jones.

Now that I had the scales removed from my eyes, I could see the mote in my own rather than the plank in Joe's. I was going home to Joe the next day, and I felt as excited as a teenager at the prospect. I couldn't wait to see him, hold him, kiss him and let him know that all was going to be well. I'd finally turned a corner, and I could trust him again.

The sixteenth arrived after what seemed like fifty-five-forevers, and I packed my car and headed out. Visions of Joe making love to me occupied my mind, and I felt this was going to be the apex of my life. I knew he'd be thrilled to see that I was finally able to put everything in perspective. At long last, little Jolly could breathe a sigh of relief. Mommy and Daddy were going to be all right, and the threat of divorce would no longer be looming over the horizon.

I even went so far as to hide my car when I got there, because I really wanted it to be a surprise. I parked on the side of the house where he never went, and my small Miata was easy to hide. I unlocked the house, then I went in and locked it behind me. I busied myself in the bedroom while I waited for him to come home.

When I heard the dogs bark, my heart pounded with anticipation. I was trying to figure out the best way to reveal myself when I realized he hadn't come inside yet, at least not into the den. I looked outside and saw that he'd come in through the sunroom and had gotten some birdseed to fill up the feeders. God, he looked so good and so sweet tending to the birds—always my caring Joe.

I backed into the hallway again, waiting for that perfect moment to surprise him. The door slammed, and the dogs started moving in my direction. I just knew they were fixing to blow things, but lucky for me the phone rang and Joe didn't notice what they were doing. Since I wanted to have his full attention directed at me, I decided to wait until he got off the phone to show myself.

"Hey, Hon, how was your day?" His voice was so strangely sweet and silky sounding that it almost didn't sound like Joe. There was a pause before he spoke again. "Yeah, I talked with her last night."

Nothing unusual about that. People were always calling to see how I was doing down in Mobile. I had honed in that the "Hon" may have been Jolly's calling her dad. But the next sentence let me know that whoever was on the phone with him was no friend of mine.

"I really appreciate the way you understand what I'm going through. It's like my e-mail said—I don't know what I would have done without you. Listen, I've got to feed the animals and do some things around here before dark. I'll call you back at nine o'clock."

My blood turned to frost, and my breath caught in my throat. My brain, however, was working good enough that I knew to back into Jolly's room and hide. When I heard him get up as the wooden computer chair made its sighing squeak as the castors rolled across the wooden floor, I almost didn't want to go over to the computer to find what I knew I was going to find.

He had cheated on me the first time by using the Internet, and it sure sounded as if he were up to his old tricks again. At last, I heard the trailing off of the dogs barking in their let's-go-outside excitement. I knew he would be busy for a while. I knew what he would be doing and how long it would take him to feed all the animals on the farm. Lucky for me he had already turned on the computer while he was on the phone and had gotten online as soon as he hung up. Yeah, he was all ready to go, wasn't he?

He used EarthLink the same as me. I opened Outlook Express and scrolled down. It looked innocent enough at first since all the incoming messages were from me, but then I looked at the sent items and my heart stopped.

"God, please let this be anything but what I think it is. Please, God." I prayed as I pointed the cursor over the subject line and clicked to open it. Imagine my shock when I saw that he'd written this two days before on January fourteenth, the night he'd promised to be faithful to me.

Carolyn,

Thanks for being so understanding about the name. I don't know exactly why but after talking to you tonight, I felt like a fraud for not telling you my real name. I don't want to lie to you, and I hope that you know it wasn't intended to be that way. I damn sure don't want to get off on the wrong foot with you. God you sound so good, and your laugh was like the sweetest sound I have ever heard. Thank you so much for letting me have someone to talk to who will understand. I could have laid on the bed and talked all night and never would I have gotten tired of hearing your voice. I know that you are as beautiful as you sound. When I talk to you, I picture a sunrise with the wonderful colors of a new day bursting from the edge of the earth. The true beauty of the light will be the first time I get to see you in person. The magic of the warmth will be the first time I get to hold your hand. The glory of the new day will be the first time I get to kiss your lips. That is maybe all I could endure for one day. I look so forward to seeing you, getting to know you, and you me. Perhaps in a couple of weeks we will take that walk on the beach, and watch the stars come out. Perhaps we will lie on a blanket and count them together. Perhaps we will finally come to that one star that will lead us to other things far more pleasurable. Could be that we will set and watch the waves. You in front leaning back with my arms around you to keep you warm and safe. Yes, it could be.

I love you,
Joe

I heard the door and the footsteps. I don't know which of us had the most surprised look on our faces—Joe or me. Because he was a master at lying, he actually walked in and acted as if he were pleasantly surprised to see me and didn't care that I was on the computer.

As he walked toward me, I said in as nonchalant of a voice as I could muster, "Who's Carolyn?"

"Carolyn? I don't know a Carolyn, unless you're talking about your friend Carolyn."

"No, Joe. This Carolyn is your friend. I don't know her at all."

I couldn't believe he actually had the nerve to get that confused look on his face! He could see the e-mail message I had been reading, yet he still played it dumb. I don't know which made me madder—that he'd cheated again or that he thought I was still stupid enough to buy his lies again.

"I mean this Carolyn, you idiot. The one you want to hold and kiss and find a special star for more pleasurable things. Don't insult my intelligence!"

He still acted as if I were going crazy and spouting off something he had no clue about. He was actually trying to play it cool so he could try to convince me I wasn't seeing what was there. The old me would have been fooled. That me had been in such denial about Joe and his lying. However, this me was furious. When he leaned over my shoulder and started reading the e-mail as if it were something he had never seen before, I snapped.

"You lying son of a bitch! You dumb-acting motherfucker! You know damn well who the fuck Carolyn is! I hate you, Joe—I hate you! I can't believe you've done this to me again. What are you? Some kind of sadist? Do you get off on tormenting and torturing me? What have I done to you that I deserve this? Why tease me with your love?"

"It isn't anything like you think. Calm down, I can explain th–"

Before he finished the sentence, I jumped out of the chair. It made this moaning sound as it rolled across our oak floors, but the sound only echoed the screams inside my head. I was close enough to Joe that I could smell the stale cigarettes and coffee on his breath. His clothes also had that peculiar smell of a paper mill that's like a stopped up toilet. Think of that—his breath really had to stink for me to smell it above the paper mill stench. He was supposed to have quit smoking, another thing he'd lied about as he'd done in the past. He'd sneak around to smoke, but when I found a pack of cigarettes or asked him if he were smoking, he'd act hurt and deny it while looking me straight in the eyes. I believe he used the smoking as a test run on his other deceptions. He perfected it with something small and inconsequential in preparation for the big betrayal.

When I came out of the chair, Joe lost that calm, cool and collected look on his face, because he knew I was ready to hurt him. He knew I'd kicked up into a black mania, and God only knew what I was fixing to do. Before he could block me, I reached for his face. I wanted to pull that lying, dumb-acting expression right off of it. I took my right hand and grabbed hold of his left cheek, then I pinched and raked my fingernails down his face, bruising him and drawing blood as well. He slapped me twice.

"Stop it, you crazy bitch!"

Joe had hit me a couple of times before in some of our fights, but it was funny that I never bruised or showed a mark when I was mad. Damn, living with him had sunk me to common trailer trash.

"You sorry, low down, lying, cheating son of a bitch! How could you swear you were being faithful that night and then type this right after you hung up the phone? God, you are so pathetic!"

"Shut the fuck up, Lee. You make me sick, and I want you to get out of my life. You chased me off by bitching and constantly bringing up the affairs. When I came down for my birthday on the seventh, you told me then that you hated me. What did you expect me to do after that?"

He said this as he slapped me in my face, but I didn't even feel the impact. I didn't even hear what he'd said to me, because there was a roar in my head as my manic thoughts disintegrated into a thousand splintered sensory impressions. Like a room filled with a dozen radios all tuned to a different stations blaring as loud as they would go, my mind reeled with the chaos and clutter of racing thoughts. Nothing was clear to me for about twenty seconds. I couldn't see, hear, smell, or feel. All I could do was simply be.

When I looked up into those deep-set hazel eyes and saw the betrayal in them again, I knew this time things were going to be different. On the drive up there that day, I'd had a strong premonition that the trip was going to be a major turning point between us, and I hadn't been wrong.

The phone rang, it was Jolly calling her dad. I answered the phone though.

"Jolly, this is mom. Your dad just hit me. We're in a big fight. I caught him again!"

"Mom, don't do anything stupid. I love you."

"Yeah, Jolly, I hit her! I'm sick of her!"

"I have to go. God, I hate him now!"

"Try to remember that I don't. He's still my dad." That only made me madder. I hung up the phone and turned again to Joe who showed his hatred in his eyes now.

"Joe, you told me you didn't love me back in 1998 then you changed your mind and begged me to take you back. I allowed your feelings of confusion and took you back. You at least owe me the same courtesy. But no, you can't take the rejection. All this time you've expected me to accept everything you did. You actually loved another woman. What a two-faced hypocrite with a double standard you are."

By then we'd taken the argument into the living room. We both screamed and cursed until I called the police. Hell, I wanted him arrested for hitting me. The town's one police officer came over, but Joe denied hitting me. Naturally, there he was bleeding and bruised while I was the one with the stupid skin that wouldn't even register that he'd touched me. Of course, the call with Jolly was before the cop was elicted.

We finally agreed that Joe would go to the marriage counselor with me on Friday. I already had an appointment because his counselor had wanted to talk to me about Joe's sexual addiction. We agreed to go together and not press charges against each other.

Chapter Thirty-Two

At Dr. Porter's office the next day, I told him what had happened the night before. Although Joe was supposed to arrive right after me, he never showed up. Of course, I hadn't really expected him to. His message was loud and clear—things were over between us.

I went home hoping that he was there and just being an asshole, but he was gone. He also wouldn't answer his cell phone. He'd left me. I knew he had gone to be with Carolyn. I brought the e-mail message back up on his computer and read it again, and I absolutely wigged out.

I went to my studio and got a hammer, then I walked back to the computer and hit the monitor as hard as I could. I called my psychoanalyst who was treating me for dissociative identity disorder, because Dee Dee wanted to let him know I was out of the picture.

"Dr. Diamond, this is Dee Dee. I caught him doing it again. He skipped out on us, and Lee's going crazy. That bastard isn't getting away with it this time. I'm in control."

Dee Dee started trying to disconnect the computer. It was a much nicer computer than Lee's computer. Dee Dee decided to take it back to Mobile with us. Unfortunately, Lee had the computer savvy, not Dee Dee.

"Fuck him! I can't get this son-of-a-bitch computer disconnected! I'm going to show that mother. God, I hate him."

Dee Dee had a screwdriver in my shaking hands, working on undoing the printer from the hard drive, lost as how to undo it easily. She screamed into the phone, cursing both the computer and Joe.

Poor Dr. Diamond was trying to get me to calm down, but I had switched into a manic rage. Because of my child-like personality, it would have been impossible for six men to control me physically at that moment. I finally disconnected the damn thing, then I hoisted the monitor over my head and threw it as hard as I could across the room. There was a dull thud followed by a ringing sound as it hit our oak floors and the glass shattered all over them.

Before I left, I went and grabbed the ceramic plaque I'd given to Joe the day he had gotten back from cheating the first time with Jane. Jolly and I had been at the state science fair, and we'd stopped at a Cracker Barrel on the way home. The plaque read Let's go over the hill together and showed a horse and a mule going over a rise. I'd bought it for Joe as an "I love you" gift. What a joke.

Thinking about that damn fight and Joe not showing up for the appointment made me madder than hell, and I no longer felt the least bit sleepy from the Ambien I'd taken. My eyes popped open, and my hands started shaking after finishing the cup of coffee I'd reheated. Joe still hadn't called me yet, so to spur me on and keep my anger level up, I picked up where I'd left off in the memory.

I never even hung up the phone with Dr. Diamond that day. I gathered up my clothes and loaded the car, but before I went to Mobile, I went to West Point, Georgia where Joe and I had our checking and savings accounts. I cleaned out both of them, then I went to J.C. Bradford and cleaned out the small savings account we had there before driving to Opelika and cleaning out our third savings account. I left Joe with exactly $14.65 total in all four of the accounts.

Then I went to see my lawyer and got him to draw up legal separation papers. Hell, I started to believe that Joe had manipulated me into doing exactly his bidding. He'd purposely left that e-mail message on his computer, because he figured I'd probably kill myself. I'd given him his ticket to do whatever he wanted, just as Regina had done twenty years earlier.

Well, that was it. Today was going to be a turning point all right. Finally, I saw Joe for what he was—a lying, cheating, manipulative, abusing husband. He loved me conditionally at best, and if things didn't suit him, he justified stopping his love for me and did whatever he pleased, to hell with anyone or any hearts that got broken in the process—Jolly's or mine or even the women he preyed upon. What he wanted always came first.

The fool didn't even know what real love was, but finally I had the courage to stand up to him and do something besides trying to kill myself. Mobile had given me the strength to live. Maybe I'd done Joe's bidding by going to the lawyer, but I'd also told myself that I deserved better than the likes of him. Yes, I had been right. I had reached the apex of my life.

My lawyer told me the romantic e-mail message was not legal proof that Joe had cheated on me, so later in the month I hacked into his Yahoo account and read his mail. Sure enough, there was a message from Daryl talking about how much Ginger had enjoyed having sex with Joe on January second—the night Joe had claimed he'd gone to Georgia to take some photographs at a state park and had gotten sick on the way home. I remembered my conversation with him when I finally got him on the phone after being worried. My stupid pill had sure worked that night. After discovering the e-mail message to Carolyn on his computer, I knew I had to get him good if I wanted to get my house and the farm, and I did. That damning e-mail message from Daryl got copied and pasted straight into a message I sent to my lawyer. Since I'd moved to Mobile, Joe knew that finding out he'd cheated on me again would either cause me to kill myself, or I'd run away and leave everything to him as I'd done when I left William, but I did neither. I fought back.

My lawyer wrote Joe a letter that said he had proof that Joe had been committing adultery with Daryl and Ginger, and if he didn't want to drag them into an ugly court scene, he'd best quick deed the farm and house back over to me. Joe knew I had him by his yammers but good.

In February, I moved back home to Senora.

I felt myself smile at the memory of pulling off that coup de grace. It was getting close to midnight. Why the hell hadn't Joe called me yet?

He was never going to abuse me again, either emotionally or physically. Whenever I was like this—when I couldn't read a calendar and make sense of it, my precursor to a psychotic episode—consequences didn't matter, only pain did. Stopping the pain I felt now was all that had any influence over me. I reviewed the only two options I felt I had: I could either end my life or his.

I chose his.

Memories flooded me as my mind jumped around, trying to make sense of what was fixing to happen next. Because of my mental illness, that was something I spent the bulk of my life doing anyway—thinking and living inside my head, right or wrong.

Madness made me restless. I walked back to my bedroom, opened the drawer, and made sure the gun was still there. I felt the cool metal underneath my gloves. I went back to the living room to wait for him.

Thoughts still plagued my mind. He'd schmoozed me with his kindness and caring, I'm-your-friend ways. Women frequently made the first sexual overtures, and I had been no exception. We'd both divorced our respective mates and married each other after Joe asked me to have his baby. I'd never considered being a mother until then. Something had clicked inside my biological clock, and I'd had a passionate drive to reproduce.

Once I had my IUD removed, I was pregnant within two weeks. I knew I was pregnant the day I'd conceived ten days earlier. I'd been able to detect within my sensitive body a slight buzz as the cells were dividing inside me. I had to confirm it with a blood test, because the urine test wouldn't pick it up that early.

Jolly was born on July 1, 1984, as perfect a child as anyone could want. She was smart, sweet, imaginative, creative, and she had common sense as well. Beautiful on the inside and outside, she had been my godsend. When she was born, I didn't think any couple could have loved their child or each other any more than Joe and me.

When I left the mill in 1988 and went back to school to get my master's degree, things changed between us. God, at first I was so intensely in love and happy, but being a mother, going to school at night and teaching during the day put the first damper on our marriage.

"You never seem to want sex with me anymore," Joe told me. "You used to be sensuous and always desired me. What I wouldn't give to see that passion in your eyes again."

He is so damn immature.

"Grow up, Joe. I meet myself coming out the door. When I get home at night from class after working, I'm exhausted. When I have any extra time, I feel as if I need to spend it with Jolly. I make time for you, but I can't do it every day like it used to be before we became parents. That's normal. Jolly needs me, and you need to appreciate the time I put in with our daughter rather than putting me down for it."

I realized now that Joe had never deserved me, and that fueled my anger again. We came from two different worlds, two different classes of people with two different educational levels.

Feeling the Ambien again, I wobbled my way back to the kitchen sink to rinse out my coffee cup. Good, every thought was firing my anger.

In 1988, I caught Joe corresponding with an old girlfriend he'd knocked up while in high school whose parents had forced her to put up the baby for adoption. Joe's mom had given her our unlisted phone number. Under the guise of looking for their long lost son, they had started an emotional relationship. Joe told me they were looking for their son but hid the fact that they'd been writing letters to each other.

I discovered it one day when he left one in his coat pocket. In the letter, he had been lying and bragging about owning a Harley Davidson bike and a farm. All he had was a big Honda. We certainly didn't have a farm. I guess he figured the Harley made him sound sexier than the old-family-man Honda Gold Wing. We also lived in a mobile home at that time, because we'd recently lost our house when I left the mill and started back to college full time.

I wondered why he was trying to impress her unless something was building. She admitted in her letter that she had a secret post office box to hide their letters from her husband, and of course Joe had been hiding his from me. I took Jolly and left him that night, and I gave him an ultimatum to cut out all contact with her if he wanted me to come back. I guess I had more sense back then. He seemed to have chosen fidelity and me over Donna Sue, but it changed our marriage. Things were never the same between us.

I had my first euphoric high episode in 1997 when I blew through over one hundred thousand dollars, most of it spent on Joe. I bought him a string of horses, a new F-350 Dooley truck with a matching four-horse trailer as well as a tractor with all the attachments, including a trailer to haul around the equipment. When Joe snapped his fingers and asked for something, I went out and bought it.

Believe it or not, he resented me for being able to do all that and put up a profile on an online dating service right after we returned from Austria in March of 1997. He swore later that he never had sex with any of the women, but I don't believe that. His idea of love was that phony lust and infatuation. When it got serious and less exciting, he felt as though the love part was gone.

Back in 1998 when I still had some guts, I'd tried leaving to divorce him. I became wild and mad as well as bold when I caught him cheating. The night I found the bag of proof in his truck, I'd decided I no longer wanted Joe as my husband. The next day, I packed up mine and Jolly's things to go find an apartment where we could finish out the school year.

Jolly had a different idea. Being thirteen, she really didn't understand what he was putting me through when I discovered his infidelity. She climbed a huge magnolia tree and refused to come down. I was tempted for the first time in my life to leave her. Once again, my pain did the talking, but my love for her was stronger than the pain.

I went back inside, unpacked, and told her I wasn't going to leave her dad. A week later, when I caught him in another lie, I grabbed her up and said we were going to Meridian, Mississippi to visit my sister and get my head straightened out. She cried all the way across the state of Alabama, begging me not to divorce her daddy even though she knew by then that he'd cheated on me.

Joe saw Jane one more time while we were in Mississippi. Not even the threat of losing his child could keep him away from his mistress. Jolly now tells me she wished I had left him for good then. He killed something in me when I crawled back to him. I felt unwanted, unloved, ugly, and unappreciated. Yet I couldn't hurt my child.

Tonight, I couldn't factor Jolly into my plans. I'd let my concern for her feelings mess me up once in my life, but it wasn't going to happen this time. Although I planned to kill Joe, I knew I still loved him, and I realized we had much more serious problems than either of us had expected.

What a contrast that was to only nine months earlier when we were swinging, when everyone who'd met us thought we were the happiest, most loving couple they knew. My mind went back to two nights ago when I'd tried killing myself and almost made it, thinking that was the solution. At long last, I'd thought there would be peace. Then I'd thought about Jolly and realized what a huge mistake I'd made. Joe really wasn't worth doing this to Jolly or myself.

After taking too many anti-convulsive pills, sleeping pills, and anti-anxiety pills, I had wanted to get up and either make myself throw up or dial 911, but my brain was the only part of me still operating. Chartreuse spots had begun to form in front of my eyes, and the room had begun to blur when the phone rang. I guess the sharp noise acted on my reflexes, because I managed to pick up the receiver and slur out a "Thello."

Thank God it was Jolly. I'd be able to tell her I loved her.

"Sholly, I, uh . . . wanthed to, uh . . . I wanthed to they I lof you . . . I'm thorry . . ."

Then I dropped the phone and was back in a state of not being able to figure out how to move or talk. I was slipping into total darkness fast. I had the sensation of a large spiral track with a metal ball going down it. With wide circles at its top, the ball went slowly, but as it narrowed and the circles became smaller, the ball began spinning faster and faster, until I felt as though it was going to hit me in my own heart. I had a fleeting moment of feeling myself die before everything went to nothingness. There was no black. For a millisecond, I saw nothing.

Those memories determined exactly what I was going to do now. I sat down in the recliner, waiting to call Joe. When twelve o'clock chimed on the mantel clock in the den, a cold chill let me know I wasn't in this alone anymore. Ray, the ghost who lived in our house, was right there with me.

Recently, I'd started thinking of Ray as my guardian angel and protector. In fact, I believed that he would do something to Joe if I needed him to help me tonight. Realizing that Ray hovered there made me start thinking about this whole Dance with Destiny I was planning. Maybe Ray was my dance partner.

I continued to put this puzzle together in my mind as I headed back to the bedroom to call Joe from there, since the portable phone's battery was low.

Even then, my thoughts drifted back to an earlier time. My small, muscular body had been what attracted Joe to me back in the summer of 1982 when we'd become lovers. He'd destroyed that love all too easily.

When I thought about Joe and what he'd done to me, I became violently angry again. Just thinking about him made my heart start pounding in my chest. Back in 1982, he'd made it pound from excitement, anticipation, and passion. How sad that it was only anger now that fueled this adrenalin rush. I could feel the blood as it raced to my head and warmed my face. The flush crawled along my features, tickling my skin as it did so.

One dimly lit lamp created strange shadows in my bedroom. I tried to convince myself that fate sealed my actions as I sat on the bed and remembered why I was upset. I thought about my next action and tried to figure out why I was destined to do what I believed needed to be done. Again, I experienced a chill, reminding me that Ray was close by.

I remembered when we'd first discovered that our house in Senora was haunted.

Chapter Thirty-Three

When Joe and I first moved into the house back in 1992, our living room had been empty. In fact, many of the rooms had been empty, because we'd moved from our small home in Georgia to a large one in Alabama—at least it had been our definition of a big house.

The first night we went to bed in it, our oak floors squeaked as if a person were walking down the hall toward the bedroom. Joe got up to check on things. Of course, he saw nothing and came on back to bed. Earlier, I had locked all the doors and later checked them before I went to bed. By habit, Joe always went behind me to check and made sure everything was locked up tight.

Between the creaking floors and the train going by at two and again at four in the morning, we didn't sleep well. When Joe got up to make the coffee, he discovered some strange things. Figuring I had to be behind it all, he wasn't too worried. He fixed me a cup of coffee, and I heard him walking toward our bedroom to wake me so I could finish the house.

"Lee, did you by any chance get up last night to look for something?"

"No, why?" I answered as I groped for the cup of coffee he offered to me. That was one of the things I enjoyed the most—if Joe were home and not at work, he made the coffee and always brought me a cup. He said he loved pampering me.

"Good morning, beautiful."

"Hello, handsome. Now what were you saying?"

"Well, when I got up this morning, all the cabinets were wide open, including the ones above the refrigerator and the sink. I couldn't imagine what you would've been looking for in any of them, since we just moved in and haven't even finished unpacking yet."

He brought my robe to me and held it while I put it on. He winked when I turned to face him then kissed me—an endearing ritual of ours.

"But, then again," he added, "nothing you do would ever surprise me. It's just like you to remember something, get out of bed in the middle of the night and not stop looking everywhere you could think of until you finally found it."

"Nope, I didn't do that." I was still too sleepy to understand the implications of what Joe was saying.

"Okay, then did you get up to let the dogs out and forget to lock back up?"

"Uh-uh." I shook my head.

The strangeness of what he was saying finally began to dawn on me.

"Are you saying that you checked the doors last night before you came to bed and they were locked, but you found them unlocked this morning?"

"Yes, and I know all of those cabinets in the kitchen were closed as well. But that isn't even the strangest thing that happened last night."

"It isn't?"

"No. I woke up this morning, and one of the kitchen chairs was over by the front window, facing like someone sat there to look out."

"Oh, silly," I said. "Jolly probably did all of this, the little monkey. There has to be a logical explanation for all of it. Doesn't there?" I sipped my coffee slowly, savoring its taste. Joe knew exactly how to make my coffee.

Jolly awakened that morning and knew nothing at all about any of the strange things that had happened. The three of us concluded that either one of us was a sleepwalker, or there was a ghost in the house.

When we bought the place, we hadn't realized how the man who'd built it had died. We found out later that Ray had been in a terrible car wreck. A semi was pulling one of those extra-wide loads across a bridge, and for some strange reason, Ray decided to go on across the bridge. The escort car for the semi had been too far ahead for it to do any good.

I heard through the grapevine that Ray wasn't even recognizable after the wreck. I shudder to think about that. His wife, Debra, had inherited a huge life insurance policy, and the money was hers to keep as long as she never married again. Well, we heard that Debra shacked up with some men right here in this house.

We suspected that Debra's actions had pulled Ray's spirit into a restless mode of trying to get back at her because he was angry. Gossip alleged that he ran her out of the house after about two months. She finally moved back in, but only long enough to fix it up in order to sell it. Enter one Joe and Lee Thames.

At that moment, I had a delusional feeling that Ray played an active role in my plans for Joe. Sure enough, the phone rang and it was him.

"I know you hate me and can't stand to call me," I told him, trying to keep my voice calm, "but I need you, Joe. I'm feeling suicidal, and you're the only one who can help me. Jolly lives too far away, and I can't afford to call 911 again and run up another hospital bill. Please come over and sit with me until my sleeping medicine takes effect. I did take some extra so it will knock me out, but I'm trying something new and don't know exactly how it works. It may be too much. That's why I need someone here with me."

"I'm really tired," he said. "I don't think I can come. Besides, why should I help you?"

"Don't do it for me, do it for Jolly. What if I took too much and I died? I swear I'm not trying to kill myself. I'm actually trying to save myself. Can you live with that? Please, Joe. For Jolly's sake, come over. Please!" A little groveling wasn't beneath me—anything to get him over here so I could end my problems.

"Damn it, Lee. I can't get away from you, can I?"

"I'm sorry, Joe. I really am, but you said you'd be there for me when I needed you, even with us separated. I really need you tonight. I don't want a repeat of the other night. I almost made it. Tom had to kick the doors down to rescue me. I truly wanted to die then because the emotional pain is overwhelming sometimes. Jolly had to save me, and I don't want to do that to her again. Do this favor for her, okay? Don't put her through that again."

"Okay," he said reluctantly. "Give me a few minutes to shower the stink off of me. I'll ride my motorcycle over. At least that will be enjoyable."

What a dig. I didn't care.

"You be particular on that bike," I said sweetly.

He was coming over! The Ambien was making me sleepy again, and I'd learned that when I fought the Ambien, it put me in a twilight state where I could do things and had no memory of them. It totally erased any inhibitions. Perfect. I could claim I didn't know what I was doing because of my bipolar and being under the influence of that drug. For the first time in nearly five years, I felt at peace.

I headed back to the kitchen and poured one more glass of tea. I wanted to be ready. I literally waltzed into the living room, humming "Lady in Red," another song of ours. I sat back in the chair, sipping my tea and waiting to hear the motorcycle. I felt my lids getting heavy. Yes, the Ambien was starting to kick in, but my adrenalin at what I was fixing to do would take care of everything.

Joe would use his key he still had to the place to get inside. I'd be in the recliner, no wait. I'd go on back to the bedroom. When I heard him open the door, I'd slur my words and invite him back. He'd tuck me in good and I'd call him back just as he was leaving, having tip toed to the dresser. I'd have the gun already out of the drawer and ready to shoot him at close range—no way could I miss. I'd claim I'd heard someone coming down the hall and thought it was a prowler.

Ah, it was working too perfectly. By the time Joe arrived, it'd be after midnight. No ex would be coming to see his wife that late. Since he had called me, there wouldn't even be a telephone record of our conversation. I'd already deleted the e-mail message to him. Yes, it was all falling into place beautifully. I kept listening for the sound of the cycle as I leaned my head back feeling more and more relaxed. My head felt heavy, and I could barely keep my eyes open.

Chapter Thirty-Four

Soon, a noise startled me awake. I heard the door open and heard him calling my name.

"I'm coming, hold your thorses," I slurred. With great effort I arose from the bed. The room started spinning and I sat back down. "Thang on, I'm coming!" For a minute, I was confused. Who the hell could it be this late at night?

Again, I positioned myself into standing up. I wobbled toward the bedroom door and unlocked it.

"Joe, what are you doing here?" I'd forgotten everything.

"You asked me to sit with you. Something about taking enough sleeping pills to knock yourself out but not enough to kill you."

"Oh, yeah. Will you truck me back into bed?" It started coming back to me.

"Yeah. But I don't have a lot of time. I'm expecting a phone call." Yeah, that was a dig, flaunting his latest girlfriend.

"You woke me upth. I shoudph go back to sheep. Tanks, Shoe." He could tell that I was drunk, and he grabbed my elbow and guided me to the bed. He was the Joe of old and pulled back the covers. I was still dressed, so he took my clothes off, leaving me nude. Of course, in days gone by, that would have led to our having sex. Not tonight, he picked me up and put me down on my side of the bed. He pulled the cover up and leaned over, probably out of habit, and kissed me on my forehead. My thinking was clearer than my actions. I could barely move.

"Tanks, Shoe. . ." I felt my eyes lose the battle and close.

I heard footsteps getting softer as he walked down the hall back into the living room. I knew I had something to do, so I fought the Ambien's hold on me and drug myself out of bed. I wobbled over to the dresser, opened the drawer and took out the gun." It felt like it weighed twenty pounds. It took both hands to pull it out of the drawer and lift it.

"Shoe, caaaan use come there?" I listened to hear his footsteps coming down the long hall.

Finally, he answered me, "What do you want now?" I heard the fromp as the recliner closed, then the footsteps. When I estimated he was half-way down the hall, I opened the bedroom door and stepped out with the gun pointing straight ahead. I fired wildly and blindly and emptied the chamber. Somewhere amidst the noise of the shots, I heard his body hit the floor. I didn't want to help him or check on him. What I wanted was sleep. I let the gun drop out of my hand. I couldn't fight the sleep anymore. My mind went blank as I passed out.

I slept late the next day. I awakened and found myself on the floor half way in the hall and half way in the bedroom. The hallway was dark. I got up to make my way to the kitchen to put on my coffee. I stumped my toe on the gun. I wondered how it had gotten out of the drawer. I picked it up and returned it to the drawer, shrugging my shoulders. When I re-entered the hall, I stepped into something sticky. I turned on the light and screamed. A trail of blood smeared down the long hall disappeared around the corner into the den. There was Joe curled up in the fetal position, on his right side. The blood had pooled in his face and stomach and he looked grotesque.

"Oh, my God! What have I done? Joe, baby, Joe, please don't be dead." I rushed to him. He was cold to the touch and a pool of blood had turned black. Blood oozed out of his mouth, nose and ears. I knelt down and picked up his head and let out a wail.

"Joe, darling, please wake up!" Blood now soaked my nude body. How did this happen? I had no recall. Ambien often did that to me. I would get up after taking it and cook or call Jolly then have no recall of talking to her. I wouldn't remember cooking, but I'd find dirty dishes and pots and pans in the sink. But this. Was I capable of doing this? How did Joe get to the house? I knew I needed to call Tom. I dialed 9-11.

"Hello, this is Lee Thames. I think I've killed my ex-husband. I don't remember doing it. The last thing I remember was going to bed after taking two of my Ambiens."

"Stay on the phone, Miss Thames. An officer will be there shortly."

"I'm naked. Let me put on a robe." I sat the phone down and walked to the closet and pulled out my floor link aqua colored robe trimmed in Navy blue. "I'm back. Oh, my God. What have I done?"

"Ma'am, don't hang up. Calm down. An officer is on his way." As she said that, I heard a knock, then heard Tom's voice.

"Lee, it's me. I'm coming in. Put the gun down."

"I don't have a gun I don't know what happened."

I heard Tom's footsteps stop. I watched him bend down to check for a pulse, although it was obvious that Joe was dead. Tom had his gun drawn and trained on me.

"Lee, put your hands up in the air."

I did as he said. Tom got up and walked over to me, gun still drawn. "Put your hands behind your back." I did as he said. I felt him cuff me.

"Lee, wuh wuh why did you do it?"

"I don't know. I don't remember shooting him. I swear to you. I don't remember anything. I just remember going to bed. No, wait a minute. I remember hearing a noise in the hallway. I must have gotten up and shot, thinking it was a prowler."

At that point in time, that is what I truly believed.

"You're going to have to come with me down to the station. I'm going to un-cuff you so you can get dressed."

I felt uneasy as I disrobed in front of him. He couldn't let me out of his sight. I hurried and put on a pair of jeans and a sweatshirt.

"You have the right to remain silent, anything you say can and wuh wuh will be used against you in a court of law. . ."

I couldn't believe this was being said to me, especially by Tom. He steered me around Joe's body. I started crying when I saw Joe again. To my horror his belly and chest had been shot the most and I realized he had bled internally. He'd died a slow, painful death.

"Oh, Tom, what have I done? I loved him. He was my soul mate. I'd never kill him." I sobbed with huge uncontrollable tears. "I deserve to die if I did this."

"Don't wuh wuh worry, Lee. I think everything is going to be okay. I know you wuh wuh would never shoot Joe on purpose."

Chapter Thirty-Five

After grilling me for hours at the police station, which felt like fifty-five forevers, the police were convinced it had been an accident and allowed me to return home. Tom brought me back to the house. In all honesty, I had no memory of shooting Joe. I was drunk and confused, forgetting I had taken so many sleeping pills.

The coroner had removed Joe's body, but the blood was everywhere. Again, I cried because I mourned his death. I knew I needed two people to be with me, Jolly and my sister. I called Jolly first.

"Jolly, something horrible has happened. I must have gotten the gun back from Jessica because I used it last night and killed your dad. I thought he was a prowler and I shot him out in the hall. I'd taken my Ambien, and I have no memory of what happened. Please come home and help me make the arrangements."

I heard Jolly scream and that jarred my heart and my mind. Something inside me told me to get her to my house as fast as possible. A dread came over me. What HAD I done?

"Mom, oh my God! What have you done? Are you planning on hurting yourself? Please don't do anything like that. I'm on my way. I love you, Mom. I'll take care of everything."

"Jolly, all I want to do is sleep. I'm going on to bed. Hurry home. God, I'm so sorry." I stared into the dresser mirror and an image that seemed evil stared back at me. Tears distorted the image and that old mirror distorted it too making me look ghoulish.

Hang on old girl. Don't go crazy now, Jolly needs you.

My brave, practical Jolly was saving me once again.

Next I called Margaret. Crying again by that time, I felt my face's drawn look and the tension in my brows, aching physically and mentally.

"Margaret, I've killed Joe. I thought I had a prowler last night, and I accidentally shot him. Please come be with me and give me strength to get through this."

"I'll have to cancel a club meeting at my house today, but I'll come as soon as I can."

"Thank you, Margaret. I don't know where to begin. I can't go to the funeral home today. I'm too upset. I'm going to take something to help me sleep until you and Jolly arrive. I'm taking the phone off the hook and I'm not going to answer the door. Jolly will be here before you. She has a key."

I dreaded the next call. I knew I'd need to let his parents know that Joe was dead.

My hands shook as I punched in their number.

"Hello," answered Joe's mama.

"May Maw, Joe is dead. I accidentally shot him last night. I thought he was a prowler." I cried as I said that to her. "I loved him. Oh, my God, what am I going to do with him being gone forever?" That phrase triggered another memory. I remember wanting him to be gone forever.

Could I have shot Joe on purpose? I've never killed anything except an ant or two or maybe a roach. I'm not capable of killing someone I love.

Maw Maw's scream brought me back into the present. Hearing her cry and scream made me cry harder.

"Listen, I've been to the police station and released since it was an accident. I'm emotionally spent. Please don't come over until tomorrow. I can't deal with this. My sister is coming to help me make the arrangements. Jolly is on her way home too. I'm fixing to go to bed until Jolly gets home. I'm taking the phone off the hook and I'm locking up and not answering the door. I can't deal with people right now."

"Where is his body? We want to drive up and go see him. We'll buy him a dress suit to put on him."

I didn't like that as it was so not Joe. But he was going to be buried in their family plot at their Baptist Church. Joe hated that church, but we didn't have a burial plot, so this was the only practical thing to do. Let them have their way. I was too tired to argue with her.

"Thanks,

"May Maw, I'm sure he'd appreciate that. He is over in the Peaceful Valley Funeral Home in Cusseta. Don't come by here, I mean it. Jolly will take care of everything. She'll get up with you by phone and y'all work things out.

As soon as I hung up the phone, it rang.

"I just heard about things. I knew better than to let you have that gun. I feel guilty and like it's partly my fault. You said you were going straight home and give it to your sister. Lee, did you murder him?"

"Jessica, I don't remember anything. I'd taken two Ambiens and thought I'd gone on to bed. Apparently, I didn't. Jessica, I've fucked up now. How will I live with myself?"

"I'm coming over to sit with you. I don't think your mental health can handle this. You need to be watched in case of being suicidal."

"Jessica, the gun is at the police station. I'm going to knock myself out.

Margaret and Jolly are going to make all of the arrangements. I just want to be left alone right now and go back to bed and sleep this horror away."

I'd told Jessica the truth because Margaret and Jolly were going to make arrangements today. I had a nagging voice in my head that insisted on not allowing Jessica into the house today.

"Okay, I know sleep is probably what you need the most today. I'm glad Margaret is there with you and Jolly is on her way." That remark stirred my memory. I'd told Jessica to give me the gun because I was going to give it to Margaret.

Good, by the time Jessica makes it over to the house, Margaret and Jolly would both be here. Jessica would never ask Margaret what had happened. She'd be that courteous in case it had traumatized her too.

Bits and pieces were coming back to me. The puzzle I was putting together did not make a pretty picture. Good to my word, I downed two more Ambiens and a Klonapin just to make sure I was knocked out for the rest of the day.

Everything I figure out happened just as I wanted it to. Margaret and Jolly made funeral arrangements. When Jolly saw the dress suit that had been left to put on him, she nixed it.

"My daddy never wore a suit that I remember. He's a khaki shirt and blue jeans man. He'll be buried in one of his work shirts. That is where he spent most of his life during my lifetime."

Joe's parents visited and there had not been a confrontation. Since Jolly was Joe's child, what she said carried more weight than what his mama had said. He was buried in a work shirt and his favorite pair of jeans. Jolly got things ready for him. I was pretty much in a non-state as I stayed full of sleeping pills and slept most of the time. I headed into a deep depression. However, I knew that I couldn't go to a mental hospital and face that truth. I promised myself to wean myself off the sleeping pills.

The funeral had been small and held in the family's Baptist church. That is something else Joe would have hated. He would have preferred our Episcopal church for his service. I couldn't make decisions due to my severe depression. So, I went along with everything.

Jessica had the good manners to never bring up the gun again. I did give it to Margaret to take back to Meridian with her after Jolly got it back from the police. The stipulation was to give it to Jolly when she was legally of age to own a gun. In my mind, it had been an accident because that is what everyone else said. Their thoughts filled in the holes in my memory of what had happened. However, I'd awaken many a night knowing I was a murderer but never realizing I had it in me to be so despicable. That burden would be my albatross around my neck for the rest of my life.

Dr. Hopkins listened to me and probably noted the one thing I refused to talk about. Knowing how fragile my mental state was, he never pushed me to deal with it and allowed me to grieve by burying my feelings. If only he knew the truth.

Epilogue

———————————

A soft knock awakens me. The room is dark, and my eyes can barely see the door. I roll over on my back and ask, "Who is it?"

"Jolly. Mom, I've brought you some Ensure to drink. You keep on losing weight." A middle aged woman walks through the door carrying a bag of groceries. She is petite and pretty. She looks vaguely familiar, but I haven't a clue who she is."

"I'm not hungry. Who did you say you were?"

"Jolly. Mom, your daughter."

"I don't have a daughter. William and I can't have any children. You have mistaken me for someone else." I point to the door to show her the way out.

"Mom, don't you remember? William died last year. You aren't married to him and haven't been for nearly thirty years now. You married my dad, Joe Thames. I'm Jolly Thames except I'm married and go by a different last name."

"Then, who are you? I don't know any Jolly or Joe Thames."

"Mom, about ten years ago, I had to put you in Pinecrest Nursing Home. Please look at me and recognize me. I love you so much."

She took the bag and put something in my small refrigerator in the room. I looked around and couldn't recognize where I was.

"Where's William? What happened to our dining room table?"

"You are in a nursing home." A tear slid out of her eye.

She came over to me and I screamed, "Get away from me. I don't know you! Help, somebody help me. William, come here. Where has he gone?"

About that time, the door opened again and a nurse came in. "Mrs. Thames, calm down. It's your baby girl. She is so good to you. Don't act like that. Don't you remember her?"

I lay back in the bed. Somewhere in the back of my mind was a memory about a daughter and a husband. Something unpleasant about the husband. For a second, I thought I knew the young lady. But it was fleeting and I turned my head away from her.

"Get out. Leave me alone. I don't have a daughter."

"God, Mom, this is killing me. You used to love me so very much. Please don't tell me to get out. I just want to help you."

I had my head turned away from her. "Nurse, make her go away. I never had any children. Why is she doing this to me?"

"Mrs. Thames, now, now...don't be mean like that. Jolly just wants to make things better for you. She loves you. I think you'd better, leave now, Jolly. She's having a really bad day today."

The nurse had turned off the TV and the lights. "Go to sleep, Mrs. Thames. Maybe tomorrow will be a better day."

About the Author

N. L. Snowden has written an astonishingly powerful novel. It grabbed me from the first page and didn't let go. Don't miss this one.
Cassandra King, *author of the New York Times best seller, The Sunday Wife.*

"The book tells a story that never gets told. Booze and infidelities often lead to madness in the spouse.
I travel throughout the mental health system as a peer all over the United States. This is true of the people in our system. Many are abused and mistreated women who are shelved. Snowden tells her story for herself and all women. If you want to understand what is really happening today in America and mental health read this book."
Moe Armstrong, *founder of peer advocacy in the mental health and veterans administration, has been on Good Morning America, Sixty Minutes, and Nightline advocating for mental health and veterans.*

Dee Jordan, a retired schoolteacher, had her first novel published under the pen name N. L. Snowden. This novel, *In and Out of Madness,* is available on Amazon and Kindle. She wrote a column about the life of a published author for a California e-zine called *Active Voice*. She also did book reviews for the *Alabama Writers' Forum Online Reviews*, and she wrote articles dealing with mental illness for the newspaper, *New York City Voices* in NYC. She has had short stories published in two literary magazines and in four different anthologies. One story won first place at the Baldwin County Writers Fiction contest. Presently she is working for SOMI Club *Survivors of Mental Illness* an adult drop in center for the mentally ill in recovery. When she is not at work, she is squirreled away in her apartment working on her second novel.

www.ingramcontent.com/pod-product-compliance
Lightning Source LLC
Chambersburg PA
CBHW070803280326
41934CB00012B/3035